The Teacher Development Series

Sound Foundations

Living Phonology

Adrian Underhill

MACMILLAN
HEINEMANN
English Language Teaching

Macmillan Heinemann English Language Teaching Oxford
A division of Macmillan Publishers Limited

Companies and representatives throughout the world

Heinemann is a registered trademark of Reed
Educational & Professional Publishing Limited

ISBN 0 435 24091 9

© Adrian Underhill 1994

Design and illustration © Macmillan Publishers Limited 1998

First published 1994

All rights reserved; no part of this publication may be reproduced,
stored in a retrieval system, transmitted in any form, or by any means,
electronic, mechanical, photocopying, recording, or otherwise,
without the prior written permission of the publishers.

Designed by Mike Brain

Illustrated by Nick Hardcastle

Author's acknowledgement

Many people have been involved in the development of this
approach, most particularly the teachers and learners at International
House Hastings and at International House schools, ILC schools and
many other language institutes around the world. Their experience
and feedback has helped to shape this approach to teaching and
learning phonology.

Of the many personal influences in this area of work the most
significant has been that of Dr Caleb Gattegno whose *Subordination of
teaching to learning* is as radical and relevant as it was twenty years ago.
I have been inspired by his work on pronunciation and on the
education of awareness, and am trying to make this more widely
accessible.

Printed and bound in Great Britain by the Bath Press

Other titles in the series

Inside Teaching
Tim Bowen & Jonathan Marks

Learning Teaching
Jim Scrivener

The ELT Manager's Handbook
Graham Impey & Nic Underhill

2003 2002 2001 2000 1999
12 11 10 9 8 7 6 5

Contents

The Teacher Development Series   v

Introduction to *Sound Foundations*   vii

Ideas behind the phonemic chart   viii

Key to phonemic symbols   xii

Part 1
Discovery toolkit

Level 1   **Sounds in isolation**   2
            1 Introduction   2
            2 Vowels: monophthongs   5
            3 Vowels: diphthongs   22
            4 Consonants   29

Level 2   **Words in isolation**   48
            1 Introduction   48
            2 Joining individual phonemes to make words   49
            3 Stress in words   51
            4 Unstress in words   53
            5 Primary and secondary stress   54
            6 Where do you put the stress in words?   55
            7 Intonation and word stress   57

Level 3   **Connected speech**   58
            1 Introduction   58
            2 Overview   58
            3 Sounds and simplifications in connected speech   60
            4 Rhythm in connected speech   69
            5 Intonation   74

Part 2
Classroom toolkit

Level 1   **Sounds in isolation**   96
            1 General applications of the chart   96
            2 Using the pointer   98
            3 Introducing and integrating the chart   99
            4 Seven modes of chart usage   100
            5 A first lesson with the chart   107
            6 Four ways of giving models   110
            7 Developing your internal imaging of sounds   114
            8 Developing your use of mime and gesture   115
            9 Working with individual sounds   118
           10 Working with mistakes   132

Level 2 **Words in isolation** 145
  1 Establishing the sound flow 145
  2 Working with the spelling–pronunciation link 146
  3 Word stress: working with words of two or more syllables 151
  4 Word stress and Cuisenaire rods 154
  5 Finger correction 160
  6 Integrating the learner's dictionary with pronunciation work 166
  7 Lip reading, ventriloquism, pronunciation and vocabulary 169

Level 3 **Connected speech** 171
  1 Overview 171
  2 Simplification and reduction of sounds in connected speech 173
  3 Stress, prominence and rhythm in connected speech 176
  4 Intonation 194
  5 Some integrative activities and suggestions 202

Appendix 1 Further thoughts on using the cassette player, blackboard, and pointer 205
Appendix 2 Phonemic charts for other languages 207

  Further reading 208

  Index 209

The Teacher Development Series

TEACHER DEVELOPMENT is the process of becoming the best teacher you can be. It means becoming a student of learning, your own as well as that of others. It represents a widening of the focus of teaching to include not only the subject matter and the teaching methods, but also the people who are working with the subject and using the methods. It means taking a step back to see the larger picture of what goes on in learning, and how the relationship between learners and teachers influences learning. It also means attending to small details which can in turn change the bigger picture. Teacher development is a continuous process of transforming human potential into human performance, a process that is never finished.

The Teacher Development Series offers perspectives on learning that embrace topic, method and person as parts of one larger interacting whole. We aim to help you, the teacher, trainer or academic manager to stretch your awareness not only of what you do and how you do it, but also of how you affect your learners and colleagues. This will enable you to extract more from your own experience, both as it happens and in retrospect, and to become more actively involved in your own continuous learning. The books themselves will focus on new treatments of familiar subjects as well as areas that are just emerging as subjects of the future.

The series represents work that is in progress rather than finished or closed. The authors are themselves exploring, and invite you to bring your own experience to the study of these books while at the same time learning from the experiences of others. We encourage you to observe, value and understand your own experience, and to evaluate and integrate relevant external practice and knowledge into your own internal evolving model of effective teaching and learning.

Adrian Underhill

About the author

Adrian Underhill

I work at International House in Hastings, where I am Director of the Teacher Training Institute. I travel quite frequently, meeting and working with teachers and learners in different countries. I am particularly interested in the human sides of teaching and learning and it seems to me that no matter how marvellous the materials and the conditions, in the end it is the person of the teacher that counts. This conclusion has formed the basis of much of my work on our programme of teachers' courses in Hastings, and led me to founding the Teacher Development Group (the first Special Interest Group of IATEFL) in 1985.

I became interested in pronunciation when I discovered that it had the power to engage and upgrade learners' attention in a definite and tangible way, and that this could even affect the rest of their language studies. I sometimes run intensive workshops on teaching pronunciation, as well as on such topics as facilitation skills, presence and performance for teachers and trainers, and humanistic approaches in education.

Introduction to *Sound Foundations*

SOUND FOUNDATIONS is about understanding and enjoying phonology. It is about integrating phonology learning into all other class activities, and developing the skill and confidence to challenge learners creatively.

Sound Foundations is made up of two complementary parts, each of which comprises a set of simple tools that enable you to carry out a large number of specific tasks quite easily. The tools themselves are made up in varying proportions from three ingredients: awareness, technique, and knowledge.

The first part of this book is the *discovery toolkit*, which is for you to do yourself. The tools you will find here will enable you to discover through direct experience how your own pronunciation works, what the variables are and how to affect them. Your work here is guided by the discovery activities and by the commentaries. You will probably find that as you make discoveries yourself you can use the activities in class to help your learners make the same discoveries.

The second part is the *classroom toolkit*, and this contains activities to do with your learners. In working with these classroom activities and commentaries your learners will develop trust in their own capacity to learn, and you will develop the ability to respond directly and effectively to your learners' pronunciation needs as they arise.

Linguistic descriptions of phonology usually follow a two-fold division of the subject matter into *segmentals* (ie phonemes) and *supra-segmentals* (ie intonation and rhythm). This framework was not constructed for language learners or teachers and does not necessarily provide the most useful basis on which to build learning activities.

Sound Foundations is designed specifically for learning and teaching pronunciation, and is based on a three-fold division, which seems to provide a more practical way of understanding phonology and a more useful and precise set of pedagogic tools. The three divisions are:

Level 1: Sounds
Level 2: Words
Level 3: Connected speech

Both the *discovery toolkit* and the *classroom toolkit* focus on each level in turn.

In studying individual sounds and words we do not lose sight of the fact that our main purpose is the promotion of fluent speech. Nevertheless sounds and words are the building blocks for connected speech, and specific and detailed work can be done at these levels without losing touch with the fluent speech from which the parts have been abstracted. *Sound Foundations* offers ways of moving elegantly and immediately from connected speech to words to sounds and back again, and of noticing, examining and constantly refining connected speech.

I hope you find pleasure and success in working with this material, and in improving it by making it yours.

Adrian Underhill
Hastings
January 1994

Ideas behind the phonemic chart

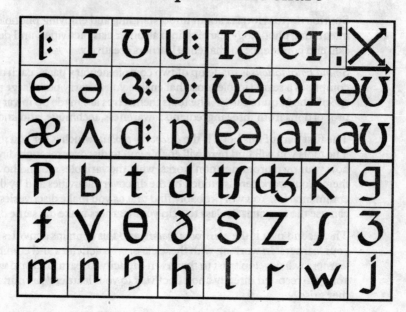

Looking at the chart

The phonemic set

Every spoken language has its own set of sounds. A characteristic of this set is that all the sounds within it exist in some sort of relationship to each other, each sound helping to shape the contours and boundaries of its neighbours. I refer to this set as the *phonemic set*. This chart shows the phonemic set of English as a complete and consistent system, to be worked with as one organic and interacting whole.

Why these symbols?

The symbols which are used on the chart to represent the sounds of the English phonemic set are taken from the International Phonetic Alphabet. These are the symbols used by most learner dictionaries, so working with them will also help learners develop the skills of finding for themselves the pronunciation and stress of any word in a learner dictionary.

Phonemes and allophones

A *phoneme* is the smallest sound that can make a difference in meaning. So if you change one phoneme for another you change the word. The word *mine* changes to *pine* and to *shine* if you change the phoneme /m/ to /p/ to /ʃ/. There are forty-four such significant sounds, or phonemes, in standard British English.

Each phoneme has a variety of *allophones*, slightly different and acceptable ways of saying the sound without changing the meaning. In this sense allophones are not significant. For example, /p/ has spread lips in *peel* and rounded lips in *pool*, but both varieties are regarded as being the same phoneme.

The layout of the chart

The forty-four phonemes of standard English are presented on the chart in a significant visual relationship to each other. Built into this design are references to **how** and **where** in the mouth each sound is produced, and so there are many clues in the design that can help in recognizing, shaping, correcting and recalling the sounds. Each symbol has its own box and pointing to this box selects that particular sound for attention. It can be useful to think of the box as containing all of the allophones of the sound.

The stress and intonation symbols

The primary and secondary stress symbols as used in most dictionaries are shown in the top right-hand corner of the chart, and beside them the five basic discourse intonation patterns (ie fall, rise, fall–rise, rise–fall and level) are shown in one composite symbol.

Sample words and decorations or a sparse chart?

I have received from teachers a number of decorated versions of the phonemic chart. The additions and decorations usually include one or two of the following: some include sample words within each phoneme box (eg *tree* in the /iː/ box), some have a picture instead of the sample word in the phoneme box (eg a picture of a tree in the /iː/ box) and some sculpt the symbol itself into an object whose English name contains that sound (eg the /iː/ symbol shaped into a tree). Some use colour, either at random for decorative effect, or to convey particular information (eg different colours for 'more difficult' sounds, or to indicate sounds 'not occurring' in the mother tongue of a particular learner group).

I encourage teachers and learners to find what works best for them, but I prefer to keep the chart sparse. There are drawbacks to including sample words or pictures on the chart:

- Sample words can be mispronounced or learned inaccurately in the first place.
- If the sample word contains an awkward sequence of sounds for certain mother tongue speakers then other sounds in the sequence may be distorted.
- Each phoneme can have a number of individual variations (allophones) depending on the phonemic context. A single sample word supplies only one of those variations, whereas a symbol represents a whole family of variations.
- The learner is tied to a sample word once it is printed on the chart. This can discourage them from choosing different and more relevant models as they become more discriminating.
- Pictures have additional problems in that they can be culture bound as well as ambiguous.

For these reasons I am reluctant to associate a phoneme permanently with one sample word, though temporary associations are of course helpful. The sample phoneme list inside the front cover is useful as a starting point, and for reference, but I hope and expect that learners will grow out of it quite quickly. Exercises in which learners find their own example words and then list them in their notebooks, or on the board, or on a poster, or even stick them temporarily on the chart, can all be helpful and illuminating as temporary measures.

An aim of this approach is to help learners to form their own images and develop their own associations with the chart, rather than find the chart already loaded with someone else's associations. In this respect providing less may allow for more.

Using the chart

Permanent display of the chart

The chart is designed for permanent display at the front of the classroom, so that it can be referred to at any moment during any lesson, and for a variety of different purposes (eg presenting, practising and diagnosing learners' perceptions of sounds, reshaping sounds, etc).

The chart as map

The chart is not a list to learn, but a map representing pronunciation territory to explore. Like any map it can help in two ways: it can help travellers to become more familiar with areas they have already visited; and it can help travellers to be clear about which areas they have yet to explore.

Learn sounds not symbols

The symbol is not the sound, just as a church or a lake on a map is not actually a church or a lake! The aim of this approach is to experience sounds and sequences of sound in a personal, physical, muscular way, and to use the phonemic symbol as a visual hook for that physical and auditory experience. It is sounds that are being studied, not symbols.

Activating the chart

You and your learners can activate the chart by touching the sound boxes singly or in succession with a pointer. This is either to initiate sounds or speech from others, or to respond to sounds or utterances made by others. The basic rule is either *point then speak* (ie someone points out sounds or sequences of sounds after others have said them), or *speak then point* (ie someone speaks while another tries to point out all or part of what they have said). You can establish these two basic patterns within the first few minutes of using the chart. On pp100-106 you will find seven modes of using the chart. The even number modes correspond to *point then speak*, and the odd number modes correspond to *speak then point*.

Three levels of study

The *Sound Foundations* approach enables the focus of pronunciation work to move elegantly, and on a moment-by-moment basis, between individual sounds, individual words, and connected speech. Thus micro and macro work can be integrated in precise response to the pronunciation needs of the lesson as it unfolds.

Level 1: Sounds

This level aims to develop in teachers and learners a deep and internally experienced awareness of how they produce sounds by manipulating their vocal musculature, and how the internal sensation of using the muscles relates to what is heard through the ears. The development of this awareness enhances learners' ability to change and modify how they use their musculature to produce new or different sounds.

Level 2: Individual words

Words spoken in isolation consist of a 'flow of sound' which is different from the sum of the individual phonemes. Neighbouring sounds modify each other as the vocal muscles join them together and take short cuts. Also, in multi-syllable words, distribution of energy across the syllables creates an energy profile, called *word stress*, that is typical and generally characteristic of a particular word when spoken on its own.

Level 3: Connected speech

Words flow together to make a stream of speech that is different from the sum of the individual words. Sounds are simplified and reduced, and the energy profile is extended from individual words to groups of words, that is from word stress that is relatively fixed to prominence (emphasis) and intonation (music) that is chosen by the speaker. This energy package, held together by the pattern of pitch and prominence, is called a *tone unit*.

Each of the three levels invites a different focus of attention and each can be called on separately or in combination to meet the needs that arise at any moment in a lesson.

Which model of English?

The phonemic symbols on the chart are generally taken to refer to British English Received Pronunciation (RP). Where the target for learners is a modified RP or a different accent then the relevant symbols can be changed or given different values.

Conventional pronunciation materials

The chart is designed to be used without conventional pronunciation materials, by exploiting material from the coursebook and from classroom interaction for use in pronunciation work. However you can easily integrate the use of the chart with conventional pronunciation materials, thereby adding a new dimension to such work.

Guiding principles

For language learning and teacher training

The phonemic chart is designed for use with learners and teachers of English at all levels. It is also designed to help you, the teacher, to develop your own awareness of pronunciation, and to discover new and practical ways of perceiving, diagnosing and responding to your learners' pronunciation needs.

Multisensory

Pronunciation is the physical side of language, involving the body, the breath, the muscles, acoustic vibration and harmonics. When attention is paid to this fact, studying pronunciation can become a living and pleasurable learning process. This approach is holistic in that it allows learners to work from their individual strengths and to develop their own more vivid learning styles. Pronunciation can become physical, visual, aural, spatial, and affective as well as intellectual.

Assumptions and values

The values and beliefs about learning and about people that underpin this approach are essentially humanistic, holistic and positive in their view of what learners are capable of under the right conditions. The *Sound Foundations* approach to teaching and learning goes beyond content and technique, and takes into account the psychological dynamics of learning and the creation of an atmosphere conducive to learning. An assumption in this book is that motivation and enjoyment arise naturally when the deep-seated human predisposition to learn, to experiment and to search for order is creatively engaged.

Key to phonemic symbols

iː	see	/siː/	e	egg	/eg/	æ	cat	/kæt/		
ɪ	sit	/sɪt/	ə	away	/əweɪ/	ʌ	up	/ʌp/		
ʊ	good	/gʊd/	ɜː	her	/hɜː/	ɑː	ask	/ɑːsk/		
uː	two	/tuː/	ɔː	four	/fɔː/	ɒ	on	/ɒn/		

ɪə	here	/hɪə/	ʊə	cure	/kjʊə/	eə	there	/ðeə/
eɪ	eight	/eɪt/	ɔɪ	boy	/bɔɪ/	aɪ	my	/maɪ/
			əʊ	no	/nəʊ/	aʊ	now	/naʊ/

p	pen	/pen/	f	five	/faɪv/	m	me	/miː/
b	bee	/biː/	v	very	/verɪ/	n	nine	/naɪn/
t	ten	/ten/	θ	thing	/θɪŋ/	ŋ	long	/lɒŋ/
d	do	/duː/	ð	this	/ðɪs/	h	house	/haʊs/
tʃ	chair	/tʃeə/	s	so	/səʊ/	l	love	/lʌv/
dʒ	just	/dʒʌst/	z	zoo	/zuː/	r	right	/raɪt/
k	can	/kæn/	ʃ	she	/ʃiː/	w	we	/wiː/
g	go	/gəʊ/	ʒ	pleasure	/pleʒə/	j	yes	/jes/

Part 1
Discovery toolkit

Level 1 Sounds in isolation   2
Level 2 Words in isolation   48
Level 3 Connected speech   58

Introduction to the discovery toolkit

The benefit of a working knowledge of how sounds are made, and of how they merge into words and connected speech, is in being better able to perceive what learners are doing. This enables us to guide them in the most useful and engaging direction.

When a learner produces a not-quite-right sound only one of several variables may need attention. The questions are *which variable?* and *what shall we do?* Without practical knowledge of phonology you may lack the criteria for deciding on the best procedure, or, when your learner tries again and produces a different not-quite-right sound, you may not know whether that is a step in the right direction or not.

The discovery toolkit enables you to discover the theory for yourself in a personal and permanent way through your own perception and experience. This will have many benefits on the ways you help your learners.

Level 1   Sounds in isolation

1 Introduction   2

2 Vowels: monophthongs   5

3 Vowels: diphthongs   22

4 Consonants   29

1   Introduction

As you can see, the phonemic chart (Fig. 1) has three main sections. The vowels are shown in the upper half, monophthongs /mɒnəfθɒŋz/ on the left, and diphthongs /dɪpθɒŋz/ or /dɪfθɒŋz/ on the right. The consonants /kɒnsənənts/ are shown in the lower half. The colon by five of the vowel symbols indicates length. The box in the top right-hand corner contains stress and intonation symbols.

Fig. 1: The phonemic chart

Sounds are all produced in the vocal tract. The vocal tract refers to the parts of the body that contribute to the production of vocal sounds: the lungs, larynx, oral cavity (mouth), lips and nose.

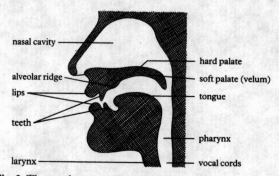

Fig. 2: The vocal tract

To facilitate the learning of the phonemes of standard English, we need to know:

- **how** each sound is produced within the vocal tract (referred to as *manner of articulation*);
- **where** in the vocal tract each sound is produced (referred to as *place of articulation*).

The phonemic chart is arranged to convey much of this information visually.

The first two discovery activities focus on distinguishing monophthongs, diphthongs and consonants. After that they are investigated in more depth.

Discovery activity 1 Distinguishing consonants from vowels

Here we make a first exploration of how and where the sounds are produced, and at the same time distinguish vowels from consonants.

Focusing on your mouth, say these pairs of words slowly, both aloud and whispered, and notice how you make the difference between the two words.

1 eee /iː/   key /kiː/
2 ooh /uː/   two /tuː/
3 or /ɔː/   nor /nɔː/
4 er /ɜː/   sir /sɜː/
5 ah /ɑː/   bar /bɑː/

Commentary ■ ■ ■

In each case the first word consists of a single vowel sound, and the second word consists of the same vowel preceded by a consonant. Notice that the vowel sound on its own has no particular restriction to the air flow, though it does require a particular 'posture' of the tongue, jaw and lips. The second word of each pair begins with some kind of restriction to the air flow which you then release as you move into the following vowel. Most consonants have their own restriction to the flow of air, which is what gives them their unique sound. (The exceptions are at the right of the bottom row of the chart. We'll return to these later.) ■

Discovery activity 2 Distinguishing two kinds of vowel

Now we'll subdivide the vowel sounds. These pairs of words have the same initial consonant, but different vowels following. What happens in your mouth? Observe carefully your tongue, jaw and lips, and notice how you make the difference between the two words.

1 key /kiː/   kay /keɪ/
2 two /tuː/   toe /təʊ/
3 nor /nɔː/   now /naʊ/
4 sir /sɜː/   sigh /saɪ/
5 bore /bɔː/   boy /bɔɪ/

Commentary ■ ■ ■

What I hope you notice is that in the second word of each pair the tongue/jaw/lip posture changes during the sounding of the vowel, while in the first word there is no such movement. If this is what you found then you are observing the general difference in articulation between monophthongs and diphthongs*. The distinction is particularly important in English and has some very practical classroom implications. ■

*These two words are from the Greek for (respectively) one sound and two sounds: *mono* one; *di* two; *phthoggos* sound or voice.

Learning from the discovery activities

The aim of the first two discovery activities is to make sure that you have noticed *in your own vocal tract* the difference between consonants, monophthongs and diphthongs. If you are uncertain about this distinction you could study Fig. 3, or go back over the discovery activity.

	WHERE	HOW
Monophthongs	The distinguishing quality of each vowel is produced by the shape and size of the resonant space in the mouth. This is controlled by the position and shape of the tongue, lips and jaw.	There is no obstruction to the escape of air through the mouth, and they are all voiced, ie the vocal cords vibrate in the air flow.
Diphthongs	As for monophthongs the distinguishing quality is produced by the tongue, lips and jaw. The difference is that there is one mouth posture at the beginning of the vowel sound, and another at the end. The resulting glide between these two tongue and lip positions gives the diphthong its characteristic 'two-sound' quality.	As with monophthongs there is no obstruction to the escape of air through the mouth, and they are all voiced, ie the vocal cords vibrate in the air flow.
Consonants	The restrictions to the air flow that make the characteristic consonant sounds are made at one of the points of contact between the various speech organs such as tongue, teeth, lips, roof of mouth, etc. All consonants involve some sort of restriction to the air flow except /w/ and /j/.	Restrictions to the air flow can be made in various ways, each giving a different characteristic sound. Restrictions can be produced by friction applied to the air flow, or by a momentary blocking of the air flow followed by a sudden release, or by diverting the air flow through the nose. The use of voicing and unvoicing also characterizes consonant sounds.

Fig. 3: The *how* and *where* for monophthongs, diphthongs and consonants

In general the aim of each discovery activity is to experience the auditory, visual and physical aspects of sounds. To make this experience more vivid there are three kinds of feedback you can give yourself in the discovery activities:

- kinesthetic feedback: the internal physical sensation of touch and of muscle movement in your throat, mouth, tongue and lips, etc;
- auditory feedback: what you hear, externally through the air, and internally through your head (you can enhance the latter by blocking your ears with your fingers when you speak);
- visual feedback: any physical movement connected with the production of the sound that you can see in yourself or in others (it is very helpful to have a pocket mirror available).

You can also deepen your observations in each activity by making use of three kinds of voicing, each of which reveal different aspects of articulation:

- speaking aloud;
- whispering;
- mouthing silently.

2 Vowels: monophthongs

In the production of vowel sounds, the vocal tract is open so that there is no obstruction to the air flow escaping over the tongue. The characteristic sound of a vowel depends on the shape and size of the resonant space in the mouth. This is determined by:

- the horizontal tongue position (front–centre–back);
- the vertical tongue position (high–mid–low);
- the lip position (rounded–neutral–spread).

And there is a fourth characteristic of vowels which is not dependent on tongue or lip position:

- the typical length or duration of the vowel (long–short).

In this section we'll examine these four variables in turn, and through the discovery activities you will be able to see how you are using these variables when you make vowel sounds. This is important if you want to build up your repertoire of precise and positive techniques for helping learners to shape or reshape their vowel sounds. You will also see how these variables are incorporated in the design of the chart.

The horizontal tongue position

Discovery activity 3 Horizontal tongue position

Say /iː/ as in *tea*, and now /uː/ as in *two*. Alternate the sounds /iː ... uː ... iː ... uː ː.../. Try this slowly at first and then more rapidly. What internal physical movements do you notice? What do you hear? What can you see in a mirror? It may help you to focus attention on the internal movement if you whisper rather than say the sounds aloud.

Try the same thing with /e/ as in *pen*, and /ɔː/ as in *door*, alternating them /e ... ɔː ... e ... ɔː ... /. With these two sounds the jaw is a little more open than before, and the tongue correspondingly a bit lower. What movement does your tongue make as you slide between these two sounds?

Finally, try the same activities with the pair /æ/ as in *cat*, and /ɒ/ as in *pot*, alternating them /æ ... ɒ ... æ ... ɒ ... /. The tongue is even lower in the mouth and the lip position is more open, but you will still be able to notice the horizontal forwards and backwards movement of the tongue.

Commentary ■ ■ ■

You probably notice two distinct areas of movement: the movement of the lips from a spread position to a rounded position, and the movement of the tongue sliding backwards and forwards in the mouth. For the moment it is the tongue movement we are interested in, and it will help if you try to distinguish between the internal sensations of the tongue and the lip movement.

The next discovery activity helps you to mask off the sensation of lip movement. ■

Discovery activity 4 Isolating your perception of the tongue movement

Say the sound /iː/, and as you do so put the tip of your finger (or a pencil) in contact with the tip of your tongue. Now gradually slide towards the sound /uː/, maintaining the contact between finger and tongue. Alternate the sounds /iː ... uː ... iː ... uː ... /. Try this a few times and you should find that your finger has to move further into your mouth if you are going to keep contact with your tongue.

Another way to focus on your perception of tongue movement is to adopt the mouth position for /iː/. Place a finger along the line of your open lips, gently touching both the top and bottom lip. Now alternate /iː ... uː ... iː ... uː ... / paying attention to the movement of your tongue. The finger on your lips may help you to mask out the sensation of lip movement.

You can also register where your tongue is on the front–back continuum by first saying the vowel and then moving your tongue vertically to touch the roof of your mouth. This sense of contact may indicate how forward or back your tongue is with different vowels.

Try each of these ways of masking off the sensation of lip movement using the other two pairs /e ... ɔː ... e ... ɔː ... / and /æ ... ɒ ... æ ... ɒ ... /.

Commentary ■ ■ ■

The aim of these activities is to highlight the role of the backwards and forwards movement of the tongue in determining the vowel sound. We have explored three pairs of vowels, each pair consisting of a vowel with the tongue forward in the mouth and a vowel with the tongue back in the mouth. The vowels produced with the tongue forward are called front vowels, being produced by the front part of the tongue in the front of the mouth. The other vowel in each pair is called a back vowel, being produced by the back of the tongue in the back of the mouth. In Fig. 4 you can see how this relates to the layout of the chart. ■

Fig. 4: Front and back monophthongs

Discovery activity 5 Locating the in-between vowels

Say the sound /iː/, and slowly glide towards the sound /uː/. Listen to the changing quality of the vowel sound, while noticing the movement of the tongue and lips.

Now repeat the glide /iː ... uː/, but this time stop along the way to see what other vowel sounds you arrive at on the continuum between /iː/ and /uː/. In theory there are many sounds possible, but two in particular correspond to English phonemes.

You may find a point soon after starting where you have a sound that corresponds approximately with /ɪ/ as in *it*, and you will have to shape it and shorten it to make it English. As you draw your tongue further back along the continuum you'll find a sound close to /ʊ/ as in *put*. You'll have to make it short to give it its English quality.

You can find other English monophthongs as you move on the continuum between the other front–back pairs. Take the continuum /e ... ɔ:/. As your tongue slides back from /e/ you may be able to locate /ə/ as in *ago*. For this the tongue is in a neutral position, and the tongue and mouth are relaxed. The sound is short and uses relatively little energy. The next sound on this line is /ɜ:/ as in *her*. You may find this in the same place as /ə/, or you may sense that the tongue is slightly further back. This sound is the longer, stressed cousin of /ə/. Again the tongue and mouth are relaxed, but the sound itself has more force. As you move the tongue to the back position, you should find a sound close to /ɔ:/. Here you may get a sensation of the back of the tongue being pulled to the back of the mouth, while the lips are pushed forward.

And now try the continuum /æ ... ɒ/. Here the tongue is in low position and the jaw is open. As you move the tongue back from /æ/ towards /ɒ/ you should find that you pass quite close to /ʌ/. In fact if you stop the tongue at a certain point, and make a very small adjustment, then you should have the sound /ʌ/. Can you find that point? What small adjustment, if any, do you have to make? As your tongue proceeds on its backward journey you will find yourself in the region of /ɑ:/. Again, see what adjustments are necessary.

Finally at the end of that continuum you have /ɒ/, which in English is short.

Commentary ■ ■ ■

In this activity we have found a rough and ready way of discovering vowels lying more or less on a line between other vowels. This is achieved by moving the tongue along the front–back continuum as shown by the three horizontal lines of vowels shown on the chart. (See Fig. 5.)

The aim of this activity is also to help you to become aware of which sounds are neighbours to which others, and exactly what you have to do to change one sound into another. Lip position is also important to 'tune' the sound made by the tongue position.

Fig. 5: Front, back and central monophthongs

You probably find that the movements involved are very slight, and at first give you little internal sensation. But as you keep your attention on it, you will find that it becomes more perceptible. Our aim is to gain insights that will qualify us to guide our learners. ■

Summary

Tongue position is the most important variable in determining the sound of a vowel. For each of the twelve English monophthongs the tongue is curved in some way, such that one part of the tongue is closer to the roof of the mouth than any other part. This raised part may be the front of the tongue, raised towards the hard palate; or the centre of the tongue, raised towards the juncture of hard and soft palate; or the back of the tongue, raised towards the soft palate. The resulting vowels are correspondingly referred to as *front, centre* or *back* vowels.

The vertical tongue position (high–mid–low)

To complete the description of a vowel, it is also necessary to fix the position of the tongue on a vertical axis – in other words, to state how far from the roof of the mouth the raised part of the tongue actually is. To describe this the labels *high, mid* and *low* are used. *High* denotes that the raised part of the tongue is relatively close to the roof of the mouth, and above the level it holds in 'neutral' position. *Low* denotes that the tongue is relatively distant from the roof of the mouth, and below the level it holds in neutral position. *Mid* indicates a neutral or middle position between these two extremes.

In the next discovery activity we'll explore this vertical positioning, and observe its effect on the mouth shape and on the resulting vowel sound.

Discovery activity 6 Vertical tongue position

Say the sound /iː/ and hold it. Slowly close the gap between the front of your tongue and the roof of your mouth (or more exactly the alveolar ridge, behind the top front teeth). Do this again whispering, and repeat until you have a clear sensation of the inner movement. You'll notice that as soon as you start to raise the tongue from the /iː/ position you start to get friction against the top of the mouth, and if you raise it any further, you stop the sound and the air flow altogether.

What this shows is that in the position for /iː/ the tongue is as high as it can be without causing audible friction.

Now take the position for the sound /æ/, and again close the gap between the front of your tongue and the roof of your mouth, and see how far it is this time. You should find that the gap is much wider than for /iː/. In fact for /æ/ the tongue is low in the mouth. If you can distinguish the physical sensation of these two tongue positions then you are noticing the difference between *high* and *low* tongue position.

Now look at the second vertical column in the monophthong section of the chart, /ɪ/ to /ʌ/. Say each sound in turn, both aloud and whispering. While saying each sound in turn close the gap between your tongue and the top of your mouth. Notice the size of the gap, and also where on the roof of your mouth your tongue touches.

Do the same investigation for the third column, /ʊ/ to /ɑː/, and for the fourth column, /uː/ to /ɒ/.

Commentary ■ ■ ■

In this activity we have explored four high–low pairs of vowels. The first of each requires the tongue to be high, that is as close as possible to the roof of the mouth without actually causing friction, and the second requires the tongue to be low, that is relatively distant from the top of the mouth, and below the neutral point of the tongue. (See Fig. 6.)

You will also have noticed that when your tongue moves between high and low, your jaw tends to move with it from a more closed position to a more open one. We'll investigate this further in discovery activity 9. ∎

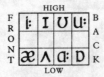

Fig. 6: High and low monophthongs

Discovery activity 7 Finding the in-between sounds in the vertical continuum

Take the first monophthong column on the chart, /iː/ to /æ/. Say /iː/, and gliding slowly towards /æ/, listen carefully to the changing vowel quality as your tongue lowers and your jaw opens. Stop at several points along the way, and see what vowel you have discovered. In theory there are many possibilities. In practice only one is English. About halfway between /iː/ and /æ/ you can isolate the sound /e/. Here the tongue is in mid or neutral position vertically, and in a front position horizontally. Try this both aloud and whispering.

Do the same with the second monophthong column, /ɪ/ to /ʌ/. Glide slowly from /ɪ/ to /ʌ/ while saying the sound, and notice the other 'in-between' vowel sounds that you can make if you stop the movement at any point. About halfway down this vertical glide, when the tongue is in mid or neutral position, you should find a sound which when made short, and with tongue and mouth relaxed, sounds like /ə/. This is known as a centre vowel because the tongue, jaw and lips are all in a relaxed, neutral posture.

Try the same sequence of experiments for the third vertical column, /ʊ/ to /ɑː/. At a point roughly midway you should find /ɜː/, which needs some length, and again requires your mouth, tongue and lips to be relaxed. This is also a centre vowel, and you may find that your tongue is in the same position as for /ə/, or it may be just a little further back.

Try the same sequence of experiments with the fourth vertical column, /uː/ to /ɒ/. At a point roughly midway between /uː/ and /ɒ/ you should find /ɔː/, which needs length, but also needs your tongue to be well back, giving the sensation of being bunched up at the back of your mouth. Rounding the lips is also important to achieve the exact acoustic quality. (More about this in the section on lip position, following discovery activity 11.)

Commentary ∎ ∎ ∎

In this activity we find that there is a position approximately midway between *high* and *low* where a third English vowel is produced. These *mid* sounds are shown in Fig. 7 on p 10. Lip position is also important to 'tune' the sound made by the tongue position. ∎

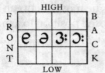

Fig. 7: The mid-vowels on the vertical continuum

Fig. 8: Summary of tongue positions: front–centre–back and high–mid–low

The traditional vowel box and the *Sound Foundations* phonemic chart

Traditionally the front–back and high–low co-ordinates of tongue position have been shown on a vowel box (Fig. 9a). A great number of different vowel sounds are possible within this vowel box, yet each language makes use of only a few of them, dividing up the space available to suit its own requirements.

The traditional vowel diagram (Fig. 9a) is transferred to the *Sound Foundations* phonemic chart (Fig. 9b) to give the layout shown in Fig. 9c. Fig. 9d shows how the chart relates to the mouth.

Fig. 9a   Fig. 9b   Fig. 9c

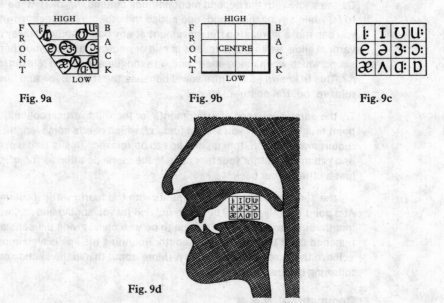

Fig. 9d

Discovery activity 8 Experiment with all the monophthongs

Look at the monophthong part of the phonemic chart.

1 Take any horizontal or vertical row and:

- say the sounds aloud, slowly, registering their inner physical movements;
- whisper the sounds;
- adopt the tongue postures, but without sound or exhalation.

2 Take symbols at random and say the corresponding sound both aloud and whispered.

3 Close your eyes or look away and think of monophthongs at random. Find the tongue posture, notice it, whisper and voice the sound. Then look back at the chart and locate the sound.

4 Look away and visualize the monophthong section of the chart in your mind's eye. Start anywhere. Visualize the symbol. Can you hear the sound in your mind's ear? And can you link that to a sensation of the muscular movement?

Schwa: a note on a special sound

The central vowel /ə/ can claim to be the 'smallest' English vowel sound and yet it is the only phoneme with its own name. It is by far the most frequent vowel sound in continuous speech, though it never carries stress. It is its unstressed nature that contrasts with stressed vowels to contribute to the rhythmical nature of English. ('You can't have stress without unstress' – more on this in Level 2 of the discovery toolkit.) Its correct use is crucial to the smooth rhythmic quality of spoken English. /ɜː/ is its longer, stressed equivalent.

Discovery activity 9 Sensitivity to jaw position

Place your forefinger on the bridge of your nose and the thumb of the same hand on the point of your chin. Say /iː/ and glide slowly to /æ/. Notice the downward movement of your jaw indicated by the increased distance between thumb and forefinger.

Try the movement /iː ... æ ... iː ... æ ... / several times both aloud and whispering to confirm the link between tongue lowering and jaw opening. Try the same activity with the other three vertical columns of monophthongs /ɪ/ to /ʌ/, /ʊ/ to /ɑː/ and /uː/ to /ɒ/.

Commentary ■ ■ ■

This illustrates that jaw position and tongue position are interlinked, so that when the tongue is relatively high or close to the roof of the mouth the jaw is usually relatively closed, while when the tongue is low the jaw is usually relatively open. This makes good mechanical sense as a more open jaw enables the tongue to move further (lower) from the roof of the mouth.

In some systems of vowel description the terms 'close–open', referring to jaw position, are used in place of the terms 'high–low', referring to tongue position. On the monophthong section of the phonemic chart, jaw position could be indicated as in Fig. 10. ■

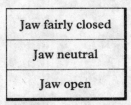

| Jaw fairly closed |
| Jaw neutral |
| Jaw open |

Fig. 10: Jaw positions for monophthongs

Discovery activity 10 High–low and close–open

In connected speech some speakers tend to use fairly minimal jaw movement while still producing the required vowel sounds. It will be helpful later to have experience of this.

Say a high vowel aloud, and glide to its opposite low vowel without opening your jaw any further. You may find that you can lower the tongue sufficiently to approximate the open sound without actually opening the jaw, though it probably sounds a little strangled.

Commentary ■ ■ ■

Now try it the other way: say the open vowels and try to glide towards the closed vowels by raising your tongue while keeping your jaw open. Not so easy is it! But store this experience in your memory for future use when working with learners who need to co-ordinate tongue and jaw movement. ■

Energy in the jaw

Another relevant aspect relating to the jaw is the energy stored and released there during the articulation of vowels. The setting of the jaw muscles for English is characteristically less tense than for some other languages (French, German, Italian, Spanish, for example).

Discovery activity 11 Energy and tension in the jaw muscles

Take monophthongs at random, and try increasing and decreasing the amount of energy you use in the jaw postures and movements. What do you change? How do you do this? What is the internal sensation? Does this provide any insight into your learners' difficulties?

Say a sentence in English and concentrate on the movement of your jaw. Try to register the sensation of tension and energy. Try the same experiment in another language. What do you notice? What implications could this have for your learners?

Commentary ■ ■ ■

So the relaxation or tension of jaw muscles provides another 'hook' for the development of awareness, and a variable that can help in 'getting the feel' of a language. ■

Lip position

We have been investigating the way in which the posture of the tongue affects the resonant space in the mouth. The lips can further modify the size and shape of the resonating space, and provide a kind of acoustic tuning to the fundamental vowel sound produced by the tongue position. Lip movement is easier to detect visually, and for many people easier to sense internally than the movement of the tongue.

In the following activities you can enhance your awareness of what you are doing:

- through the internal sensation of muscle tension and release in your lips;
- through your external sense of touch, using your fingers as described;
- through visual observation of your lips using a small mirror.

Discovery activity 12 Lip position

1 Say the sound /ɜː/ as in *sir*, and notice the position and shape of your lips. They should be relaxed and in a neutral position. If you detect any tension in lips, tongue or jaw, then try to let go. This lip posture is characteristic of English vowels where the tongue is in a central position.

2 Say /iː/ as in *me*. You'll notice that the lips spread, with some muscular tension, as if towards a half smile. This lip posture is characteristic of English vowels where the tongue is in a high–front position. Now exaggerate the lip position into a full smile, noticing the change in internal sensation, and in the sound produced.

3 Say /uː/ as in *too*. You'll find that your lips become rounded, as if towards a whistling position. Notice the internal sensation of the muscle tone. This lip posture is characteristic of English vowels where the tongue is in a high–back position. Try exaggerating the lip position by rounding them more tightly and pushing them further forward. Notice the different sound linked to the different muscular sensation.

4 Say /æ/ as in *sad*. Your lips should be open and spread. This lip posture is characteristic of English vowels where the tongue is in a low–front position.

5 Say /ɔː/ as in *door*. The rounding of your lips is probably not as tight or as forward as for /uː/ but nevertheless very obvious, and helps to obtain the right sound. Notice the contrast in this vowel position between the forward posture of the lips and the back posture of the tongue. This lip posture is characteristic of English vowels where the tongue is in a mid–back position.

6 Now try these activities again, but this time:

- whispering the vowel. Your ear still picks up the unvoiced characteristics of the vowel which you can relate to lip positions;
- silently. Removing the sound entirely may help you attend more fully to the internal sensation of muscle tone in your lips;
- using a mirror to compare the visual movement of your lips with the internal sensation of movement.

Commentary ■ ■ ■

Try to make the connection between the sensation of the lip muscles in different positions and the effect on the sounds that you hear. It's important to become sensitive to all the visual clues of pronunciation, because they will help you to know what your learners are trying to do, which in turn will help you to help them. See if you can relate your own lip positions in discovery activity 12 to the examples shown in Fig. 11. ■

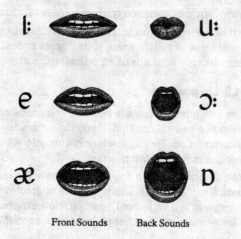

Front Sounds   Back Sounds

Fig. 11: Examples of lip positions for front and back vowels

Discovery activity 13 Lip rounding and spreading

1 Start with the sound /iː/. Touch the tip of your thumb gently against one corner of your lips, and the tip of your forefinger against the other corner. Now change /iː/ very gradually to the sound /uː/. Slowly alternate /iː ... uː ... iː ... uː ... / letting thumb and forefinger follow the movement of your lips. This should tell you that your lips are alternating between spread and rounded. Now exaggerate the lip movement. Notice the internal sensation.

2 Using your fingers in the same way, what lip rounding and spreading can you detect when moving between these pairs?

/e ... ɔː ... e ... ɔː ... /
/æ ... ɒ ... æ ... ɒ ... /

Commentary ■ ■ ■

The aim of this activity is to sharpen the sensation of lip rounding and spreading by providing external tactile evidence. ■

Discovery activity 14 Forward and backward lip movement

1 Start with the sound /iː/. Touch your forefinger lightly against the front of your lips. Now change /iː/ very gradually to the sound /uː/. Slowly alternate /iː ... uː ... iː ... uː ... / while maintaining contact between finger and lips. You should get a clear indication that your lips are moving forward when rounded and backward when spread.

2 Try the same thing with these pairs:

/e ... ɔː ... e ... ɔː ... /
/æ ... ɒ ... æ ... ɒ ... /

3 Try the same activities silently, attending to the sensation of lip movement on its own.

Commentary ■ ■ ■

This activity is intended to illustrate that forward movement of the lips is part of the lip-rounding movement, and that backward movement of the lips is part of the lip-spreading movement. Fig. 12 contains this information.

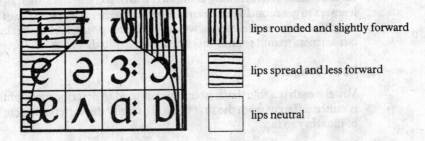

lips rounded and slightly forward

lips spread and less forward

lips neutral

Fig. 12: Lip position superimposed on the monophthong chart

However, the correspondence between back vowels and rounded lips, and between front vowels and spread lips, is not necessarily a tendency in other languages. Now that you can change tongue position and lip position independently and at will, you can also try producing front vowels with lips rounded and back vowels with lips spread. This results in interesting non-English sounds, and gives further insights into difficulties some learners may have and how to help them. The next discovery activity goes into this. ■

Discovery activity 15 Doing the 'opposite' lip movements

This activity involves doing the opposite of what is indicated in Fig. 12.

1 Say /iː/ with the lips spread as usual, but then round your lips while holding the tongue position constant. What happens? First the posture may feel awkward and unfamiliar (if English is your mother tongue), and second you probably get a sound you recognize from several other languages (including French, Swedish, and German, but not English). What you have is the non-English combination of forward tongue with forward, rounded lips. This is a good illustration of how the lip position can fine-tune the resonating space created by the tongue to make up the overall sound.

2 Try the corresponding activity. Say /iː/ with the lips spread as usual, and then hold the lip position constant while moving the tongue back in the mouth towards /uː/. Think /iː/ with your lips and /uː/ with your tongue, and what do you get?

3 Say /e/, and holding the tongue position constant gradually round your lips. How does that alter the sound? Try the same with /æ/.

4 Say /e/, and hold your lip position constant while moving your tongue back. Notice the resulting rather nondescript vowel sound. Try the same with /æ/.

5 Try the following activities, and notice the non-English vowels you invent:

- Say /uː/, hold the lips constant and move the tongue forward.
- Say /uː/, hold the tongue constant while you spread the lips.
- Say /ɔː/, hold the lips constant and move the tongue forward.
- Say /ɔː/, hold the tongue constant while you spread the lips.
- Say /ɒ/, hold the lips constant and move the tongue forward.
- Say /ɒ/, hold the tongue constant while you spread the lips.

Try these aloud, whispered, and silently.

Commentary ■ ■ ■

Perhaps these activities have reminded you of some of the attempts by your learners to get round a new sound. If we as teachers can be aware of these variables within ourselves, we will be in a better position to understand and help our learners to find sounds that are unfamiliar to them. ■

Vowel length

Vowel length is a fourth variable which is used to describe monophthongs, and it is rather different from the first three. To clarify this difference here's a summary of the story so far:

Vowels get their characteristic sound quality from the shape and size of the resonant space in the mouth, and this resonant space is determined by:

- the horizontal tongue position (front–centre–back);
- the vertical tongue position (high–mid–low); and
- the lip position (rounded–neutral–spread).

Each of these variables affects the acoustic quality of the sound itself, while the fourth variable, vowel length, concerns not the quality, but the quantity, or length, or duration of the monophthong.

Discovery activity 16 Making monophthongs longer or shorter

Look at the monophthong section and say each vowel:

1 as you normally say it;
2 making it last longer than usual, though not changing the quality of the sound;
3 giving it the briefest duration you can, but not changing the quality of the sound.

iː	ɪ	ʊ	uː
e	ə	ɜː	ɔː
æ	ʌ	ɑː	ɒ

Fig. 13: Monophthong section

Commentary ■ ■ ■

Are there any which seem more 'comfortable' when short, or when long? You may find that some vowels are easier to lengthen or shorten, and that you have distorted the quality of others. This may relate to habitual associations you make between certain tongue postures and length, and other postures and brevity. ■

Discovery activity 17 Five long vowels

In English there are five vowels usually designated as being relatively longer than the others, and these are indicated by a length mark (a colon) after the symbol. They are /iː, uː, ɜː, ɔː, ɑː/.

Say them aloud, and note your subjective feel for the length of each of them as said in isolation. Do the ones with length markers /iː, uː, ɜː, ɔː, ɑː/ in fact seem to you relatively longer?

Commentary ■ ■ ■

Two points to note about length:

1 English vowels are traditionally referred to as long or short. A long vowel tends to have a longer duration than a short vowel in the same context. But length is not an absolute attribute of any vowel.

2 A second point to note is that length is not the only thing that distinguishes long vowels from short ones. Monophthongs differ from each other in the quality of the sound regardless of whether they are longer or shorter. ■

Discovery activity 18 Length in identical contexts

Say these words several times over. Ignore the difference in the quality of the vowels and try simply to observe the length of each vowel compared to the others. The consonants are identical in each case in order to make it easier to compare the vowels:

/hiːt/	heat
/hɪt/	hit
/huːt/	hoot
/hʌt/	hut
/hɑːt/	heart
/hɒt/	hot
/hɜːt/	hurt

Commentary ■ ■ ■

What you should find is that on the whole the vowels with length marks are longer than the others. If you don't notice this it could either be that you are not making any difference in length, or that you are making the difference but you do not notice it. In either case don't despair, but try the next activity! ■

Discovery activity 19 Reversing length in identical contexts

Say these four words, and again try to notice the relative length of the vowels:

bead	/biːd/
bid	/bɪd/
bard	/bɑːd/
bud	/bʌd/

Now try each 'English' word with normal vowel length (below, left-hand column) and compare it with another 'non-English' word with reversed vowel length (right-hand column). If the symbol is normally long, then you shorten it; if normally short, you lengthen it. Phonetically you try to say this:

'English' (normal vowel length)	'Non-English' (reversed vowel length)
/biːd/	/bid/
/bɪd/	/bɪːd/
/bɑːd/	/bad/
/bʌd/	/bʌːd/

Try this several times until you can distinguish each of these eight 'words' from each other. If you find you can't distinguish them, don't worry. I find it difficult too! But at least try to understand what the activity is demanding.

Commentary ■ ■ ■

Notice that /iː/ is not just a long /ɪ/, and that /ɑː/ is not just a long /ʌ/. Note also that the vowel symbols in the right-hand column are not on the phonemic chart.

These experiments may run counter to your habitual manner of speaking, and this in a nutshell is the problem of learning a new pronunciation. An aim of these activities is to make ourselves conscious of what we are doing habitually, so that we can intervene and change things at will. Then we will be able to help our learners to do the same. That is why I see this approach to pronunciation as being based on awareness, or consciousness, rather than on mechanicity (eg non-aware repetition), which seems to be the implicit basis of some approaches. ■

Discovery activity 20 Length in non-identical contexts

1 Say each of these words:

/biːt/	beat
/biːd/	bead

Say them quickly as well as drawn out. Can you notice any difference in length? If not, then shorten the duration you give to each vowel until you find a point at which one of them still sounds acceptable, while the other has become too short to be identifiable. Which is which?

What you may observe is that /iː/ in *bead* tends (or needs) to be a little longer than /iː/ in *beat*. Don't be put off by the fact that you can also give them both the same length!

2 Here's the same experiment with /ɪ/:

/bɪt/   bit
/bɪd/   bid

Say each word aloud and whispered. Can you notice any difference in length? If not, then shorten the duration you give to each word until you find a point at which one of them still sounds acceptable, while the other has become too short to be identifiable.

Even if you can't find any difference, the action of trying to observe length more accurately will help develop your sensitivity to the variables of sound production. In my opinion it is your sensitivity rather than your accuracy that ultimately facilitates your learners' learning.

3 Now compare the relative length of /iː/ and /ɪ/ in this context:

/biːt/   beat
/bɪd/   bid

Here you may find that the long and the short vowel are roughly the same length. So, what is going on?

Commentary ■ ■ ■

The general tendency you may have observed in these examples is that vowels are shortened in stressed syllables closed by a *fortis* consonant, eg /p, t, tʃ, k, f, θ, s, ʃ/, and are given more length in stressed syllables closed by a *lenis* consonant, eg /b, d, dʒ, g, v, ð, z, ʒ/. (*Fortis*, meaning strong, describes consonants characteristically produced with a strong breath force. In English these are coincidentally the unvoiced consonants. *Lenis*, meaning gentle, describes consonants characteristically produced with a weaker breath force. In English these are coincidentally the voiced consonants. We will study this further in discovery activity 34.) ■

This tendency (and it is a tendency not a rule) operates on both long and short vowels (ie with or without length marks), so that in the previous activity you may have found that a long vowel /iː/ before an unvoiced consonant can be approximately the same length as a short vowel /ɪ/ before a voiced consonant.

Length marks do not indicate that a vowel is absolutely longer all the time. Length is quite a variable matter, depending particularly on whether the syllable is stressed or not (which we'll examine in the discovery toolkit Level 2), and on the quality of the neighbouring sounds.

Summary

Some vowels tend to be characteristically longer or shorter than others, and other factors such as speed of speech, phonemic context, stress, etc further modify vowel length. If you learn to notice this as it occurs then you'll be in a good position to help your learners make changes when necessary. The essence of this approach is not primarily to learn or remember rules about phonology, but to become more sensitive to the experience of what is happening in the vocal tract, as it is happening. In other words to know it from the inside, not just from the outside.

HELP If you're not clear about this, or if you're wondering how relevant it is, then stay with it! For the moment take my word that it will become clear, and that you will find it relevant to the creation of your own classroom toolkit for working with pronunciation.

Discovery activity 21 Observing length in the special case of /æ/

Although traditionally indicated as a short vowel, /æ/ often has special length, particularly before a *lenis* (or voiced) consonant, eg /b, d, dʒ, g, v, ð, z, ʒ/, when it may become as long as any of the five traditionally long vowels.

1 In which of the columns does /æ/ seem longer?

/mæn/ man	/mæp/ map
/bæd/ bad	/bæk/ back
/sæm/ Sam	/sæt/ sat
/ræg/ rag	/ræt/ rat

As before, you can explore the contrast by lengthening and shortening the pairs, and you may find a point where the words in the first column feel uncomfortably short, while the words in the second column still seem viable. The point here is that /æ/ is likely to be considerably longer before *lenis* consonants (for example those in the left column above).

2 So let's compare the length of /æ/ when it's in a long context (ie a syllable closed by a *lenis*, or voiced, consonant) with a traditional long vowel in the same context.

/mæn/ man	/miːn/ mean
/bæd/ bad	/biːd/ bead
/sæm/ Sam	/siːm/ seem

Commentary ■ ■ ■

The point here is that /æ/ is often as long as a long vowel, especially before a *lenis* consonant. You don't need to remember exactly when or why, but it would be useful to begin to notice it in your own speech and that of your learners. ■

Summary

Here are the key points on vowel length.

1 The length mark indicates that a vowel may be relatively longer in the same phonemic context than one without such a mark.

2 It is useful to develop sensitivity to vowel length differences when practising vowel sounds in isolation, and artificial lengthening and shortening of vowels can be a useful awareness-raising exercise. This is explored further in the classroom toolkit, 'Working with individual sounds'.

3 In stressed syllables, vowels and diphthongs tend to be shorter when followed by a *fortis* (or unvoiced) consonant and given more length when followed by a *lenis* (or unvoiced) consonant.

4 /æ/ in particular is given special length before *lenis* consonants, and practice of this characteristic may help learners to distinguish more clearly between /æ/ and its neighbouring short vowels on the chart, /e/ and /ʌ/.

5 With the possible exception of /ə/ and /ɜ:/, there are no pairs of vowels distinguished from each other solely by length. The traditional pairs /i:/ and /ɪ/, /u:/ and /ʊ/, /ɔ:/, and /ɒ/ all have differences in tongue position as well as length differences. In fact, since length is relative and variable according to context, the difference in quality between these pairs may be of more importance in distinguishing between them.

Discovery activity 22 Overview of the chart layout

Experience for yourself the logic behind the arrangement of the monophthong vowels on the chart:

1 Take the first horizontal row of sounds on the chart, /i:, ɪ, ʊ, u:/, and say them in order from the left of the chart to the right (ie from the front of the mouth to the back). Notice how the raised hump of the tongue rolls along from front to back.

2 Now take the same sequence, but glide smoothly and without stopping through all four vowels, making one continuous and drawn-out movement, and again notice the tongue moving back and the lips moving forward for rounding.

3 Now try both experiments with the sequence in reverse, /u:, ʊ, ɪ, i:/, ie from the back of the mouth to the front, or from the right of the chart to the left.

4 Do the same three experiments for the second row, /e, ə, ɜ:, ɔ:/, noticing that the jaw is a little more open, that the tongue again moves between front and back and that there is considerable lip rounding for /ɔ:/.

5 And now try the same three experiments for the third row, /æ, ʌ, ɑ:, ɒ/, noticing that the jaw is now relatively more open, and that the tongue makes a corresponding front–back movement though further from the roof of the mouth.

6 Now take each of the four vertical columns in turn, /i:, e, æ/, /ɪ, ə, ʌ/, /ʊ, ɜ:, ɑ:/ and /u:, ɔ:, ɒ/. These show movement from high to low tongue position, ie from top to bottom on the chart.

First say each of the three sounds separately, then as a continuous glide, and then in the reverse direction.

Also focus on the changing distance of the tongue from the roof of the mouth, on the movement of the jaw, and on the relationship of these two variables to the position of the lips.

7 Glide quickly and then slowly between any two neighbouring sounds on the chart. Can you find a sound which is in-between the two, neither one nor the other? Your learners are probably quite good at that! It can be very instructive to find these midway points, and to sense keenly the minute muscular change required to make it clearly one sound or the other.

Commentary ■ ■ ■

Bear in mind that our aim is not primarily to 'learn the theory', but to become more aware of the subtle muscular sensation of each sound. If we can do this we will be in a better position to appreciate what our learners are doing, and in a better position to help our learners to be more aware of what they are doing, so that we can find the best strategies to help them. ■

3 Vowels: diphthongs

Diphthongs are the result of a glide from one vowel to another within a single syllable. The diphthong in *game* has the phonemic symbol /eɪ/, indicating a glide from /e/ to /ɪ/. These represent the two extremes of vowel movement; the starting point, or *first element*, /e/, glides towards the *second element*, /ɪ/.

A diphthong is perceived as one phoneme not two, and therefore as one syllable not two, so each diphthong occupies a single box on the chart. Thus *say* /seɪ/ is one diphthong and one syllable, whereas *seeing* /siːɪŋ/ is a sequence of two monophthongs occupying two syllables. In the activities that follow, experiment with lengthening and shortening both the first and second elements, and with putting the stress on either element. But as a general rule the first element is slightly longer than the second, and has more emphasis. (We will investigate length and stress in diphthongs more fully in activities 29 and 30.)

The diphthong section of the chart shows eight diphthongs grouped in three vertical columns according to their second element.

ɪə	eɪ	
ʊə	ɔɪ	əʊ
eə	aɪ	aʊ

Fig. 14: Symbols for glides in the diphthong section

The first column has /ə/ as the second element. These three diphthongs are called *centring* diphthongs, as the glide towards the second element is towards the central vowel /ə/.

The second column has /ɪ/ as the second element, and the third column has /ʊ/ as the second element. The five diphthongs in these two columns are called *closing* diphthongs, as the glide towards the second element is towards the high or closed vowels /ɪ/ and /ʊ/.

In the next activities we will investigate the closing diphthongs first and then the centring diphthongs.

Discovery activity 23 Three diphthongs gliding to /ɪ/

1 Each of the following word pairs contains a monophthong in the first column and a diphthong in the second. Say each pair, and compare the movement of your lips and tongue in relation to the vowel sound produced.

debt /det/	date /deɪt/
bore /bɔː/	boy /bɔɪ/
hut /hʌt/	height /haɪt/

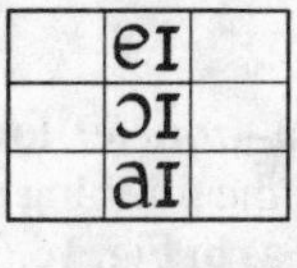

Fig. 15: Glides to /ɪ/ in the diphthong section

Commentary ■ ■ ■

Notice that in the first pair the monophthong symbol in the first word, /e/, is also the first element of the diphthong symbol /eɪ/ in the second word. The same is true of the second pair except that /ɔː/ loses its length mark in the diphthong symbol /ɔɪ/. However in the third pair you'll notice that the diphthong symbol is /aɪ/ and not /ʌɪ/. I'll explain this in the next activity. ■

Discovery activity 24 Focusing on the glide to /ɪ/

If plotted on the monophthong section of the chart these three diphthongs would look like this:

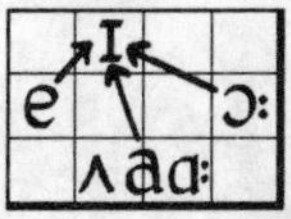

Fig. 16: Glides to /ɪ/ shown in the monophthong section

1 Say /e/ and /ɪ/ separately to locate them. Now join them smoothly by gliding from /e/ to /ɪ/. Try this several times and notice the upward movement of your tongue and closing of your jaw. Try it aloud, whispered and silently. You should have /eɪ/ as in *date*.

2 Say /ɔː/ and /ɪ/ separately, and then join them with a glide. This gives the diphthong /ɔɪ/ as in *boy*. Notice the lip movement from rounded to spread and the forward and upward movement of the tongue. Try to make a link between this inner muscular sensation and the corresponding change in sound. As already pointed out, the diphthong symbol /ɔɪ/ does not retain the length mark from /ɔː/.

3 There is a third diphthong that has /ɪ/ as its finishing point. Establish /ʌ/ and /ɪ/ separately and then join them with a glide. This gives you the diphthong /aɪ/ as in *height*. We have already observed that the symbol used is not notated as /ʌɪ/. According to phoneticians the first element of this diphthong is a sound that can be notated as /a/, but which in standard English does not exist as a phoneme on its own. If it did it would be somewhere between /ʌ/ and /ɑː/, which is where I have shown it in the diagram. For practical purposes I use /ʌ/ as the first element, and I help learners to build these two diphthongs by first pointing to /ʌ/ on the chart. The results are always entirely satisfactory.

Commentary ■ ■ ■

These three glides start in three different places, mid–front /e/, low–centre /ʌ/ and mid–back /ɔ:/, and all converge on /ɪ/, high–front, as the finishing point. They can be plotted on the monophthong section of the chart as in Fig. 16. The monophthong section provides a good worktable on which to introduce, revise, or repair diphthongs (see classroom toolkit 1, 'Working with individual sounds'). You can also use the monophthong section of the chart to invent other non-English diphthongs as a creative exercise. ■

Discovery activity 25 Two diphthongs gliding to /ʊ/

1 Each of the following word pairs contains a monophthong in the first column and a diphthong in the second. Say each pair, and compare the movement of your lips and tongue in relation to the vowel sound produced.

sir /sɜː/   so /səʊ/
done /dʌn/   down /daʊn/

Fig. 17: Glides to /ʊ/ in the diphthong section

Commentary ■ ■ ■

In the first pair (*sir* and *so*) the monophthong symbol /ɜː/, which is the long version of the central vowel, changes to the shorter version /ə/ in the diphthong. In the second pair (*done* and *down*) you'll see that again the diphthong symbol is /aʊ/ and not /ʌʊ/.

Both starting points, /ə/ and /ʌ/, have the tongue at approximately the same point on the front–back axis. However, /ʌ/ has the tongue lower and the lips and jaw more open. In a sense it has a more definite and energetic muscular posture. /ə/ has a mid-tongue position, with tongue and lips relaxed. ■

Discovery activity 26 Focusing on the glide to /ʊ/

If plotted on the monophthong section of the chart, these two glides would look like this (Fig. 18):

Fig. 18: Glides to /ʊ/ shown in the monophthong section

1 Establish separately the two sounds /ə/ and /ʊ/ and then join them with a smooth glide. Check that your glide does not distort the starting or finishing points. Try it several times, noticing the tongue and lip movement. The tongue moves from a neutral central position upward and backward to /ʊ/. The lips move from a relaxed posture to a more rounded posture. The target sound is /əʊ/ as in *no* and *home*. Try exaggerating the movement slightly, and get tactile and visual feedback on the movement by touching your finger to your lips, and by looking in a mirror.

2 Locate the two sounds /ʌ/ and /ʊ/ in your mouth, and then join them with a glide. This will give you the sound /aʊ/ as in *now* and *town*. Once again this is written as /aʊ/ and not as /ʌʊ/. As discussed above, the first element, /a/, is a sound that does not exist as a phoneme on its own. If it did it would be somewhere between /ʌ/ and /ɑ:/. See if you can locate /a/. Take the two sounds /ʌ/ and /ɑ:/ and glide slowly between them. With a little practice you'll be able to find a point between them: /a/.

For classroom purposes, as I have said, I use /ʌ/ as the first element, and I help learners to build these two diphthongs by first pointing to /ʌ/ on the chart, and then to the second element.

Commentary ■ ■ ■

Notice the similarity between /aʊ/ and /əʊ/. Both converge on /ʊ/, though do not usually reach that position, and both have the tongue starting at approximately the same point on the front–back axis. However /a/, or /ʌ/ as I use, has the tongue lower and the lips and jaw more open. /ə/ has the mid-tongue position, with both tongue and lips relaxed. Can you see the difference between these two sounds in a mirror? ■

Discovery activity 27 Discriminating /aʊ/ and /əʊ/

Try alternating the two diphthongs /aʊ/ and /əʊ/. Focus on the difference in the internal muscular sensation and relate this to the different acoustic sensation. Notice that a small shift in starting point makes a clear difference to the sound. This contrast can be seen in the following words:

no	now
phoned	found
tone	town
a rose	arouse

Discovery activity 28 Three centring diphthongs

We have experimented with the five closing diphthongs used in standard English. In this activity we'll look at the three which glide towards a central rather than a closed sound. For this reason they are called *centring* diphthongs.

Each of the following word pairs contains a monophthong in the first column and diphthong in the second. Say each pair, and compare the movement of your lips and tongue in relation to the vowel sound produced.

bid /bɪd/   beard /bɪəd/
put /pʊt/   pure /pjʊə/
dead /ded/   dared /deəd/

Iə		
Uə		
eə		

Fig. 19: Symbols for centring glides in the diphthong section

First pair (*bid* and *beard*). Identify /ɪ/ and /ə/ separately and then join them with a smooth glide. Notice the downward movement of your tongue and your jaw. This may be very slight, so you could try magnifying the movement just to see what is going on. Try it aloud, whispered and silently. You should have the diphthong /ɪə/ as in *ear* and *dear*.

Second pair (*put* and *pure*). Establish the individual sounds /ʊ/ and /ə/ and then join them with a glide. This will give you the diphthong /ʊə/ as in *cure* and *pure*. Notice the lip movement from rounded to neutral, and the downward movement of the tongue. There seems to be an on-going tendency in RP to replace /ʊə/ with /ɔː/. I myself certainly say /ʃɔː/ rather than /ʃʊə/ and though I still say /pjʊə/ and /kjʊə/ I feel quite comfortable with /pjɔː/ and /kjɔː/.

Third pair (*dead* and *dared*). Start with /e/ and glide to /ə/. This gives you the diphthong /eə/ as in *air* and *hair*. Notice the tongue movement, which again can be quite slight. Tongue height is mid for both elements, and the movement is back towards the centre. It is not so much the body of the tongue that moves back, though this is quite possible, but the raised part. You can check this by putting your finger or a pen on your tongue while making this glide. My own observation is that this diphthong is frequently reduced to a composite monophthong, something like a long /eː/.

Commentary ■ ■ ■

Many learners find these three diphthongs less obvious, or more elusive, than the other five. I think this is partly because it is hard to find good examples. Not only are they less frequent than the other five, but as we observed above, the realization of two of them in RP is frequently 'monophthongized'.

But I think there is another possible and interesting explanation. When you plot them on the monophthong section of the chart (Fig. 20) you see that the component monophthongs are much closer together than is the case with the other two sets of diphthongs. In fact all three are immediate neighbours, thus restricting the amount of glide that is possible in any case. These diphthongs involve less movement between first and second elements than some others. In this sense perhaps they can be seen as 'weaker', and therefore less likely to survive in the use of the language. Compare Fig. 20 with Figs. 18 and 16. ■

Fig. 20: Centring glides shown in the monophthong section

Length and stress in diphthongs

Both of these features are important in determining how 'English' a diphthong sounds. Although length and stress are related, it can be helpful to focus on them separately, especially when working with learners who are trying to relax the grip of their mother tongue phonemic set. So we'll consider them separately in the next two activities.

Discovery activity 29 Length in diphthongs

1 Take any diphthongs (for the moment let's use these three):

/eɪ/ as in *take*
/əʊ/ as in *bone*
/ɔɪ/ as in *coin*

Try to make the second element longer than the first, and make the first deliberately short. Do this with each diphthong on its own, and then in the context of the given word. If you have managed to make the second element longer than the first, and if you try the glide in the context of words, you should find that it sounds distinctly 'unEnglish'.

2 Now make the first element longer than the second. Again try several diphthongs both in and out of context. You should notice that they sound more English.

Commentary ■ ■ ■

As a general guide you can think of a diphthong as having about the duration of a long vowel, and most of this duration is focused on the first element. This characteristic is different in English from many other languages.

As with so much else in pronunciation, in order to get it right it can be helpful to do consciously what is not right. A good illustration of this is the activity you have just done, where deliberately putting the length on the second element helps you to know what is involved in putting the length on the first element. We'll do this in the following activity too. ■

Discovery activity 30 Stress in diphthongs

This is really the same as the previous activity, but with a different focus. You'll see why as soon as you try it.

1 Take the same three diphthongs:

/eɪ/ as in *take*
/əʊ/ as in *bone*
/ɔɪ/ as in *coin*

Try to give the second element more stress than the first, and make the first deliberately less stressed. Try this with the diphthongs on their own, and then with the words. Once again this should make the diphthong and the word sound definitely 'unEnglish'.

2 Now give the first element more stress than the second. Adjust the amount of stress until it sounds about right for English.

3 Now that you have the stress on the first element sounding about right, say the words normally and pay particular attention to the way in which you unstress the second element, and to how this affects the quality of sound of the second element. Notice too that you do not have to arrive fully at the position of the second element, but just 'head in that direction'.

Commentary ▨ ■ ■

The point to notice is that a diphthong is one syllable, yet with two sounds, of which the first is usually longer and more stressed. You'll also have noticed the close relationship between duration and stress, something examined more fully later on. ■

The visual aspect of diphthongs

As you did the previous activities, you may have been struck by the degree to which the mouth movements of diphthongs are visually detectable. Any movement from one vowel to another must involve a movement of the tongue, and quite possibly a movement of the lips and jaw as well. This can provide a useful teaching and learning instrument. The visual side of pronunciation is examined in depth in the classroom toolkit, Level 1. Here is a useful preparatory activity.

Discovery activity 31 The visual clues of diphthongs

1 Say each of the diphthongs and, using a hand mirror, just observe the movements.

2 Now exaggerate the movement of each diphthong while observing in the mirror, and also listening to the quality of the sound.

3 Which glides seem to you to have the most movement, and which the least? Try miming the diphthongs silently. Which sounds can you 'see' clearly? Remember that deaf people lip read proficiently in all languages!

4 Try a few words containing diphthongs. Can you lip read yourself? Well, try with a colleague.

4 Consonants

Here are two definitions of consonants, both of them useful in adding to the background of insight from which we can help our learners to help themselves. The activity that follows enables you to test the definitions against your experience.

Definition 1

Consonant sounds are made by restricting or blocking the air flow in some physical way, and this restriction, or the release of the restriction, is what gives the consonant its characteristic sound. By contrast, vowels require the vocal tract to be open so that the air stream escapes unobstructed.

Commentary ■ ■ ■

This distinction between consonants and vowels is useful as far as it goes, but it is not watertight because there are two consonants, /w/ and /j/, that are made without any restriction to the air flow, and in this sense are like vowels (they are in fact also called semi-vowels). ■

Definition 2

Consonants, either singly or in clusters, mark the beginnings and ends of syllables. Vowels occur as the centres or focal points of syllables, either between consonants or on their own.

Commentary ■ ■ ■

This definition takes account of /w/ and /j/ because these sounds can mark the boundaries of syllables in the same way as the other consonants do, eg *wet, yet, lower, layer.*

Both definitions are useful, but number 2 is the *functional* or *phonemic* definition that is usually used to distinguish vowels from consonants. According to this definition English has twenty-four consonant phonemes, though not all of them can function at both the beginning and the end of syllables. ■

Discovery activity 32 Distinguishing consonants and vowels

This activity is a simple practical test of the two definitions above.

1 Take any words at random (I suggest you take the sentence you are reading now), say them slowly and aloud, and focus your attention on how you make each successive sound.

Do you notice that for each consonant there is some kind of restriction on the air flow, while for the vowel there is no restriction but simply a tongue posture that tunes your voice to the vowel required? If so, you are finding evidence for definition 1.

Say the first sentence again, and pay particular attention to the initial sound of *words* and *you*. Do you notice that in each case there is no block or restriction to the air flow, but simply a shape of the tongue and lips not unlike a vowel? If so, then you are finding the exceptions to definition 1.

2 Now take the same sentence again and focus on the way in which the consonants mark the beginnings and ends of syllables, even in the case of /w/ and /y/. If you can observe this, then you are finding evidence for definition 2.

Commentary ■ ■ ■

Don't worry if you can't find these distinctions. They will become clear during the next activities. What's important is that by trying to notice what you do, you are gradually strengthening your power of observation.

Describing the twenty-four consonants

All consonants (with the exceptions of /w/ and /j/) involve a restriction to the outflow of air, and it is the precise place and manner of this restriction that gives each consonant its unique sound. We can describe the uniqueness of each consonant quite well using these three variables:

1   voiced or unvoiced;
2   place of articulation (**where** the sound is produced in the vocal tract);
3   manner of articulation (**how** the sound is produced in the vocal tract).

Here are a few words about these three variables:

Variable 1: voiced or unvoiced

A sound is said to be *voiced* if it requires the vocal cords to vibrate, and *unvoiced* if it does not. In English the voiced/unvoiced distinction tends to coincide with gentle and strong aspiration (also referred to as *lenis* and *fortis*). This means that voiced consonants may be uttered with weaker breath force, while unvoiced consonants may be uttered with stronger breath force. (This is partly because voiced sounds take energy from the breath in order to drive the larynx, and partly because unvoiced sounds need to compensate for their lack of voice with force and clarity in their articulation.)

Variable 2: place of articulation

The place in the vocal tract where the physical restriction or block to the air flow takes place is referred to as *place of articulation*, ie **where** the characteristic component sounds of that consonant are initiated.

Variable 3: manner of articulation

The nature of the physical restriction to the air flow is referred to as *manner of articulation*, ie **how** the characteristic component sounds of that consonant are initiated.

By combining these three variables we arrive at a practical working description of how each consonant is produced. And since the consonants are arranged on the phonemic chart according to these three variables, understanding the layout will give you a useful grasp of how the consonants are made and how they can be altered.

P	b	t	d	tʃ	dʒ	K	g
f	v	θ	ð	s	z	ʃ	ʒ
m	n	ŋ	h	l	r	w	j

Fig. 21: The arrangement of consonants on the chart

Discovery activity 33 Voiced/unvoiced distinction

1 Look at Fig. 22. It is the same as Fig. 21 but focuses on different aspects of the sounds. The + signs indicate that the sound is voiced, ie that the vocal cords are vibrating. The – signs show that the sound is unvoiced, ie that there is no such vibration. What is the pattern behind the distribution of +'s and –'s?

–	+	–	+	–	+	–	+
–	+	–	+	–	+	–	+
+	+	+	–	+	+	+	+

– unvoiced and *fortis*
+ voiced and *lenis*

Fig. 22

2 Look back to Fig. 21 and say any of the consonant sounds whose symbols you recognize. Refer to Fig. 22 to see whether you agree that the sound is voiced or unvoiced. You will have to say each consonant with a vowel, so you could try long ones such as /iː/ or /uː/ or /ɜː/. Try the consonant both before and after the vowel.

Commentary ■ ■ ■

You'll have noticed that in the first two rows the +'s and –'s alternate. Each pair of one plus and one minus indicates a pair of consonants whose only difference is that the first sound of each pair is unvoiced and *fortis*, while the second is voiced and *lenis*: for example, /t d/, /f v/, /s z/. The bottom row consists entirely of voiced sounds except for /h/.

The distinction *fortis* and *lenis* is very useful when working with learners. It involves the degree of muscular effort and breath force used to produce the consonant. In this respect we can divide consonants roughly into strong and weak. The next activity draws attention to this. ■

Discovery activity 34 Strong and weak consonants

1 Use the list of paired words below. Say each pair aloud, checking that the sounds are the same except for the voiced/unvoiced distinction.

2 Whisper the same pair. Try to hear and feel the difference in the force of your breath. If you put your open palm close to your lips you can also feel the difference in the force of the expelled air. For example:

pea	bee
tea	dee
chore	jaw
came	game
fire	via
three	then
sue	zoo
mission	measure

Commentary ■ ■ ■

You should find that even when you whisper you can still distinguish between the consonants on the left and those on the right. The question is how did you make that difference? You probably found that you made the consonants on the left with a relatively stronger muscular effort and force of exhalation, and those on the right with a relatively weaker degree of muscular effort and exhalation. The terms used to describe this are respectively *fortis* (strong) and *lenis* (gentle).

In conclusion, then, voicing and unvoicing is not the only difference between these pairs of consonants. There is the additional and separate choice of putting more or less energy into the breath. It happens that in English it is the voiced consonants /b, d, dʒ, g, v, ð, z, ʒ/ etc that are *lenis*, or weaker in their force of exhalation, and their unvoiced counterparts /p, t, tʃ, k, f, θ, s, ʃ/ etc that are *fortis*, or stronger in their force of exhalation. Of these unvoiced consonants it is particularly those in the first row on the chart that are given this stronger exhalation.

When the voicing distinction is reduced or absent, as for example when you whisper, then the *fortis/lenis* distinction may be the only remaining contrast between a pair of consonants.

The link between voiced and *lenis*, and unvoiced and *fortis*, that is natural to the native English speaker may not be natural to learners whose mother tongues may have voiced *fortis* consonants and unvoiced *lenis* consonants. The difficulties they may face are simulated in the next activity. ■

Discovery activity 35 Reversing *fortis* and *lenis*

In this activity you are going to try to make consonants that are not English.

We'll use the list of paired words from discovery activity 34, but this time put stronger breath force on the consonants in the right column, and weaker breath force on the consonants in the left column. (This means working against your habit, but you need to be an expert on that since it is what you are helping your learners to do.) Put your open palm in front of your lips to give you feedback on when you have successfully reversed the *fortis/lenis* distinction. Do this aloud, not whispered.

pea	bee
tea	dee
chore	jaw
came	game
fire	via
three	then
sue	zoo
mission	measure

Commentary ■ ■ ■

The amount of energy and the degree of breath force is a subtle but significant variable which happens to coincide with voicing (in English) and so often gets lost behind it. One practical point here is that guiding learners to vary the amount of muscular energy and breath force they use in speaking English can be very helpful. I have found this to be true both at the level of individual sounds and at the level of connected speech in general.

In the next section we will look at the other two variables, which concern the manner of articulation and the place of articulation. The layout of the phonemic chart is configured to contain these variables, so it is useful to consider one row at a time. ■

Row 1 plosives and affricates: /p, b, t, d, tʃ, dʒ, k, g/

Variable 1: voice and breath

For the sake of completeness, here is a diagrammatic summary of the first row in terms of voice and breath force variables.

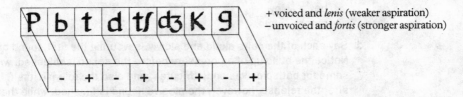

+ voiced and *lenis* (weaker aspiration)
− unvoiced and *fortis* (stronger aspiration)

Fig. 23: Consonants, row 1

Variable 2: manner of articulation

This concerns the way in which the air flow is restricted to make the characteristic sound of a consonant. The next activity will help you to focus on this and to identify how you make each sound.

Discovery activity 36 The plosive consonants

1 Take each of the consonants in the first row, and choose a vowel to follow it. You could use these words:

pie by too do cheer jeer course gorse /p, b, t, d, tʃ, dʒ, k, g/

Say each one aloud slowly, and try to notice the first audible signal of each of the consonants. What are you doing in your mouth at that point? What internal movement coincides with the very beginning of the consonant sound? Try this several times until you can focus on the precise point. You need to ignore the following vowel, perhaps even omit it, in order to focus on the consonant.

2 Do the same again but this time whisper and notice two things: what happens in your mouth immediately *prior* to the onset of the consonant, and what happens immediately *at* the onset of the audible consonant?

Commentary ■ ■ ■

You probably notice that there is a build-up of air just before the sound starts, and that there is a sort of pop as the air is released and the consonant sound too is released. Sounds made by such a build-up and release, like a mini-explosion, are called *plosives*. For plosives, the air stream is completely blocked by the tongue or lips, held momentarily, then the pressure is released explosively. A plosive in a final position is called a stop when the air pressure is stopped but not released. For example, you can say *stop* either releasing or not releasing the air pressure after /p/.

All of the eight consonants you tried in the first row are produced in this way, with a slight variation on the fifth and sixth sounds /tʃ/ and /dʒ/. These two sounds also begin with a build-up of pressure, but the release stage is a little slower, producing a more fricative noise. Hence these two sounds are termed *affricates*, which we can treat as a subdivision of plosives. Try the next activity just to clarify this. ■

Discovery activity 37 Contrasting plosives and affricates

On the left are words beginning with plosive sounds and on the right words beginning with the two affricate sounds.

tease	cheese
pin	chin
boy	joy
dump	jump

1 Say each of the pairs aloud and slowly, savouring the first sound of each word. Notice the build-up of air pressure before the sound is released, which is the same for both plosives and affricates, and also the release itself. Immediately after the release, however, the plosive sound is finished, while the affricate sound still has a short audible friction to follow.

2 Try whispering the pairs. What other contrast can you notice?

3 Try miming the words. If you exaggerate slightly, is there a purely visual difference?

Commentary ■ ■ ■

You can see from the phonemic symbols of the affricates that they are composed of two consonants merged together, /tʃ/ = /t/ + /ʃ/ and /dʒ/ = /d/ + /ʒ/. However, these are not glides between two sounds as with vowel diphthongs, but mergers of two sounds so that they happen almost at the same time. In each case the first symbol represents the plosive part and the second the fricative part. (More on fricatives from discovery activity 39 onwards.) ■

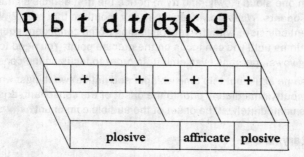

Fig. 24: The first consonant row showing voiced/unvoiced and manner of articulation of plosives and affricates.

Variable 3: place of articulation

In discovery activity 36 we found that the consonants in the first row are produced 'plosively', that is by building up and then releasing air pressure. The next question is where exactly in the mouth does this build-up and release occur?

Although there are eight phonemes in this row, there are only four places in the mouth where the air block is made. These four places give four different and characteristic sound qualities, and the voiced/unvoiced contrast in each place gives a total of eight sounds. The next activity will help you to experience this.

Discovery activity 38 Where the plosives and affricates are produced

1 /p/ and /b/. Say the words *pie* and *by*. Where in your mouth do you block and release the air flow? You'll find that your two lips come together to block the air stream, hence the technical term *bilabial* (*bi* + *labial* = two + lips) to describe this place of articulation.

If we include manner of articulation, then the pair are called *bilabial plosives*, and to distinguish between them we can use the full description:

unvoiced bilabial plosive = /p/
voiced bilabial plosive = /b/

Both /p/ and /b/ can occur in both initial and final position, eg /pɪn/, /nɪp/ and /bɪn/, /nɪb/.

2 /t/ and /d/. Say the words *too* and *do*. Where in your mouth do you block and release the air flow? Contrast this place with /p/ and /b/ as in *pie* and *by*. Notice that /t/ and /d/ are formed a little further back, when the front part of your tongue (the 'blade') makes contact with the bony ridge immediately behind your upper front teeth.

At this point the block to the air stream is both made and released. The technical term to describe this manner of articulation is *alveolar* (*alveolum* being the Latin name for this ridge). If we include manner of articulation then this pair are called *alveolar plosives*, and to distinguish between them we can use the full description:

unvoiced alveolar plosive = /t/
voiced alveolar plosive = /d/

Both /t/ and /d/ can occur in both initial and final position, eg /tiːn/, /niːt/ and /diːn/, /niːd/.

3 /tʃ/ and /dʒ/. Say the words *cheer* and *jeer*. Where in your mouth do you block and release the air flow? Contrast this position with the position for /p/ and /b/ and /t/ and /d/. Notice that /tʃ/ and /dʒ/ are formed a little further back, when the blade of your tongue makes contact with the junction between the alveolar ridge and the hard palate, and the body of the tongue is slightly raised towards the hard palate.

The technical term for this place of articulation is *palato-alveolar*, and so we can call this pair *palato-alveolar affricates*. We can distinguish between the pair by including voicing:

unvoiced palato-alveolar affricate = /tʃ/
voiced palato-alveolar affricate = /dʒ/

Both /tʃ/ and /dʒ/ can occur in initial and final position, eg /tʃɜːtʃ/, /dʒʌdʒ/.

4 /k/ and /g/. Say the words *course* and *gorse*. Where exactly do you block and release the air flow? Contrast this position with the position for /p/ and /b/, /t/ and /d/, /k/ and /g/ and notice that /k/ and /g/ are formed still further back. The air stream is blocked when the back of your tongue is in contact with the soft palate.

The technical term for this place of articulation is *velar* (*velum* = veil, ie the soft tissue hanging at the back of the palate, also called soft palate). So we can call this pair *velar plosives,* and we can distinguish between them by including voicing:

unvoiced velar plosives = /k/
voiced velar plosives = /g/

Both can occur in both initial and final position, eg /kɪk/, /gɪg/.

5 The front–back continuum. Say the unvoiced sounds in the sequence /p ... t ... tʃ ... k/. Notice that the place of articulation moves progressively back in the mouth. Try the voiced sequence /b ... d ... dʒ ... g/.

Commentary ■ ■ ■

We have now explored the first row consonants in terms of the three variables that characterize the way they are produced (voicing, manner and place). Fig. 25 summarizes this. ■

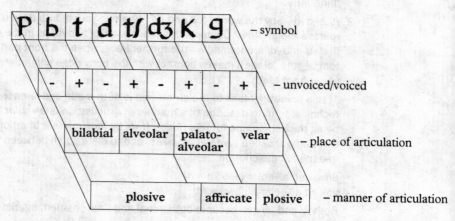

Fig. 25: Diagrammatic summary of plosives and affricates

The information in Fig. 25 can be merged to give the standard technical description of each of the sounds (Fig. 26). The references to places of articulation are illustrated in Fig. 27 on p 37.

unvoiced bilabial plosive	voiced bilabial plosive	unvoiced alveolar plosive	voiced alveolar plosive	unvoiced palato-alveolar affricate	voiced palato-alveolar affricate	unvoiced velar plosive	voiced velar plosive

Fig. 26: Standard technical description of consonants in row 1

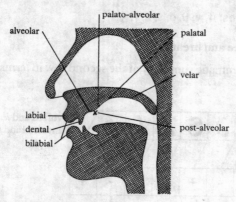

Fig. 27: Places of articulation

Glottal stop

Though frequently used by speakers of RP the glottal stop is not considered a significant sound in that it cannot change the meaning of a word. Thus it is not given phonemic status and does not figure on the *Sound Foundations* phonemic chart. But since it is quite frequent, especially in rapid colloquial speech, I would like to describe it at this point.

The glottal stop is a plosive produced by a complete block to the air stream at the glottis. The air pressure is then suddenly released. The stop itself is perceived as a silence beginning with the sudden cessation of the previous sound and ended by the sudden onset of the following sound. It can be described as an unvoiced glottal plosive (or stop), and is denoted by the symbol /ʔ/.

The glottal stop can be used:

1 to give emphasis to a syllable beginning with a vowel, eg *Am I?* /ʔæm aɪ/ *Excellent!* /ʔeksələnt/ *It's easy!* /ɪtsʔ iːzi/
2 between adjacent vowels belonging to different syllables (instead of a glide), eg *co-operate* /kəʊʔɒpəreɪt/;
3 to avoid an intrusive /r/, eg *I saw it* /aɪ sɔːʔ ɪt/ (See discovery activity 67 for intrusive /r/);
4 to replace or reinforce an unvoiced plosive /p, t, k/ at the end of words, eg *what* /wɒʔ/, *shock* /ʃɒʔ/, *sip* /sɪʔ/.

You and your learners will notice the occurrence of /ʔ/ in authentic listening material and amongst some native speakers. It is worth practising in context at the same time as practising the articulation it is replacing. This will give insight and help listening comprehension. When working with the glottal stop you can write the symbol /ʔ/ in a box either on the board or on a square of paper beside the chart.

Row 2 fricatives: /f, v, θ, ð, s, z, ∫, ʒ/

Variable 1: voice and breath

Here is a diagrammatic summary of the second row in terms of voice and breath force variables.

+ voiced and *lenis* (weaker aspiration)
− unvoiced and *fortis* (stronger aspiration)

Fig. 28: Consonants, row 2

Variable 2: manner of articulation

This concerns the way in which the air flow is restricted to make the characteristic sound of a consonant. The next activity will help you to focus on this and to identify how you make each sound in row 2.

Discovery activity 39 The fricative consonants

1 Take each of the consonant sounds in the second row, and choose a vowel to follow it. You could use these words:

fire via three then sue zoo shore measure /f, v, θ, ð, s, z, ∫, ʒ/

Say each one aloud slowly. What movement in your mouth coincides with the first audible sound of each consonant?

2 Do the same again but this time whisper, and notice two things: what happens in your mouth immediately prior to the onset of the sound, and what happens immediately at the onset of the audible sound?

3 Try miming the words. If you exaggerate slightly can you see visual clues for each consonant?

Commentary ■ ■ ■

For these eight consonant sounds the air flow through the mouth is not completely blocked, though it is restricted. (If it were blocked a plosive sound would be produced.) Even before the sound begins there may be a slight 'air leak' through this restriction.

At the beginning of the sound you'll notice an increase in the pressure of air behind the restriction, producing an audible friction which provides the characteristic sound of that consonant. Sounds produced by this kind of friction are called *fricatives*, and, unlike plosives, fricatives can be sustained and given longer or shorter duration. ■

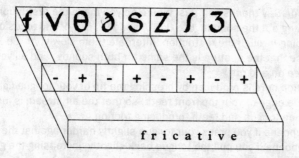

Fig. 29: The second consonant row on the chart contains the eight fricative consonants in their unvoiced/voiced pairs. The diagram also indicates manner of articulation.

Variable 3: place of articulation

In activity 39 we found that the second row of consonants are produced by friction, which involves restricting the air flow through the mouth. Although there are eight phonemes in this row, there are only four places in the mouth where the restriction to the air flow is made, each place yielding two phonemes, one voiced and one unvoiced. These four places give four different and characteristic sound qualities, and the voiced/unvoiced contrast in each place gives a total of eight sounds. The next activity will help you to experience this directly.

Discovery activity 40 Where fricatives are produced

1 /f/ and /v/. Say the words *fire* and *via* aloud. Where in your mouth do you make the restriction that causes the friction?
Draw out the sound of /v/, and notice where you feel the vibrations.
Adopt the posture for /f/ and inhale instead of exhale. Does the incoming air help to locate where the friction occurs?
Alternate the two sounds slowly /f ... f ... v ... v ... f ... f ... v ... v/ and notice that the position is the same for them both: the only change is that you turn your voice on and off. Observe how you use a certain muscle in the throat to turn the voice on and off. Observe also how the breath force increases when you turn the voicing off.

You should find that you are producing the friction for this consonant by pressing your bottom lip lightly against the edge of your top front teeth. The technical term for this place of articulation is *labio-dental* (*labio* = lip, *dental* = teeth). This pair are therefore *labio-dental fricatives*, and to distinguish between them we can include the voicing variable:

unvoiced labio-dental fricative = /f/
voiced labio-dental fricative = /v/

/f/ and /v/ can occur in both initial and final position, eg /flʌf/, /vælv/.

2 /θ/ and /ð/. Say *thanks* and *this*. Where do you make the restriction?
Try drawing out the sounds /θ ... θ ... θ/ and /ð ... ð ... ð/ and focus on how the air
is escaping through the restriction. Alternate them slowly: /θ ... ð ... θ ... ð ... θ ...
ð/. Notice that the posture is the same for both sounds, and all you do is turn
your voice on and off.
The friction here is produced by pressing the tip of your tongue lightly against
the inside edge of your top front teeth, so that the air stream is just able to flow
in between tongue and teeth, producing friction.
What happens if you press your tongue slightly harder against the teeth? And
what happens if you pull the tongue back slightly, increasing the gap between
tongue and teeth?
These two sounds are referred to as *dental fricatives*, so the full description of
each is:

unvoiced dental fricative = /θ/
voiced dental fricative = /ð/

/θ/ and /ð/ can occur in both initial and final position, eg /θɜːd/, /fɔːθ/, /ðɪs/,
/smuːð/.

3 /s/ and /z/. Say *Sue* and *zoo*. Where do you make the restriction to the air flow
and the resulting friction?
Draw out the sounds /s ... s ... s ... / and /z ... z ... z ... / and alternate them
slowly. Notice that the posture is the same for both sounds; all you have to do
is turn your voice on and off. Notice how you do this, how voicing may in turn
also affect the breath force.
The friction is produced by pressing the blade of your tongue lightly against the
alveolar ridge, and so these two are referred to as *alveolar fricatives*. /s/ is
unvoiced and *fortis*, while /z/ is voiced and *lenis*, so:

unvoiced alveolar fricative = /s/
voiced alveolar fricative = /z/

/s/ and /z/ can occur in both initial and final position, eg /zuː/, /praɪz/, /saɪ/, /aɪs/.

4 /ʃ/ and /ʒ/. Say *fashion* and *fusion*. Where do you produce the friction?
Draw out each of the sounds, and then try alternating them on their own: /ʃ ... ʒ ...
ʃ ... ʒ ... /. Once again, notice how they both have the same mouth and tongue
posture, and you make the difference by turning your voice on or off.
The friction here is produced with the tongue at a point slightly further back from
/s/ and /z/, so that the blade of the tongue is roughly opposite the join between
the alveolar ridge and the palate. In addition, the centre of the tongue is raised
towards the hard palate, the air flowing with some friction between the raised
tongue and the hard palate. The term used for this place of articulation is *palato-
alveolar*, and these two sounds are known as *palato-alveolar fricatives*:

unvoiced palato-alveolar fricative = /ʃ/
voiced palato-alveolar fricative = /ʒ/

/ʃ/ can occur in both initial and final position, eg /ʃɪp/, /fɪʃ/.
/ʒ/ does not occur initially, and very rarely finally, eg /ɡærɑːʒ/, but is frequent
intervocalically, ie in the middle of words, eg /pleʒə/, /vɪʒən/.

5 The front–back continuum. Say the unvoiced sounds in the sequence /f ... θ ... s ... ʃ ... / and notice that the place of articulation moves progressively back in the mouth. The same goes for the voiced sequence /v ... ð ... z ... ʒ .../.

Commentary ■ ■ ■

We have now explored the second row consonants in terms of the three variables that characterize the way they are produced (voicing, manner and place). Fig. 30 summarizes this. ■

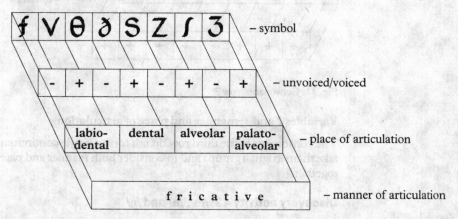

Fig. 30: Diagrammatic summary of fricatives

Notice how the spectrum from front to back is featured in the chart layout.

The information in Fig. 30 can be merged to give the standard technical description of each of the sounds (Fig. 31).

unvoiced labio-dental fricative	voiced labio-dental fricative	unvoiced dental fricative	voiced dental fricative	unvoiced alveolar fricative	voiced alveolar fricative	unvoiced palato-alveolar fricative	voiced palato-alveolar fricative

Fig. 31: Standard technical description of fricatives

Row 3: The other consonants /m, n, ŋ, h, l, r, w, j/

Discovery activity 41 Variable 1: voice and breath

Say these words and see whether you are voicing or unvoicing the row 3 consonants: _m_ay, _n_o, si_ng_, _h_er, _l_ie, _r_are, _w_hy, _y_es. Do you agree with Fig. 32?

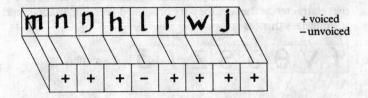

+ voiced
− unvoiced

Fig. 32: Consonants, row 3

Variables 2 and 3: manner and place of articulation

The consonants in the third row do not form a single continuum, so it is easier to take them in small groups and to consider both manner and place of articulation together.

Discovery activity 42 /m/, /n/ and /ŋ/

1 Say /m/, /n/ and /ŋ/ on their own and in the context of words, for example _may, no, sing_. What have the three sounds got in common in the way they are produced?

You probably observe that the air stream carries the sound through your nose, hence the term _nasal_ for these three sounds. You can check this by saying the sounds while at the same time pinching your nose (or catching a heavy cold). So the manner of articulation of these three sounds is nasal, and since all three are voiced the only thing that differentiates them is the place in the mouth where the air stream is blocked and diverted through the nose.

2 Sustain each of /m/, /n/ and /ŋ/ on its own. Where in your mouth are you making the block that diverts the air stream up through your nose? Where do you sense the vibrations of your voice for each sound?

For /m/ you bring your two lips together to close off the air stream through your mouth. The place of articulation is therefore _bilabial_ (two lips). You can probably feel the vibrations in your lips, and also the way your closed mouth space adds resonance to the sound. The full description of this sound is _voiced bilabial nasal._ /m/ occurs initially and finally: /mʌm/.

For /n/ you obstruct the flow of air through your mouth by bringing the blade of your tongue into contact with the alveolar ridge immediately behind the upper front teeth. The place of articulation is therefore _alveolar_. When you sustain /n/ you can probably feel the vibration in your tongue and in the bone at the top of your mouth.

Say the other alveolar sounds /t, d, s, z/. Can you observe the similarity with /n/ in the place of articulation? The full description of this sound is _voiced alveolar nasal._ /n/ occurs both initially and finally: for example, /nʌn/.

For /ŋ/ you obstruct the air stream through your mouth by bringing the back of your tongue into contact with the soft palate. The place of articulation is therefore velar. Compare /ŋ/ with the other velar sounds /k, g/. Can you observe the similarity? The full description of this sound is *voiced velar nasal*. /ŋ/ does not occur initially, but is common in final position: for example, /sɪŋ/.

Commentary ■ ■ ■

The three sounds /m, n, ŋ/ are voiced and nasal. What differentiates them is the place in the mouth at which the air stream is diverted through the nose. The three places for /m, n, ŋ / are respectively the same as for /p, b/, /t, d/ and /k, g/, with the difference that the block is complete and is maintained for the duration of the sound.

Notice that the three places of articulation form points on a continuum from front to back with bilabial /m/ at the front, alveolar /n/ further back, and velar /ŋ/ at the back. Try saying the three in sequence to notice that backward shift, which is reflected in their arrangement on the phonemic chart. ■

Discovery activity 43 /h/: manner and place of articulation

1 Say these four words slowly, and observe the posture of your tongue, lip and jaw during the sounding of /h/.

hat /hæt/
heat /hiːt/
hot /hɒt/
hoot /huːt/

You should notice that the tongue, lip and jaw position for /h/ in each word is the same as that which is required for the following vowels, in this case /æ, iː, ɒ, uː/. In other words there is no single tongue/lip posture for /h/. Rather, /h/ is produced with the mouth cavity shaped according to the requirements of the following vowel.

So if the place of articulation of /h/ is as for the following vowel, then what is the manner of articulation that is characteristic of /h/?

2 Notice the presence and absence of /h/ within each pair, and the four different ways that /h/ is produced.

/iːt/ /hiːt/
/æt/ /hæt/
/ɒt/ /hɒt/
/uːt/ /huːt/

Try it a few times and you'll probably notice a stronger expulsion of air from the lungs (*fortis*) than is required for the vowel alone, causing friction in the vocal tract (*fricative*), which is already shaped in readiness for the following vowel. So we could say that the manner of articulation of /h/ is *fortis fricative*. And since /h/ adopts the place of articulation of the following vowel it can be called an *onset* (ie taking the position of what follows). I think of this sound as being like the cuckoo – it has no place of its own, but finds its home in the nests of others.

The full description of /h/ is *unvoiced fortis fricative onset*. It occurs initially, for example /hærɪ/, but not finally.

Commentary ■ ■ ■

/h/ can be articulated in any of the twelve different mouth/tongue postures corresponding to the twelve English monophthongs. ■

Discovery activity 44 /l/: manner and place of articulation

1 Say these words and observe how you form the sound /l/: *lay, low, lie, lee, lovely*.

Notice that you can sustain the initial part of the /l/ sound indefinitely, and that while you are doing that there is a partial (though non-fricative) closure to the air stream.

2 Where exactly do you form this partial closure to the air stream? Say the example words slowly, and observe how the blade of your tongue makes contact with the alveolar ridge (the same place as for /s, z, t, d, n/, so we can say that the place of articulation is *alveolar*.

3 Say the words again and focus your attention on how the air stream escapes past this partial closure. You'll find that air escapes over each side of your tongue while the blade is in contact with the alveolar ridge. You can check this by forming the tongue position for /l/ and then drawing air in through the mouth. You can feel the cold air on each side of the tongue. This manner of articulation is *lateral* (ie the air goes over the sides).

4 If you whisper a prolonged /l/ and alternate it with a prolonged whispered /s/, like this /l ... l ... s ... s ... l ... l ... s ... s ... /, you can feel that with /l/ the tip of the tongue touches the alveolar ridge and the air escapes around the sides, and with /s/ the sides of the tongue touch the teeth, forcing the air out between the blade of the tongue and the alveolar ridge. The place of articulation for both sounds is alveolar, but of course the manner is different.

The full description, then, is *voiced alveolar lateral* = /l/.

Commentary ■ ■ ■

The sound described above is often referred to as *clear* /l/, formed when the alveolar lateral gives way to a following vowel, as the tongue breaks contact with the roof of the mouth.

Another allophone (variant) of /l/ referred to as *dark* /l/ occurs after vowels, for example /wel/; before consonants, for example /təʊld/; and as a syllable, for example /metl/. This is sometimes called *syllabic* /l/. I prefer not to use syllabic /l/ in phonemic transcription. I find it more helpful to learners to show the syllable with the vowel /ə/, thus: /metəl/.

Dark /l/ is formed in the same way as clear /l/, but the tongue does not break contact with the roof of the mouth so that the alveolar lateral sound is maintained. And in addition the back of the tongue is also raised towards the soft palate, contributing a certain velar or 'back vowel quality', while clear /l/ has a more 'front vowel quality'. The word *little* /lɪtəl/ contains clear /l/ at the beginning and dark /l/ at the end, though as I pointed out above I prefer to include /ə/ in the phonemic spelling. ■

Discovery activity 45 /r/

1 Say these words and observe how you form /r/: *rare, raw, ray, row.* Say them very slowly. Pay attention to the initial position of your tongue, and to its movement towards the following vowel. Notice that you can sustain the /r/ sound indefinitely.

2 Take any one of the example words and repeat it over and over..Notice the rhythmical movement of your tongue up and down in your mouth. What tongue movement can you see in a mirror?

In the starting position the tip of your tongue is raised close to the rear part of the alveolar ridge, but far enough from it to produce a sound that has no friction. While the tip of the tongue is curved upwards, the central part of the tongue is lowered, completing the overall sensation of the tongue being curled upwards.

3 /r/ is frictionless because the air stream escapes freely, without friction, over the central part of the tongue. You can check this by forming your tongue in the /r/ position and then drawing air in through your mouth. You should feel the cold air passing along the centre of your tongue.

4 Notice that this position is similar to the tongue position for /ʃ, ʒ, tʃ, dʒ/ except that for /r/ the tip of the tongue is raised a little further back in the mouth, behind the alveolar ridge, and for /ʃ, ʒ, tʃ, dʒ/ it is the blade of the tongue that makes the friction.

Say each of the sounds: /ʃ, ʒ, tʃ, dʒ/ and after each say /r/. You should notice that the tip of your tongue moves back over the palate, thus also increasing the distance from the roof of the mouth, ensuring that the sound has no friction. This place of articulation is referred to as *post alveolar*, ie 'a little behind' the alveolar position of /t, d/ and also a little behind the palato-alveolar position of /ʃ, ʒ, tʃ, dʒ/.

Putting all this together, we get the technical description *post alveolar frictionless continuant*. Post alveolar refers to the place of articulation. The manner of articulation is frictionless and continuant, which means that it can be sustained in a vowel-like way.

/r/ is usually voiced, though devoicing may occur in certain contexts. It occurs initially in all types of English, and finally in many types of English, eg American, Scottish, Irish (called *rhotic* varieties) but not in British RP (called *non-rhotic*). In rhotic varieties /r/ can also occur before consonants and before silence.

Discovery activity 46 /w/ and /j/

Say the words slowly and focus attention on the first sound of each:

/wet/ wet		/jet/ yet	
/west/ west		/jes/ yes	
/wu:/ woo		/ju:/ you	
/wɔ:/ war		/jɔ:/ your	
/wɜ:/ were		/jɜ:/ year	

Notice that there is no restriction to the air flow during the first sound, and so no friction or closure characteristic of most consonants. Note also that you can maintain the initial sound indefinitely.

In this way the manner of articulation of /w/ and /j/ is rather vowel-like, and they are often referred to as semi-vowels. Although semi-vowels may be phonetically described in terms of vowels, they function as consonants in that they precede the main vowel of a syllable. (See the definitions of consonants above discovery activity 32.) We'll investigate the two sounds in turn.

Discovery activity 47 /w/

Get ready to say the word *wet*, but don't actually say it. What is your tongue and lip position? Now say the very beginning of the sound, and try to freeze your tongue and lip posture at that point and maintain the resulting sound. This starting sound is close to /ʊ/, with lips rounded and tongue back. You can test this:

Repeat /wiː/ several times rapidly: /wiː ... wiː ... wiː ... wiː ... /. And now repeat /ʊiː/ rapidly: /ʊiː ... ʊiː ... ʊiː ... ʊiː ... /. They should sound very similar, especially if you keep /ʊ/ very short.

So the sound which has the symbol /w/ is in fact /ʊ/, of very short duration, gliding rapidly to the following vowel. Try the list at the beginning of discovery activity 46 above, putting a very short /ʊ/ in place of /w/ in each word: for example, /ʊet/ instead of /wet/. Do they sound the same? You may find there is a stronger lip movement with /w/.

The exact starting position depends on the nature of the following vowel, but it is usually characterized by rounded lips, hence the full description of /w/ as a *voiced bilabial semi-vowel*. /w/ occurs initially but not finally.

Discovery activity 48 /j/

Get ready to say the word *yes*, but don't actually say it. What is your tongue and lip position? Now say the very beginning of the sound, and try to freeze your tongue and lip posture at that point and maintain the resulting sound. This starting sound is close to /ɪ/, with lips neutral or slightly spread and tongue slightly closer to the alveolar ridge, creating almost a hint of friction. You can test this:

Repeat /jɔː/ several times rapidly: /jɔː ... jɔː ... jɔː ... jɔː ... /. And now repeat /ɪɔː/ rapidly: /ɪɔː ... ɪɔː ... ɪɔː ... ɪɔː ... /. They should sound very similar, especially if you keep /ɪ/ very short.

So the sound /j/ in fact begins with /ɪ/, of very short duration, gliding rapidly to the following vowel. Try the list on the right in activity 46 above, putting a very short /ɪ/ in place of /j/ in each word, eg /ɪes/ instead of /jes/. Do they sound the same?

The exact starting position of /j/ depends on the nature of the following vowel, but it is usually characterized by the tongue being close to the palate, hence the full description of /j/ as a *voiced palatal semi-vowel*. /j/ occurs initially but never finally.

Discovery activity 49 /r, w, j/ as linking sounds

The last three sounds on the bottom row of the chart are placed together as they share an important characteristic in 'stream of speech' English, namely that they link together two words, where the first ends with a vowel sound and the second begins with a vowel. Say the following phrases normally and quite quickly. Also try them slowly. Observe what happens at the boundary between the first two words. How do you link them? Do you insert another sound?

> Africa and Asia
> you and me
> me and you

You may find that you naturally introduce a 'hint' of the linking sounds:

> Africa /r/ and Asia
> you /w/ and me
> me /j/ and you

We will investigate this more thoroughly in Level 3, 'Sounds and simplifications in connected speech'.

Commentary ■ ■ ■

The bottom row of consonants contains several groupings. The nasal sounds are in order of front to back (left to right on the chart). /l/ and /r/ are together, the semi-vowels /w/ and /j/ are together, the linking sounds /r/, /w/ and /j/ are also together. The odd one out, /h/, is in the middle. ■

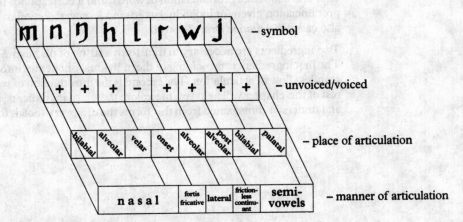

Fig. 33: Consonants (row 3) showing manner and place of articulation

voiced bilabial nasal	voiced alveolar nasal	voiced velar nasal	onset: unvoiced fortis fricative	voiced alveolar lateral	post alveolar frictionless continuant	bilabial semi-vowel	palatal semi-vowel

Fig. 34: Standard technical description of row 3 consonants

Level 2   Words in isolation

1 Introduction   48

2 Joining individual phonemes to make words   49

3 Stress in words   51

4 Unstress in words   53

5 Primary and secondary stress   54

6 Where do you put the stress in words?   55

7 Intonation and word stress   57

1 Introduction

In Level 1 we focused on the individual sounds, or phonemes, of English RP, their various characteristics and how to make and alter them. In the discovery activities we worked on the minimum understanding necessary as a basis for creative teaching.

Now, in Level 2, we put these phonemes together into sequences to form syllables and words. Level 2 pronunciation focuses on words spoken carefully in isolation. This kind of pronunciation is recognized by native speakers of English as a slow, clear and deliberate pronunciation of words, and it corresponds to the pronunciation given for individual words in a learners' dictionary. It is sometimes also called the *citation form* of a word.

Two ingredients are necessary to transform a string of phonemes into a word. The first ingredient is the joining of the individual phonemes into a single, seamless flow of articulation. The second is the introduction of word stress. The rest of this chapter will help you to explore these two ingredients, and the insight and understanding gained from this forms the discovery toolkit for Level 2.

2   Joining individual phonemes to make words

The pronunciation of a word is more than the sum of its individual phonemes. It consists rather of a flow of sound in which it may no longer be obvious exactly where one phoneme ends and the next begins. At Level 1 we stopped this flow and broke it into individual segments; we arrested the natural flow of sound in order to identify the fixed points for closer study. In doing that we necessarily made these individual phonemes larger and more tangible than they are when they occur in words. That has given us a sound foundation on which to reassemble the parts back into the whole, and what we have to remember at Level 2 is that words consist of a flow of sound rather than a sequence of fixed sounds. (The same process of melting the parts into a fluid whole is repeated again at Level 3, where words are assembled back into the greater whole of connected speech.)

Discovery activity 50   Joining sounds to make words

1   Take any word and say each of its phonemes clearly, slowly and separately. This is Level 1 pronunciation.

2   Repeat this several times, gradually joining the phonemes together to make the word. This is Level 2 pronunciation.

You can try with these words:

Level 1	Level 2	
/f...ɔː...tʃ...ə...n...ə...t.../	/fɔːtʃənət/	fortunate
/e...k...s...p...l...ə...r...e...ɪ...ʃ...ə...n/	/ekspləreɪʃən/	exploration
/p...r...ə...n...ʌ...n...s...ɪ...e...ɪ...ʃ...ə...n/	/prənʌnsɪeɪʃən/	pronunciation
/f...l...ə...ʊ...ɪ...ŋ/	/fləʊɪŋ/	flowing

Commentary ■ ■ ■

Notice how at Level 1 the sounds are separate, unconnected. As you move towards Level 2 notice how the phonemes begin to flow, or melt, into one another, affecting and changing each other, and forming a seamless flow. Notice how the phonemes overlap, so that the second phoneme is forming before the first has finished. (The technical word for this is *coarticulation*, literally 'together articulation'.) For example, with /prənʌnsɪeɪʃən/, notice how your tongue is already in the position for /r/ while your lips are making /p/.

Whereas at Level 1 there is a space between the sounds which is not part of the word, at Level 2 the movement between two sounds is incorporated into the two sounds and into the pronunciation of the word. So the pronunciation of the word is made up of the movement through each phoneme as well as the movement between each phoneme. ■

Discovery activity 51 The dancers and the dance

1 Say the words in activity 50 clearly and not too fast. Put your attention on the following:
• your tongue, and notice the complex but smooth 'dance' that it makes around the available space in your mouth;
• your lips;
• your jaw movement;
• the turning on and off of your voice.

Notice how each organ has its own dance, which is perfectly choreographed with that of the others.

2 Try this with any word you can see in this text, and with words from other languages.

Commentary ■ ■ ■

The more aware you become of this dance taking place in your own mouth, the more insight you will be able to bring to bear when working with your learners.

Although the pronunciation of a word can be represented by a sequence of phonemic symbols, the phonemes in the context of a word do not necessarily have the same sound as when they are spoken in isolation. What happens is that the phonemes are run together so that each one interacts with and modifies the quality of its neighbours. These variations of a single phoneme, resulting from the pressure of its phonetic context, are called *allophones* (literally 'different + sound'). An allophonic change does not carry any significance. Therefore it does not change the meaning, and is understood as one possible representation of the parent phoneme. ■

Discovery activity 52 Using the chart to slow down and speed up pronunciation

1 Take any word and point it out to yourself on the chart. Say each sound aloud as you do so and notice how this slows your pronunciation down to Level 1, and forces you to focus on each sound as an entity in itself.

2 Again take a word and point it out to yourself on the chart, but this time retain the sounds in your memory without saying them. When you have finished pointing, say the word aloud:
• first, as a string of isolated sounds (Level 1);
• second, as a connected stream of sounds but very slowly (Level 2, slow);
• third, connected together and at normal speaking speed (Level 2).

Commentary ■ ■ ■

This theme of slowing things down in order to shape and change the elements, and then speeding them up again in order to have fluency as well as accuracy, is one that will recur in verbal interventions used by the teacher, in the use of finger correction, and in the use of Cuisenaire rods. ■

Stress and the phonemic chart

The International Phonetic Alphabet (IPA) uses the symbol /'/ for primary stress and the symbol /,/ for secondary stress. They are displayed in the top right-hand corner of the chart, just to the left of the intonation symbols, and you activate them by touching them with the pointer at the beginning of the syllable to be stressed.

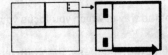

Fig. 35: Stress symbols on the chart: primary (above), secondary (below)

3 Stress in words

Word stress is the term used to describe the accent or emphasis given to a particular syllable of a word, and it is a more or less invariable attribute of that word when spoken in isolation. Words of more than one syllable contain both stressed and unstressed syllables. Learners' dictionaries indicate the stressed syllable(s) for every multi-syllable word as if it were being spoken in isolation. The stress symbol used by most dictionaries is /'/ just before the affected syllable, eg /spə'sıfık/. The location of this stress is as much a part of the pronunciation of a word as are the phonemes themselves. Sounds and stress both contribute to the acoustic identity of a word, so both need to be studied at the same time.

The following discovery activities provide insight into the different aspects of stress. After activity 54 I pull these ideas together into a working definition of stress.

Discovery activity 53 Stress and lung power

1 Repeat a sequence of any unvoiced consonant, eg /f ... f ... f ... f ... f ... f ..../ or /ʃ ... ʃ ... ʃ ... ʃ ... ʃ ... ʃ ... /.

2 Now stress alternate sounds /f ... **f** ... f ... **f** ... f ... **f** ... / or /ʃ ... **ʃ** ... ʃ ... **ʃ** ... ʃ ... **ʃ** ... / or /t ... **t** ... t ... **t** ... t ... **t**... / or /θ ... **θ** ... θ ... **θ** ... θ ... **θ** ... /. Notice the increased lung power you use to drive out the air on the stressed sounds.

3 Repeat a sequence of any voiced sound, eg /z ... z ... z ... z ... z ... z ... / or /d ... d ... d ... d ... d ... d ... /.

4 Now stress alternate sounds /z ... **z** ... z ... **z** ... z ... **z** ... / or /d ... **d** ... d ... **d** ... d ... **d** ... / or /iː ... **iː** ... iː ... **iː** ... iː ... **iː** ... / or /ʊ ... **ʊ** ... ʊ ... **ʊ** ... ʊ ... **ʊ**... /.

5 Now stress alternate syllables such as /miː ... **miː** ... miː ... **miː** ... miː ... **miː** ... / or /nəʊ ... **nəʊ** ... nəʊ ... **nəʊ** ... nəʊ ... **nəʊ** ... /.

Commentary ■ ■ ■

You probably notice that the stressed versions of each sound are louder than the unstressed ones due to the extra lung power you are using. You may also find that you are giving the stressed sounds a different pitch, probably higher but possibly lower. In addition you may have made the stressed sounds relatively longer.

There seems to be a natural physical connection between strongly stressed syllables and increased volume, change of pitch and length. But these variables do not have to occur together. ■

Discovery activity 54 All the attributes of stress

1 Make a list of words of two or more syllables. You could choose words from the list below.

2 Say each of these words several times, each time stressing a different syllable and leaving the other syllables unstressed, eg 'student/stu'dent or 'important/im'portant/impor'tant.

3 While doing this, try to be aware of the way in which you focus your lung power on the stressed syllable.

4 Try to mark the stressed syllable first with loudness, then with length, and then with pitch change. Do you naturally tend to do all three at the same time?

student	hotel
important	advert
impotent	advertise
photograph	advertisement
photo	photography
photographer	photographic
kangaroo	benefit
elementary	elephant
element	eleven

5 Now focus on the extra clarity or sharpness that you give to the stressed syllable. Notice the more exact articulation of the consonants and the clearer articulation of the vowels.

6 Focus also on the unstressed syllables. How do you alter the sounds in order to make a syllable unstressed?

7 If you make the stressed syllables fairly emphatic you can also notice an increase in muscular movement on those syllables, and if you look in a mirror you may see the visual aspect of stress.

A practical definition of stress

A stressed syllable is articulated with relatively more force than an unstressed syllable. This is due to the extra pressure of air reaching the vocal cords, caused by an increase in lung power. There are three distinguishable acoustic results. You may perceive syllables as stressed if, compared with their neighbours, they are relatively:

1 louder;

2 longer;

3 different in pitch (usually higher but possibly lower).

To this we can add a fourth variable:

4 the sounds in a stressed syllable may be more clearly articulated, and in particular the vowels may be purer.

As a result of this we can also add a fifth variable, which also provides a visual cue:

5 stressed syllables may be accompanied by larger jaw, lip and other facial movements by the speaker.

These five variables are in fact all interrelated, because they are all ways of increasing or decreasing the amount of energy in the articulation at any point. They all concern the way that articulatory energy is distributed across the word. In fact you can think of the stress pattern of a word as its *energy profile*.

Why are these stress variables important for the teacher?

These five variables, singly or in combination, constitute word stress, and since there is more than one correlate, it follows that when you are trying to help your learners to produce a clearer word stress you can choose to work on whichever feature the learner finds easiest to control, or whichever feature seems to guide the learner towards the most 'English' sound, or seems to interfere least with the clear and economical articulation of the rest of the utterance.

Whichever variable(s) appear to be operating, a syllable will only appear stressed relative to the unstressed syllables surrounding it. The practical implication of this is that it is as important for learners to work on *un*stress as it is to work on stress, since the two exist relative to each other. It is the clear contrast between stress and unstress, rather than any absolute quality of either, that gives the necessary signal to the listener. In fact, for many learners of English, the challenge of developing an adequate articulation of stress is the same as the challenge of learning to deal adequately with unstressed syllables.

4   Unstress in words

Insofar as loudness, length and pitch correlate with stress, so absence of all three can correlate with unstress. When helping learners to put less force on unstressed syllables you can again work on whichever of these three variables the learners find easiest to manipulate or whichever yields the most English-sounding results.

Regarding the fourth variable, clarity and purity of articulation, it is worth saying more about the changes that can result from unstressing the sound:

1   The consonants in an unstressed syllable may be more weakly or even incompletely articulated.

2   The vowel in the syllable may sound less distinct. This loss of sharpness in unstressed vowels is called *reduction*, and all vowel sounds can undergo greater or lesser degrees of reduction. All monophthongs reduce towards the central /ə/ sound, though /iː/ often reduces to /ɪ/ and /uː/ often reduces to /ʊ/. Unstressed diphthongs become generally less distinct, often losing their two-vowel glide quality and merging into one composite 'greyish' monophthong.

Discovery activity 55 Reducing the energy in unstressed syllables

1   Take words from the list in discovery activity 54 and say them first slowly and then quickly, paying attention to the quality of the sounds in the unstressed syllables.

2   Can you detect the absence on the unstressed syllables of any or all of the five variables given in the practical definition? Do you notice the effects of reduction on the way you are saying the unstressed vowels?

Commentary ■ ■ ■

We so easily pay attention to stress, because 'it is there', and overlook unstress 'because it isn't there'. And yet working with unstress is the key to working with stress. ■

5 Primary and secondary stress

Longer words, especially when spoken in isolation, may have more than one stressed syllable (eg *popularity*), in which case one of the stresses is given more force than the other. The strongest is referred to as primary stress and the less strong as secondary stress.

Both primary and secondary stress are in contrast to unstress. Secondary stress can be realized acoustically by duration and loudness, and through clearer articulation. It merely has less energy than its neighbouring primary stress. However the pitch change quality of stress tends to occur as an attribute of primary stress only.

Discovery activity 56 Primary and secondary stress

The following words are normally considered to have two stresses, a primary and a secondary stress: ˌinforˈmation, ˌcontroˈversial, ˌmotiˈvation.

1 Try saying these words without any stressed syllable at all. What do you have to do in order to do that?

2 Now try to stress every syllable. Notice how you do this.

3 This time, put only one stress in each word. Put that stress on each syllable in turn, making sure you keep the other syllables unstressed. How does the word sound with only one stress?

4 Now stress the correct syllables, but *reverse your placement of primary and secondary stress*. Notice how this sounds. And now put the two stresses in the correct place.

Commentary ■ ■ ■

There's a useful knack here. Whenever you are trying to decide which is the primary and which is the secondary stress in a longer word, try reversing primary and secondary stress, and say the word both ways. This may help you to recognize what the correct stress pattern is. ■

Discovery activity 57 Stress shift in words

Sometimes words with secondary stress change their stress pattern in connected speech, especially when followed by a word which is more strongly stressed.

This is how primary and secondary stress is attributed to these four words in the dictionary:

frontbench	/ˌfrʌntˈbentʃ/
regimental	/ˌredʒɪˈmentəl/
laid-back	/ˌleɪdˈbæk/
sixteenth	/ˌsɪksˈtiːnθ/

Try saying these four sentences:

The MP on the frontbench
The colours are regimental
The teacher is laid-back
It's her sixteenth

Do you find that the given stress pattern is respected? Now try these:

> The frontbench MP
> The regimental colours
> A laid-back teacher
> It's her sixteenth birthday

Commentary ■ ■ ■

You may find that you shift the primary stress to the normal position of the secondary stress.

Stress shift is a tendency not a rule, and something to observe when it comes up in the study of stream of speech class materials. ■

6   Where do you put the stress in words?

Some writers emphasize the existence of rules underlying the placement of word stress in English. Sometimes they cite the facility with which a native speaker can correctly stress an unknown word. On the other hand, some writers emphasize the lack of generative power of such rules, citing the difficulty that native speakers can encounter when trying to place the stress in an unknown word!

Both views are helpful as each describes an aspect of reality. Quite a number of rules for the placement of word stress have been described and some of them are summarized below. But there are two questions to ask in connection with such rules. How learnable are they, and how generalizable are they?

Some rules are complex to apply, and even then have many exceptions. In fact *tendency* may be a better term than *rule*. On their own these tendencies clearly do not form a comprehensive basis for the learning of stress placement, and so we need effective ways for learning the stress of each word individually while at the same time developing the kind of inner criteria that native speakers have.

I don't want learners to be sidetracked by cognitive rules with limited application. *Oh so that's how it is, good, then I needn't look out any more.* For me, and I think the learners I work with, the best rule is to be alert, to notice what you are doing and what the language is doing, and to reflect. Linguistic rules and tendencies must be used to enhance this process. So my 'charter' for learning word stress might be:

- to work with each new word as it comes up, on its own terms, consulting the teacher or coursebook or learners' dictionary as required;
- to do so in such a way as to encourage the development of the learners' intuitive learning faculties so that underlying tendencies can emerge within each learner without necessarily having to be described or explained;
- to make use of rules and observations and explanations about placement of word stress where they are useful, that is where they contain some insight and when the learners are ready to integrate that rule.

Stress in two-syllable words

There is a general tendency to stress two-syllable nouns and adjectives on the first syllable: 'many, 'function, 'spelling, 'second, 'colour, 'yellow.

Stress in two-syllable nouns/verbs

In English there are many words that can function as nouns or as verbs: for example, *transfer, suspect, progress, produce*. Where their spelling is identical, and where there are two syllables, there is a strong tendency:

- to stress nouns and adjectives on the first syllable, eg 'export, 'increase, 'permit;
- and to stress verbs on the second syllable, eg ex'port, in'crease, per'mit.

Stress in compound nouns

The chief characteristic of compounds is that they consist of two words, both of which can exist separately. There is a tendency for the words that form a compound to keep their pronunciation unchanged in the compound. Regarding the placement of stress on one word or the other, there are also some general tendencies that are worth stating though not always reliable:

- The main stress in a compound formed from two separate words is likely to be on the second word. Most of these might more accurately be termed *collocating noun phrases: town'centre, black'magic, science 'fiction, black'hole*.

- The main stress in a compound formed from two joined or hyphenated words is likely to be on the first word: '*football,* '*seaside,* '*motorway,* '*handbag,* '*greenhouse*.

Derivatives and stress pattern

A root word can form different word classes, or parts of speech, by adding a variety of suffixes. In this way a given root word may be able to form a verb, a noun, an adjective and an adverb.

Discovery activity 58 Stress in derivatives

How does the stress behave in these derivatives?

compre'hend	compre'hension	compre'hensive	compre'hensively
'photograph	pho'tographer	photo'graphic	photo'graphically
elec'tricity	e'lectrify	e'lectrical	e'lectrically
e'xamine	exami'nation		
'magic	'magical	'magically	ma'gician
i'dentify	i'dentity	identifi'cation	
il'lumine	il'luminate	illumi'nation	
'beauty	'beautify	'beautiful	'beautifully
pro'tect	pro'tective	pro'tection	

Commentary ■ ■ ■

You can see from this that there is a tendency for root words to keep their pronunciation and stress pattern unchanged when they form derivatives. But as you can see there are also exceptions, and where there is a change in stress pattern it carries significance as a grammatical signal of word class to the listener. This underlines the importance of treating stress pattern as an integral part of the aural identity of a word. It also provides a useful basis for classwork on stress and stress shift. ■

7 Intonation and word stress

We have already referred to pitch as one of the acoustic correlates of stress. This means that intonation, in the sense of simple pitch movement, has a role to play even at the level of words spoken in isolation (Level 2). We have noted that this pitch movement is associated with primary stress and not with secondary stress, and we can add a second observation, which is that pitch movement on the primary stressed syllable is usually a fall from a higher pitch to a lower pitch.

Discovery activity 59

1 Say these words which are stressed on the first syllable, and notice the pitch movement between first and second syllable.

'awesome   'lovely   'beauty   'practical   'wonderful

2 Where there are unstressed syllables before the primary stress, they will probably be voiced at a lower pitch than the primary stress. Try these and notice what you do.

a'mazing   spec'tacular   re'ality   to'night

Commentary ■ ■ ■

Intonation in the form of simple pitch movement carrying no significance other than to mark the primary stress enters the phonological scene at the level below that of connected speech (ie at Level 2). So there is an opportunity to work on awareness of pitch movement whenever learners are working on the pronunciation of isolated words. ■

Conclusion

Both the sequence of sounds and the stress pattern are essential parts of the identity of a word spoken in isolation, and both affect the way a word will behave in the stream of speech (more about this at Level 3). Stress only exists relative to unstress, and so learning to unstress is as important as learning to stress. Vowel reduction is an important ingredient of unstress and it contributes to the aural recognition of words. Pitch movement is an ingredient of primary stress.

Sounds and stress should always be learned together as two inseparable parts of any one, whole pronunciation. It may be that a word spoken with not-quite-right sounds, but with correct stress pattern, is more easily understood than one with more or less correct sounds but incorrect stress pattern.

At Level 1 we considered the nature of each of the forty-four English RP phonemes. At Level 2 we have considered the nature of dictionary pronunciation, and found it to be a combination of individual phonemes moulded together into one 'flow', integrated with and modified by word stress.

The next part of the book deals with connected speech, which I have called Level 3, and we shall see that just as the individual phonemes of Level 1 are altered and added to when fused together to yield the isolated word pronunciation of Level 2, so isolated words are altered and added to when they are strung together in the stream of speech.

Level 3   Connected speech

1	Introduction	58
2	Overview	58
3	Sounds and simplifications in connected speech	60
4	Rhythm in connected speech	69
5	Intonation	74

1 Introduction

Just as at Level 2 we found that a word is not just the sum of its individual sounds, so at Level 3 we find that connected speech is not just the sum of its individual words. Continuous connected speech consists of a flow of sounds which are modified by a system of simplifications through which phonemes are connected, grouped and modified. Stream of speech pronunciation brings together the three branches of practical phonology: sounds, stress and intonation. After the following overview these three areas are examined to the degree of detail that I have found is of benefit to practical classroom work.

2 Overview

Sounds in connected speech

The modifications to dictionary pronunciation (Level 2) once isolated words are embedded in connected speech are fairly systematic and include *assimilation* (the changing of sounds), *elision* (the omission of sounds), *vowel reduction, liaison, linking* and *intrusive* sounds, and *juncture*. We will explore all of these features in Section 3 below.

Stress, accent and prominence in connected speech

Stress is an umbrella term used to cover both *accent* (or word stress), and *prominence* (or sentence stress). The former belongs to the word, while the latter is chosen by the speaker to highlight the intended meaning. Connected speech contains both word accents (in a sense *regardless* of the speaker) and prominence (*because of* the speaker). And what happens then is that individual word accent is likely to be subordinated to the speaker's choice of prominence, and these prominences form the major part of the rhythm of the whole utterance. Spoken English has a characteristic tendency to be rhythmical. We will explore this further in Section 4 below.

Intonation and rhythm

Intonation and rhythm together help to focus attention on the information structure of a discourse and to indicate 'what goes with what' in an utterance. Within the context of a particular discourse, the intonation contours chosen by the speaker may indicate attitudes, mark syntactic boundaries, highlight the relationship between the utterances, and indicate the common ground assumed between speaker and hearer.

Unfortunately, analyses of intonation have so far tended to yield descriptions which are too cumbersome for language learners. We will look at what help existing theories of intonation can offer us in the classroom, and at what we can do where theory does not help.

Connected speech learner targets

The degree of simplification of sounds depends largely on the speed and context of the utterance, as well as on the characteristics of the speaker. So a slower and more careful delivery may remain closer to dictionary pronunciation, while a faster and less careful delivery will contain a greater degree of simplification. In an idealized form these two speeds of delivery are respectively called *careful colloquial speech* and *rapid colloquial speech*, and these can serve as two useful models or landmarks to aim for in the study of connected speech pronunciation. Both forms can contain all types of simplification, the difference being largely a matter of degree.

Careful colloquial speech

This style contains all types of simplification to a moderate degree. Words remain closer to their dictionary pronunciation than with rapid colloquial speech. This style is likely to be used in a more formal setting, the speaker shaping utterances more carefully, deliberately and slowly. An internationally available example of careful colloquial RP is that of newscasters and announcers on the BBC World Service.

I suggest that this type of pronunciation is useful as a target for learners to aim at in their speaking skill, as it is clear, easy to listen to and widely understood. (There are of course many situations throughout the world where it is more useful to use the local brand of English as the learning model.)

Rapid colloquial speech

This contains more extensive simplifications, and individual words may be further from their dictionary pronunciation form than with careful colloquial speech. This style is used in less formal settings as when native speakers are talking informally to one another. Compared with careful colloquial speech, this style may be characterized by faster delivery and less care and attention to precise articulation on the part of the speaker. I suggest that this style of pronunciation is useful as a target for learners to aim at in their listening skill.

3 Sounds and simplifications in connected speech

In this section we will explore the kinds of change that can occur between Level 2 and Level 3 pronunciations. We'll cover the following:

- assimilation;
- elision;
- vowel reduction;
- strong and weak forms;
- liaison;
- contractions;
- juncture.

Assimilation

Assimilation occurs when a phoneme changes its quality due to the influence of a neighbouring sound. It changes to become more like the neighbouring sound, or even identical to it.

Discovery activity 60 Assimilation

Here are examples of the main kinds of assimilation in English. See if you can identify them. Say the following phrases first as isolated words and then several times as connected speech. Do you change any of the sounds at the word boundaries?

> ten pin bowling
> in bed
> good boy
> hit man
> tin man
> good girl
> this shop
> these shops
> have to go
> how d'you do
> don't you know

Commentary ■ ■ ■

Alveolar consonants /t/, /d/ and /n/ at the end of a word often assimilate to the place of articulation of the consonant at the beginning of the next word. Before /p/, /b/ and /m/, for example, they can become bilabial:

ten pin bowling	/ten pɪn bəʊlɪŋ/	/tem pɪm bəʊlɪŋ/
in bed	/ɪn bed/	/ɪm bed/
good boy	/gʊd bɔɪ/	/gʊb bɔɪ/
hit man	/hɪt mæn/	/hɪp mæn/
tin man	/tɪn mæn/	/tɪm mæn/

/d/ can change to /g/:

good girl	/gʊd gɜːl/	/gʊg gɜːl/

/s/ can change to /ʃ/ and /z/ can change to /ʒ/ when /ʃ/ begins the next syllable:

| this shop | /ðɪs ʃɒp/ | /ðɪʃ ʃɒp/ |
| these shops | /ði:z ʃɒps/ | /ði:ʒ ʃɒps/ |

Voicing can change too. Here /v/ becomes an unvoiced /f/ under the influence of the following unvoiced /t/:

| have to go | /hæv tə gəʊ/ | /hæf tə gəʊ/ |

/d/ and /j/ can fuse, or *coalesce*, to make a less plosive sound, the affricate /dʒ/:

| how d'you do | /haʊ djʊ du:/ | /haʊ dʒʊ du:/ |

And similarly /t/ and /j/ can coalesce to give the unvoiced affricate /tʃ/:

| don't you know | /dəʊnt jʊ nəʊ/ | /dəʊntʃə nəʊ/ |

Assimilation is the natural result of the various speech organs 'cutting corners' as they perform their complex sequence of movements, and this occurs mostly at word boundaries and affects mainly consonant sounds.

Although assimilation follows fairly regular patterns, the most common of which are set out above, it is different in different languages. Learners cannot therefore simply apply their mother tongue assimilations to English. Learners who do not assimilate at all may sound finicky, over-precise, too careful, and where their mother tongue assimilation patterns intrude they may be difficult for English listeners to follow. Lack of appropriate assimilation in the stream of speech can inhibit the use of English rhythm and intonation patterns, leading to a loss of both fluency and clarity of meaning.

I don't think it is necessarily helpful for learners to learn the rules governing assimilation. What is much more important is that you, the teacher, draw your learners' attention to examples of assimilation when they arise, either on tape or as you speak to one another. ■

Elision

Elision occurs when a sound which would be present in a word spoken in isolation is omitted in connected speech.

Discovery activity 61 Elision

It is mainly /t/ and /d/ that are elided in English, particularly when they are between two other consonants. Experiment yourself with the possible omissions in these phrases:

Omission of /t/

next please	/neks pli:z/
I don't know	/aɪ dəʊ nəʊ/
post the letter	/pəʊs ðə letə/

Omission of /d/

old man	/əʊl mæn/
you and me	/ju: ən mi:/
sandwich	/sænwɪtʃ/
stand there	/stæn ðeə/

I have given the elided versions in phonemic spelling above. But now say each phrase again without eliding any of the sounds. How different does it feel? What impression do you get?

Commentary ■ ■ ■

Like assimilation, elision is a natural result of the speech organs 'cutting corners' in connected speech, mainly at word boundaries. It applies particularly to consonant sounds, and as with assimilation, speakers who do not elide may sound over-meticulous and rather crisp in their articulation. It may also be more difficult for them to use intonation and rhythm patterns with fluency.

When learners become aware that a number of phonemes they might expect to hear are not actually produced, and when they discover that they can make these sounds disappear in their own speech, they begin to gain an insight which helps them when they listen to rapid connected English. ■

Elision and assimilation together

Learners of English often remark on the way English speakers seem to 'swallow' the sounds. Usually what they are observing is the combined action of assimilation, elision and vowel reduction.

Vowel reduction

Unaccented vowels in the stream of speech are characterized by a reduction in length, and a change in quality towards a less distinct, more central vowel sound. Most monophthongs reduce towards /ə/. This process is sometimes called *centralization* since the /ə/ sound is produced with the lips and jaw relaxed and the tongue in a central, neutral position. However, the two monophthongs /iː/ and /uː/ are often only partially centralized, /iː/ reducing towards /ɪ/ and /uː/ reducing towards /ʊ/.

Discovery activity 62 Vowel reduction

Say these two sentences rapidly, stressing the underlined syllables and unstressing the others:

<u>You</u> and <u>me</u>
I <u>wish</u> you would <u>tell</u> me

What happens to the vowels in *you* and *me* in the second sentence?

Commentary ■ ■ ■

In the second sentence the vowels in these two words are reduced, ie shorter and less clear. / 'juː ən 'miː/ becomes /aɪ 'wɪʃ ju wʊd 'tel mɪ/. This highlights the connection between unstress and vowel reduction. If you say both of the sentences as a sequence of words in isolation, you restore each sound to its full value but make it difficult to indicate your meaning since you cannot then stress the sentence properly. ■

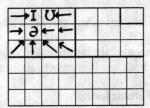

Fig. 36: Direction of reduction for monophthongs

Diphthongs are also likely to be reduced when unaccented in connected speech. The length of the glide is reduced, in fact the glide quality itself may even disappear resulting in a 'greyish' neutral diphthong in which the first and second elements are dissolved into one composite monophthong.

Discovery activity 63

Say these words rapidly, stressing the underlined syllables and unstressing the others:

1 <u>Go</u>   *go* has this diphthong: /əʊ/.
   Go <u>out</u>   How does the diphthong in *go* sound now?

2 Go <u>out</u>   Here *out* contains this diphthong: /aʊ/.
   Go out<u>side</u>   What sound does *out* contain here?

3 <u>Why</u>   *why* contains this diphthong: /aɪ/.
   Why <u>not</u>   What sound does *why* contain here?

Commentary ■ ■ ■

If you say the pairs of sentences at speed and with unstress as well as stress, you should find that in the second sentence of each pair the diphthong in question is shorter and less clear than in the first sentence. In fact it may cease to be a diphthong altogether by dropping its second element and becoming a neutralized version of its first element.

Discovery activities 60 and 61 illustrate the link between elision and assimilation and stress and unstress. Activities 62 and 63 illustrate the close link between vowel reduction and the smooth distribution of stress and unstress. Since stressing and unstressing is an important way for the speaker to indicate meaning it follows that these simplifications in the stream of speech are important aspects of expressing and communicating meaning. ■

Strong and weak forms

Vowel reduction affects the frequent monosyllabic grammar words of English, and many of them have two or more accepted pronunciations, one when stressed or spoken in isolation, the *strong form*, and one when reduced in their more usual unstressed position, the *weak form*. Learners' dictionaries list both the strong and weak forms for such words, which have the following characteristics:

- they have only one syllable;
- they act as function words;
- they usually occur in their weak forms unless the speaker wishes to emphasize them to underline the message;
- the weak forms occur in speech only and are not (usually) shown in writing;
- they are high frequency words, though few in number (about fifty).

Discovery activity 64 Strong and weak forms

Make two sentences for each of the following function words, one that contains the strong, prominent form, the other the weak, reduced form. Notice the difference in pronunciation and emphasis between the two forms. Compare your version with the forms given here:

	Strong form	Weak form
and	/ænd/	/ən/
of	/ɒv/	/əv/
you	/juː/	/jʊ/
me	/miː/	/mɪ/
she	/ʃiː/	/ʃɪ /
would	/wʊd/	/wəd/ /əd/
does	/dʌz/	/dəz/
have	/hæv/	/həv/ /əv/
must	/mʌst/	/məst/ /məs/

Commentary ■ ■ ■

In general, the greater the speed of delivery, the greater the reduction of unstressed vowels. Since reduction is a feature of unstress, and since stress and unstress exist only relative to each other, you can see that vowel reduction plays an essential role in producing the rhythmical nature of stream-of-speech English. Phoneme quality is inextricably linked with rhythm in connected speech.

The appropriate use of weak forms is essential to smooth and rhythmical speaking, to clarity of prominent and non-prominent syllables, and so to clarity of meaning. Weak forms are just as much a part of careful colloquial speech as they are of rapid colloquial speech. Working on the production of weak forms gives learners insight into the speech of native speakers, and helps to improve their listening skill and confidence. ■

Contractions

In the stream of speech a weak form can occur together with another word in such a way that it undergoes another reduction and the two words are pronounced as one, often occupying only a single syllable. This is a contraction, which has the following characteristics:

- two single-syllable words usually combine into one syllable;
- an elision (omission) of sounds occurs;
- an omission of one or two letters also occurs in the written form; their place marked by an apostrophe. This is a special case of elision in that it is indicated in the written form.

Common instances of contraction are personal pronoun + auxiliary verb and verb + *not*. For example:

I'm, I've, I'll, I'd, they're, they've, they'll, they'd, etc.
can't, couldn't, don't, hasn't, wasn't, etc.
wouldn't've, can't've, etc.

Liaison

Liaison refers to the smooth linking or joining together of words in connected speech. Of course two words can have a silence between them, but liaison is concerned with the way sounds are fused together at word boundaries.

Discovery activity 65 Liaison

Say each of the following phrases and notice how you join the words together:

in English   my uncle   far away   go away

Now say each one without joining the words together. Notice the difference.

Commentary ■ ■ ■

Fully liaised speech is characterized by a seamless, continuous quality, where final consonants are linked to following initial vowel sounds, and initial consonants to preceding final vowel sounds. Once again liaison is an essential ingredient of both rhythm and intonation.

Poorly linked speech is typically rather jerky, perhaps staccato, and the resulting lack of flow makes it more difficult for the speaker to take advantage of the stress system and so for the listener to focus on the content of the message.

Some systematic forms of liaison are described under the following headings:

- linking /r/;
- intrusive /r/;
- intrusive /w/ and /j/. ■

Linking /r/

In RP the letter 'r' in the spelling of a word is not pronounced unless it is followed by a vowel sound. But in connected speech the final spelling 'r' of a word may be pronounced or not, depending on whether the first sound of the next word is a consonant or a vowel.

Discovery activity 66 Linking /r/

Say the following phrases and decide whether the 'r' at the end of the first word is sounded on not:

> her English
> her Spanish
> car seat
> car engine
> brother and sister

Commentary ■ ■ ■

In the second and third phrases the 'r' is not sounded as the following sound is a consonant. In the first, fourth and fifth phrases the 'r' is a linking /r/ joining the first word to the second which begins with a vowel.

Note that the term linking /r/ can be applied only when the letter 'r' occurs in the written form.

The notion of linking /r/ is redundant in rhotic varieties of English that typically pronounce all 'r's occurring in the spelling form. Learner dictionaries show linking /r/ in brackets as part of the pronunciation. ■

Intrusive /r/

This refers to the /r/ sound an English speaker may insert between two words where the first ends in /ə/ or /ɔː/ and the following word begins with a vowel sound.

Discovery activity 67 Intrusive /r/

See if you make use of intrusive /r/. Say these two phrases and notice how you join the first to the second word.

> America and Canada
> law and order

Commentary ■ ■ ■

Some speakers would say /əmerɪkə r ən kænədə/, or /lɔː r ən ɔːdə/. Use of this intrusive /r/ is frequent though by no means obligatory. The only difference between linking and intrusive /r/ is that linking /r/ is reflected in the written form while intrusive /r/ is not. Intrusive /r/ does not exist in rhotic accents (where 'r' in the spelling is always pronounced). ■

Intrusive /w/ and /j/

These are also used to link certain vowel–vowel combinations at word junctions. The intrusive sound may not be distinctly heard especially where the overall vowel sequence is fairly relaxed. Nevertheless you will find it noticeable in all sorts of recorded material, and it has great value as a learning device when helping learners towards a smooth linking of words in continuous speech.

Discovery activity 68 Intrusive /w/

Say these phrases and notice how you join the words together:

> you are
> go off
> Sue always wants to eat

Commentary ■ ■ ■

You probably find that you insert /w/: /juː w ɑː/; /gəʊ w ɒf/; /suː w ɔːlweɪz wɒnts tu w iːt/. Intrusive /w/ follows a final /uː/ or a diphthong ending in /ʊ/ where the next word begins with a vowel sound. This is because /uː/ and /ʊ/ have lip rounding and form the starting point for the bilabial semi-vowel /w/. ■

Discovery activity 69 Intrusive /j/

Say these phrases and notice how you join the words together:

> he is
> they are
> she always takes my arm

Commentary ■ ■ ■

You probably find that you insert /j/: /hiː j ɪz/; /ðeɪ j ɑː/; /ʃiː j ɔːlweɪz teɪks maɪ j ɑːm/. Intrusive /j/ follows a final /iː/ or a diphthong ending in /ɪ/, where the next word begins with a vowel sound. This is because /iː/ and /ɪ/ form the starting point for the semi-vowel /j/. ■

Discovery activity 70 Four features of liaison together

Here is a sentence whose smooth articulation requires all four of the liaison features mentioned above. Can you identify them?

> You are obviously unhappy about the idea of it.

Try to say this sentence as one continuous and seamless stream of sound.

Commentary ■ ■ ■

This is one possible version: /ju w ɑː r ɒbvɪəslɪ j ʌnhæpɪ j əbaʊt ðɪ j aɪdɪə r əv ɪt/. It has one each of linking /r/, intrusive /r/, linking /w/ and three occurrences of linking /j/. ■

Juncture

Juncture is the label given to a number of features which may occur at the boundary between two words in connected speech such that, even though the two words may be fully linked together, the boundary between them is nevertheless unambiguous and clear.

Discovery activity 71 Juncture

This is a very interesting activity. Say the following pairs of phrases. Can you distinguish between them? And if you can, then how? Try them both whispered and aloud to yourself, and also with another person:

mice pies	my spies
grey tapes	great apes
send the maid	send them aid
car pit	carpet
it's an aim	it's a name
grade 'A'	grey day
ice cream	I scream
ice train	eye strain
the way to cut it	the waiter cut it
I'm 'A'	I may

Commentary ■ ■ ■

The articulatory features that are likely to enable you to distinguish the phrase in column one from that in column two are:

- the shortening or lengthening of vowel sounds on either side of the juncture;
- the delayed or advanced articulation of consonant sounds on either side;
- variations in the degree of syllable stress on either side of the juncture;
- other allophonic variations in the phonemes on either side of the boundary. ■

Conclusion

There are a number of differences in the way words are pronounced in isolation and in the stream of speech between Level 2 and Level 3 pronunciation. I have used the term 'simplifications' as a collective name for the differences and you can see that the building blocks of connected speech comprise a system that is on the whole regular and predictable. The English phonemic set affects native speakers in such a way that they generally find it more convenient to include these simplifications. Our aim can be to help our learners also to find that these simplifications are convenient.

You can help learners to use their experience to develop insight into these simplifications through regular class analysis of very small samples of English (one or two sentences), selected from whatever taped materials are available to the class, including recordings of yourself and other class members talking.

4 Rhythm in connected speech

We have seen how phonemes in isolation are moulded into words and how isolated words melt into the stream of speech through a series of phonemic changes called simplifications. We have also seen how word stress, or accent, is an invariable attribute of words of more than one syllable when spoken in isolation. Now we need to look at how stress is manifested in connected speech, and to do this we need first to introduce the notion of prominence.

Prominence and accent

So far I have been using the term *stress* to mean two things, but when dealing with connected speech we need to distinguish these two meanings with two different terms. The first use has been as in *word stress* – the emphasis on a syllable of a word that is more or less a fixed attribute of that word, and predictable enough to be given in dictionaries. From now on I am going to use the word *accent* to refer to word stress.

The second use has been as in *sentence stress* – emphasis given to any word in an utterance by the speaker in order to highlight the intended meaning. From now on I will use the word *prominence* to refer to this type of stress.

One way of looking at this contrast is to say that accent is determined by the language, while prominence is determined by the speaker.

Discovery activity 72 Discriminating accent from prominence

1 Say this sentence first as a series of isolated words with accents as marked.

> She's <u>ho</u>ping to get a <u>ta</u>xi to the <u>sta</u>tion.

If you say the words separately and without meaning you will probably put an accent on the underlined syllables.

2 Now say it with the words connected together, and with the accents, but do not superimpose any meaning or prominence of your own. In other words say the words fluently but do not 'express any meaning'.

Once again the emphasis you give to the first syllable in the two-syllable words is accent; it is there as a property of the word rather than because you decided to put it there. This is true as long as you are 'quoting the words' rather than 'expressing a meaning'.

3 Now say the sentence but put your own meaning into it, and notice where you put the main emphasis, ie prominence, in order to highlight your meaning.

4 Try putting the prominence on each of the accents in turn. One way of telling prominence from accent is that prominence also carries the main intonation change. Notice also that the other two-syllable words still retain their accents on the first syllable. You are now noticing both prominence and accent. Of course, you can also put the prominence and intonation movement on one of the single-syllable words.

Commentary ■ ■ ■

Try the activities with other sentences, and try them with your learners. Here are some guidelines that you will begin to discern:

- Prominence can be given to any word, whether lexical or not.
- Accent and prominence have different roles, but in connected speech the role of accent is subordinated to the role of prominence.
- In the case of multi-syllable words the speaker normally places prominence on the syllable that normally carries the word accent.
- In the case of single-syllable words there is clearly no choice about which syllable is to carry the prominence.
- Not all accents will be given prominence.
- Accents which are not given prominence may retain some of their emphasis but with less force than the prominent syllables, or they may receive little or no emphasis at all, along with all the other unstressed syllables.
- Unaccented vowels tend to be reduced as described above, so centralization is common.
- Prominence is articulated by any of the four variables that are used to indicate accent, namely volume, pitch, length and quality (see definition after discovery activity 54).
- Prominent syllables also highlight the speaker's message by carrying the significant pitch movement, thus the tonic syllable is always on a prominence. (See above for a definition of prominence, and discovery activity 78 on the tonic syllable.) ■

Lexical and grammatical words

Lexical words (also called *content* words) are those which carry the main part of the meaning in an utterance. They are usually nouns, main verbs, adjectives and adverbs. Grammar words (also called *function* words) may have less meaning by themselves, their function being to connect content words together in grammatical relationships. They are usually the weak forms of articles, conjunctions, prepositions, pronouns and auxiliary verbs. In general, therefore, it is the lexical words of an utterance that are given prominence and the grammatical words that are not. But any word or even any syllable can be given a lexical role and made prominent where the meaning requires it, often in a contrasting or correcting capacity.

Here are some other possible meanings you could give the sentence in discovery activity 72 by putting the prominence on one of the grammatical words:

a She's hoping to get a taxi to the station (ie contrastive stress – not from the station)

b She is hoping to get a taxi to the station (whatever you say to the contrary)

c She's hoping to get a taxi to the station (unlikely, but typical teacher talk while correcting a learner's mistake. A common use of prominence in the EFL classroom).

Stress timing and syllable timing

English is sometimes called a *stress timed* language. This refers to an underlying tendency for stressed syllables (whether prominent or accented) to occur at roughly equal intervals of time, regardless of the number of unstressed syllables in between.

Discovery activity 73 Stress timing

This activity will give you a direct insight into the idea of stress timing:

1 Say phrase a aloud and rather slowly, with emphasis on each of the four words.

a <u>You</u>		<u>me</u>		<u>him</u>		<u>her</u>
b <u>You</u>	and	<u>me</u>	and	<u>him</u>	and	<u>her</u>
c <u>You</u>	and then	<u>me</u>	and then	<u>him</u>	and then	<u>her</u>
d <u>You</u>	and then it's	<u>me</u>	and then it's	<u>him</u>	and then it's	<u>her</u>

2 Now say phrase b at the same speed, so that it occupies the same amount of time. Insert an unstressed *and* between each of the four words.

3 Now say phrase c, this time inserting unstressed *and then* between the four main words.

4 Now say phrase d with the three unstressed syllables between each main word. Try to take only the same amount of time as the first sentence.

Commentary ■ ■ ■

According to the principle of stress timing these four sentences each occupy approximately the same amount of time. The more unstressed syllables there are the quicker you have to say them in order to fit them into the beat. In other words the time taken to speak each utterance depends on the number of stresses and not on the number of syllables. This means that maintaining regular stress depends on maintaining irregular syllable length.

This is in contrast to the phenomenon of *syllable timing*, where the time taken to speak an utterance depends roughly on how many syllables there are. If English were syllable timed, then the series of four sentences you have just tried would take progressively longer to say, as each contains more syllables than the previous one, though the same number of stresses.

English, Dutch and German are examples of languages said to be stress timed. Spanish, Japanese and French are said to be syllable timed. ■

Discovery activity 74 Stress timing and syllable timing

Both of these sentences contain two stresses, but the first has three syllables and the second has five syllables.

> <u>Put</u> it <u>down</u>   (3 syllables, 2 stresses)
> <u>Put</u> it over <u>there</u>   (5 syllables, 2 stresses)

1 Say the first sentence with stress on the first and third syllables. Say it several times and establish a rhythm for it; maybe you can clap or tap the rhythm at the same time.

2 Now alternate the first sentence with the second while keeping the same rhythm and speed. When you say the second sentence you have to fit three unstressed syllables into the same space, and so the two sentences take roughly the same time to say. This is stress timing.

3 Say the first sentence with a more equal emphasis on each of the three syllables. Tap or beat this rhythm and you'll notice that it has a quite different feel to it. If you now say the second sentence with a more equal emphasis on each of the five syllables, you'll find, not surprisingly, that it takes longer to say. This is syllable timing.

Commentary ■ ■ ■

According to the rule of stress timing these sentences take the same time to say as each one has two stresses. According to the rule of syllable timing the second sentence takes longer as it has five syllables while the first has three.

Stress timing is only possible if the unstressed syllables are both weakly and rapidly articulated. This in turn requires that the unstressed vowels are reduced, perhaps with other stream of speech simplifications operating.

In a stress timed language such as English the number of words stressed by the speaker depends on the role of each word in the meaning of the whole utterance. An utterance with a high proportion of lexical words is likely to contain more stresses than one with the same number of syllables but a higher proportion of grammatical words. Either way the rhythmical nature of English will tend to be maintained.

Careful colloquial speech, tending to be slower and more deliberate, may contain more stresses than rapid colloquial speech, which, apart from being faster, is also likely to contain more false starts, stops, hesitations, repetitions, etc. All of these factors tend to obscure regular stress time, elide syllables and even give stress to apparently unimportant words.

While some people have argued that there is not strong evidence for the existence of stress timing, I am quite sure that stress timing is a characteristic of short stretches of spoken English. But more importantly I have found that practising stress timing does help learners to sound noticeably more English. Cultivating an awareness of stress timing does seem to yield significant improvements in both receptive and productive skills. We'll return to this in some practical ways in Level 3 of the classroom toolkit. ■

Discovery activity 75 Listening to the rhythms of language

1 Listen to the rhythm of different speakers of English on the radio or on tape. The following might help:

- Try not to listen to sounds, but sensitize your ear to the distribution of energy over sequences of syllables.
- Try turning the volume right down to the point where the low energy syllables are inaudible, leaving only the higher energy ones which have more volume. If you get the volume level right this can sometimes give a startling insight into a speaker's underlying rhythmicality.
- You can turn the treble tone control to minimum, and the bass control, if there is one, to maximum. You may find that this reduces the clarity of individual sounds and increases the perceptibility of prominent and stressed syllables.

2 Try the same thing with small samples of different languages on the radio, whether you understand them or not, and try to detect their rhythmicality. Do syllables tend to be the same length? Are some shorter and others longer? How does the speaker distribute energy?

3 Notice the same thing in your own speech, by listening to a recording of yourself and by listening to yourself 'live'.

4 Read the following commentary aloud and see if you can detect a tendency towards stress timing. Take it not too fast and make it full of meaning!

Commentary ■ ■ ■

My own observation is that the tendency to stress timing frequently emerges in snippets of three or four relatively equally spaced stresses, and then disappears to emerge again a few syllables later. In summary, rhythm depends on two factors: the contrast between stressed and unstressed syllables, and a relatively regular occurrence of the stressed syllables. ■

Unstress in the stream of speech

For the message to stand out clearly the more important words must be stressed and the less important words relatively unstressed. For stress to exist it is necessary that unstress also exists, and rhythm is created by the relationship between the two. For our learners this means that production and practice of stress must go hand-in-hand with production and practice of unstress, since one cannot exist without the other. It can be quite difficult to understand English speech in which the stress is either absent or wrongly placed, and learners whose mother tongue tends towards syllable timing may find stress timing and the consequent 'crowding in' of unstressed syllables rather different and cumbersome to begin with.

Discovery activity 76 Unstress in the stream of speech

1 Choose a sentence from the previous paragraph. Say it and decide where you want to place the stresses.

2 And now, without changing it, say it a few more times but focus your attention on the unstressed syllables. Notice *that* they are unstressed and notice *how* you unstress them. Notice how the vowels may be reduced.

Commentary ■ ■ ■

Though this exercise is simple it is not so easy, but it is very useful. ■

5 Intonation

'It's not what you say, but the way you say it.' What I understand by this is that in the end it's not the choice of words that conveys the speaker's intention, but rather the manner in which the words are said.

It suggests that there is a common understanding between speakers of a language (and perhaps even between speakers of different languages) about 'ways of saying things'. The way of saying something may depend on gesture, facial expression and voice quality, but usually the most significant factor is intonation. Within any given context an utterance can be given a variety of different meanings according to the intonation patterns chosen by the speaker.

Discovery activity 77 Same sentence, different meanings

1 Give the following sentence as many different meanings as you can. Keep the words the same but find different ways of saying it. You probably need to imagine a context.

    It's eight o'clock!

2 Now observe the difference between the intonation patterns you have used.

Commentary ■ ■ ■

When I try this activity I find myself paraphrasing what my intonation signals. For example, I can say 'It's eight o'clock!' with such an intonation that it can mean any of these:

    Hurry up!
    We've got plenty of time
    I'm hungry
    You're late
    You're early
    You're on time
    At last we can start!
    The bus is late!
    You didn't set the alarm clock
    Please turn on the TV!
    My, how time flies!
    We've overslept
    I wonder what's happened to Maria
    Yippee!
    He'll have had his operation by now!
    I've just eaten
    He'll be here shortly
    Be quiet

But for this to be possible there has to be a context, and an understanding of common ground or common experience between speaker and hearer. The less common ground there is then the less shared experience there is for my intonation to refer back to, and so the more limited the range of meanings it can have. ■

Where does intonation choice come from?

A further point concerns the way that intonation is chosen. While I can exercise a fairly conscious choice over my selection of words, my choice of intonation seems much less conscious. It's as if it comes from deeper within me, from another part of my brain which is less open to my conscious intervention. I think that some of the problems that teachers and learners face concerning intonation may be connected with this idea, and I will return to it later when we consider the meaning of intonation.

The same idea can be approached from the listener's point of view. What happens when a non-native speaker uses an inappropriate intonation pattern? My observation is that while within certain limits of intelligibility mistakes or inappropriacies of pronunciation, grammar and even vocabulary can be accommodated by the native listener, inappropriate intonation can at times give rise not just to obscuration of the message, but to reception of a quite different message. Once again it is almost as if intonation is received by a different part of the listener's brain, which is less able to make allowances for inappropriate use.

Intonation and learnability

Intonation refers to the patterns of pitch change over an utterance or series of utterances. Such patterns may be partly personal, but they are also conventional, and to that extent they are also systematic. Being systematic it follows that at some level there are rules according to which the speaker of a language chooses one intonation pattern rather than another. The special problem that we teachers face with intonation is to find an adequate and learnable description of these rules that learners can relate directly to their own experience.

The teaching of intonation seems to have been characterized by an even greater uncertainty and lack of confidence than the other areas of practical phonology. I think this is because we are not in control of a practical, workable and trustworthy system through which we can make intonation comprehensible to ourselves or to our learners. But then again this may be due to the nature of intonation itself, that it is somehow less perceptible and less tangible than other areas of language.

Summary

Existing descriptions of intonation seem to be incomplete, and not necessarily very learnable. However they can still help our own understanding, and so we'll make a brief survey of some descriptions of intonation to see what they offer and how far they go. The descriptions tend to agree on what the formal characteristics of intonation are, what its components are, how it's made up and how to identify it, and to differ in their answer to the question 'What is the function of intonation: what meaning does it convey?'

In what follows I'll first summarize the general area of agreement on the form of intonation, and I'll introduce six technical terms that make talking about intonation easier. Then I'll summarize the differing views on the meaning of intonation. From this we can shed some light on how far theory can guide us in the classroom, and where theory stops being of help, leaving us free to search for what *works* rather than what can be justified on theoretical grounds.

The form of intonation

The vocal cords vibrate during speech. This vibration is heard as sound, and the pitch of this sound varies according to the frequency of the vibration of the cords: the higher the frequency of vibration the higher the pitch that you hear. When you sing a pitch or note you usually hold it for a time before jumping or sliding to the next note. But in speech the pitch of your voice varies continuously so that your speech is not heard as a tune. This pitch variation extends over single phonemes, sequences of phonemes, and whole utterances. The term intonation refers to the patterns that can be found within this pitch variation, and so intonation can be defined as a 'pattern of pitch variation'. It is not the absolute pitch of any single syllable that counts, but the overall pitch pattern and the relative pitch heights within it. Prominence and rhythm are inseparable parts of intonation too.

The tone unit

In order to study these continuous pitch variations more closely it is helpful to divide connected speech into units of pitch. The phonological unit devised for this purpose is called the *tone unit* (sometimes called *tone group*). This unit enables us to isolate pitch patterns by defining where one pattern ends and the next begins.

The tone unit contains a single complete pitch pattern. The smallest possible tone unit contains only a *tonic syllable* but a tone group can also contain a *tail*, an *onset*, a *head* and a *prehead*. We will investigate the meaning of these terms in that order.

The tonic syllable

Most of the pitch change in a tone unit is concentrated onto one syllable of one word. This syllable is the *tonic syllable* (sometimes also called the *tonic* or the *nucleus*).*

Not only does the tonic syllable carry the main pitch change, but it also carries prominence. In fact a tonic syllable is by definition prominent.

Discovery activity 78 Finding the tonic syllable

What are the last few (English) utterances you made? Say them to yourself trying to recapture not just the sequence of words but your intention behind the words. Taking a short section, can you locate one syllable that has more emphasis and more pitch change than the others?

*One meaning of the word 'tonic' is 'healthy or strengthening', a good name for this syllable which brings an utterance to life and gives it shape, meaning and vividness.

Commentary ■ ■ ■

If you can locate a more emphatic syllable this is probably the tonic syllable. If you can't, run the phrase again slowly, either aloud or internally. The pitch may fluctuate over the whole phrase but will be more marked or definite on the tonic. Also the shift does not need to be big, just more marked than the surrounding pitch variation. If you find that there seem to be two tonic syllables side by side, then see which is more prominent by exaggerating the prominence first of one and then of the other. When you do this one version will sound right.

By this combination of prominence and pitch change you mark the tonic syllable or the word containing the tonic syllable as the most important in that tone group with respect to the message you want to convey. The tonic syllable is thus the focus of the tone unit. It is what the tone unit is about. A tone unit must contain a tonic syllable, otherwise it is incomplete. But it need not contain anything else. Here are two tone units, each containing the minimum of one tonic syllable:

<u>YES</u>
<u>STAY</u> ■

Note on orthographic convention

In the remainder of this section capital letters indicate a prominent syllable, and underlined capital letters indicate a tonic syllable. Word stress is distinguished with the symbol / '/. Where pitch movement is not indicated, experiment with different patterns, but put the main emphasis and most of the pitch change on the tonic syllable.

Three variables of pitch

When we examine the pitch movement in any given tonic unit there are three main variables to observe:

1 The direction of the pitch movement. Does the pitch rise or fall? Does it rise and then fall, or fall and then rise? Perhaps it is level, without significant change. Different descriptions of intonation recognize different numbers of significant pitch patterns, anything from five to over forty.

2 The degree of pitch movement. Does the pitch move a lot or a little? By how much does the pitch fall or rise, relative to each speaker's own norm?

3 The placement of this pitch movement within the speaker's own voice range. Are the patterns pitched in the higher, middle or lower part of the speaker's voice range?

Of course there are other non-pitch variables that affect our perception of the speaker's intention. Some of these are audible, such as voice quality and timbre, volume, use of pause, speed of speech, etc. And some are visual, such as the speaker's facial expression, eye movement and quality and duration of eye contact, gesture and body movement, physical posture, breathing, etc.

Discovery activity 79 Three variables in your own intonation

1 Take any short utterance or phrase that has only one tonic unit, that is one major pitch change.

2 Say it a few times and try to observe the three variables (direction, degree and placement) as described above.

3 Keeping the same sequence of words, try changing each of the three variables in turn.

Commentary ■ ■ ■

If you find it difficult to spot the variables, then try speaking and making any changes you can, listening carefully to yourself. You may find this helps you to discover the variables through trying to change them. ■

The tail

Frequently there are non-prominent syllables following the tonic syllable, and these are said to make up the *tail*.

Discovery activity 80 Finding the tail

1 In these two examples there are three syllables in the tone unit. Begin the main pitch movement on the tonic syllable, and let the tail share in the completion of the pitch movement.

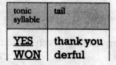

tonic syllable	tail
YES	thank you
WON	derful

2 Though the tail never contains a prominence, it may contain a word stress. Try this:

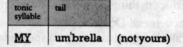

tonic syllable	tail	
MY	um'brella	(not yours)

Here the tonic is MY; it has the main emphasis and pitch movement. 'brell is the word stress normal for the word umbrella.

The onset

A tone unit must contain at least one prominent syllable, which is on the tonic syllable. Where there are two prominent syllables in the tone group, it is the second which is the tonic syllable; the first is the *onset*.

Discovery activity 81 Finding the onset

1 Try this, with prominence on PHONE and prominence and main pitch change on MOR:

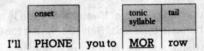

	onset			tonic syllable	tail
I'll	PHONE	you to		MOR	row

2 And now try it with the tonic syllable on PHONE and MOR as a word stress in the tail:

	tonic syllable	tail
I'll	PHONE	you to'morrow

The head

The stretch of utterance from the first prominent syllable, the onset, up to but not including the tonic syllable, constitutes the *head*. So in this example:

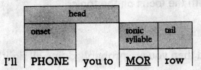

	head				
	onset			tonic syllable	tail
I'll	PHONE	you to		MOR	row

The head begins on the onset syllable, and so where there is no onset there can be no head.

The prehead

This consists of all non-prominent syllables before the onset. In this case:

		head				
pre head	onset				tonic syllable	tail
I'll	PHONE	you to			MOR	row

If there is no onset, and so no head, then any non-prominent syllables leading up to the tonic constitute the prehead. For example:

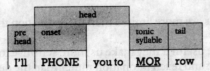

prehead	tonic syllable	tail
It was	FUN	ny

However, if the speaker inserts the word *so* and makes it prominent, it becomes the head:

prehead	head	tonic syllable	tail
It was	SO	FUN	ny

A prehead can therefore occur with or without a following head.

Discovery activity 82 Putting these terms together

Take a short utterance in English, perhaps one that you typically use in class.

1 Say it a few times and then write it down.

2 Decide which is the tonic syllable. If you think there is more than one then you may have more than one tone unit. Select only one tone unit to work with.

3 Mark the tonic syllable and the tail if there is one.

4 Are there any word stresses in the tail? If so, mark them in.

5 Are there any words before the tonic syllable? If so, is there a prominent syllable among them? If there is, then that is the onset. If there seem to be two prominences then either one is a word stress or you have got two tone groups.

6 The syllables from the onset to the tonic (including the onset but excluding the tonic) make up the head. Compare any pitch movement on the head with pitch movement on the tonic.

7 Are there any syllables before the head? If so that is the prehead. Notice how it leads into the head, or if there is no head then directly into the tonic.

8 Notice how all these (artificially separated) parts flow together into one overall pitch contour, with the focus on the tonic.

How are you doing?

If you are confused then you are probably doing all right! Let me explain.

These definitions of the divisions of the tone unit are useful if they help us become more aware of what intonation is made up of. But we must remember that our aim is to help people to use and be sensitive to intonation patterns, and not to get carried away by trying to fit what actually happens into a contrived descriptive framework. Consider these statements for a moment:

1 Descriptions of intonation have not necessarily been devised with language learners in mind.
2 The descriptions are more limited than the intonation they are trying to describe.
3 Descriptions are useful if they make us more sensitive to the phenomenon.
4 We want to learn and teach intonation rather than the descriptions of intonation.

My point is that we are examining the theories of intonation in order to find what can help us, not in order to follow them. I do not think it is helpful to try to teach all the divisions of the tone unit. Nor is it necessary for you to be infallibly accurate in your analysis of tone units. I'm not. The main aspects that help learners seem to be sensitivity to stress, rhythm, and the location of the tonic syllable. We will pick this up in the classroom toolkit.

Summary

The minimum size for a tone unit is one tonic syllable only. What may vary is the number of syllables occurring after or before it. Here are the possible structures of a tone unit, showing which parts are optional:

optional	optional	necessary	optional
prehead +	head +	tonic syllable +	tail

Prehead: all non-prominent syllables before the onset.

Head: the stretch of utterance from the first prominent syllable, the onset, up to but not including the tonic syllable.

Tail: non-prominent syllables following the tonic syllable. May contain a word stress.

Tonic syllable: the focal syllable in the tone unit. It carries the main pitch change and is prominent. For example:

tonic syllable
LOOK!

tonic syllable	tail
LOV	ely!

tonic syllable	tail including word stress
LOV	ely 'flowers!

prehead	tonic syllable	tail
What	**LOV**	ely 'flowers!

	head		tonic syllable	tail
onset				
AB	solutely		**LOV**	ely 'flowers!

		head		tonic syllable	tail
prehead	onset				
What	AB	solutely		**LOV**	ely 'flowers!

pre head	tonic syllable	tail
Oh	**THANK**	you!

		head		tonic syllable	tail
prehead	onset				
What	AB	solutely		**LOV**	ely 'flowers!

Try these examples with different pitch patterns, but put the main emphasis, and most of the pitch movement, on the tonic syllable.

Some notes

The tonic syllable is selected by the speaker as the most important syllable in the tone unit, representing the focus of information. It must therefore be made to stand out in some way, hence its special status as the syllable carrying both the main prominence and the main pitch movement.

The tonic syllable is often the last lexical item in the tone unit, owing to the tendency in English for new information or the focus of information to be placed at the end of a sentence.

The tonic syllable may be placed earlier in the tone group, where there is a word of greater importance to the message.

Occasionally the tonic syllable may be a non-lexical word, as when some contrast or contradiction is being emphasized. For example:

it <u>WAS</u> ex'pensive   (even though you don't believe me)
not you <u>AND</u> me   (one of us but not both)

In cases of correction we may even find the tonic syllable placed on a syllable not containing word stress. Perhaps the learner has said:

it's go to <u>RAIN</u>

prompting the teacher to say:

it's go<u>ING</u> to rain

The head and prehead usually form a smooth pitch contour leading up to the tonic. Any jump in pitch before the tonic may represent a separate tonic and therefore another tone unit.

The tail may complete the pitch pattern started on the tonic syllable, but any jump in pitch after the tonic syllable would again probably indicate another tone unit.

The generally smooth pitch movement on the prehead, head and tail does not generally carry as much communicative significance as the pitch movement begun on the tonic syllable. But the pitch of the onset syllable, where there is one, is significant in that it provides a standard against which the tonic syllable can be either relatively higher, lower or the same. This determines the *key* of the utterance, which also helps shape the intonational meaning. (See discussion on key following discovery activity 87.)

Pauses are less likely within a tone unit, and more likely between tone units.

The boundary of a tone unit may well coincide with a syntactic boundary, but where the unit of information crosses a syntactic boundary, it is likely that the tone unit does too.

The meaning of intonation

So far we have described the *form* of intonation. But isolating and describing the physical patterns of pitch is only a part of the task. We also need to understand the *meaning* of these pitch patterns in context. It is here that there is less agreement between the different descriptions of intonation, as we shall see.

Different descriptions of the meaning of intonation

Descriptions of intonation differ in the way they account for its meaning. One description links intonational meaning to attitude, another links it to grammar, and a third to discourse. That there are different descriptions of the meaning of intonation is not really a problem for us as we are practical people on the lookout for whatever helps us to facilitate learning. None of these descriptions is complete and each is useful as far as it goes. Ideally what we are after is a system that:

● is learnable;
● accounts for what native speakers do and don't do;
● has a limited set of rules that enables learners to develop valid generalizations on which to base their own interpretation and production.

In my view the discourse approach goes closer to satisfying these three conditions, and so I will describe it more fully after looking at the attitudinal approach and the grammatical approach.

Intonation as an indicator of attitude

This approach presents intonation as a way of expressing our attitude at the moment of speaking to the situation we are in, or to what we are talking about, or to ourselves or to our listener.

Discovery activity 83 Intonation and attitude

1 Take a short sentence and say it aloud in a number of different ways, corresponding perhaps to 'miserable', 'matter-of-fact', 'insistent', 'disbelieving', 'furious', 'optimistic', etc. You may be able to observe variations in pitch direction, range and placement within your voice range. Notice also variations in voice quality and body movement. Record yourself doing this. What else can you learn from the playback?

2 Take any taped extract of authentic speech and listen to the pitch variables while trying to ascribe an attitude to the speaker.

3 Does intonation in other languages, including ones you don't understand, sound the same?

Commentary ■ ■ ■

The attitudinal approach usually isolates certain intonation contours and gives them attitudinal labels such as 'impressed, either favourably or unfavourably', 'lighter, more casual', 'concerned, reproachful, hurt', 'flat, even hostile', 'brisk, business-like, considerate' etc.

The problem is not that a certain tone choice cannot carry a particular attitude. The problem is that such attitudinal values cannot be presented in a way that offers learners a set of rules from which they can make meaningful choices affecting their own production. Nor does it enable learners to discern their own attitudes and to select an appropriate intonation before they speak.

Moreover, the attitudes or feelings assigned to any one contour can be extended almost indefinitely. Not only are attitudes difficult to recognize in ourselves, they are also difficult to label objectively, and even if we could do both of these things, we still face the fact that a given tone choice can be a manifestation of a number of different attitudes of dubious connection. At what point, for example, does 'business-like' become 'considerate', or 'flat' become 'hostile'?

Remember, too, that expression of attitude can also be a function of the choice of lexis and syntax, the location of pause and prominence, voice quality, facial expression, gesture, eye movement, other body language, and so on. If all of these factors can help express an attitude, it may be that in some cases the intonation contour coincides with, rather than directly and solely expresses, the attitude of the speaker.

So, whatever the merits of this approach, I don't think it accounts usefully for what native speakers do and don't do, and I don't think that on its own it provides our learners with a system that is learnable or generative. ■

Intonation as a grammatical indicator

There are two aspects to the grammatical function of intonation: the correlation between intonation and sentence type, and the correlation between tone unit divisions and syntactic boundaries.

Intonation and sentence type

This view of the function of intonation notes that a small number of common sentence types are typically linked to certain basic intonation contours. For example:

• declarative	falling
• *Wh-* question	falling
• yes/no question	rising
• multiple interrogative	rising then falling
• imperative	falling
• exclamation	falling
• question tags:	
expecting confirmation	falling
less certain expectation	rising

Although there may be a tendency for certain pitch contours to coincide with certain sentence types, it can be shown that they do not always do so. It is quite possible for a *Wh-* question to have either a rising tone or a falling tone, depending on its function. 'What's her name?' with a falling tone on the last word can mean *I don't know her name, please tell me* or with a rising tone on the last word can mean *I've forgotten her name, please refresh my memory*.

In fact, almost any sentence can carry a range of intonations, each one imparting a different nuance or meaning within the context. The importance of this observation has received more emphasis with communicative approaches to teaching English. By keeping the grammatical sequence of words constant, and changing the intonation and the context, we can give a range of meanings to the words. This illustrates not only that form and function do not coincide, but that classification of intonational meaning by sentence type is a generalization that cannot yield a learnable set of rules by which learners can choose one intonation pattern against another.

Tone unit division and syntactic boundaries

From this point of view one of the most important functions of intonation is marking off syntactic structures from each other, rather like the function of punctuation in writing but with a much wider range of choices. This may help the listener to process the speech in its appropriate units and it may also help the speaker to organize her speech. By dividing one structure from the next, tone units indicate what structurally belongs to what.

There is a tendency for tone unit boundaries to occur at the boundaries between sentences, clauses and phrases, especially in more careful colloquial speech (this is not always so clear in rapid colloquial speech). It is certainly useful for learners to try to exploit this tendency in their speaking and listening. But the links between tone units and syntactic boundaries are very far short of offering a full account of intonational meaning, since the link essentially focuses on the gaps between tone units rather than on the pitch contours themselves.

Discovery activity 84 Intonation and grammatical structure

1 Take a dialogue from a play or from a coursebook you are using, or improvise a dialogue or monologue with yourself. Once you settle into it try to notice to what extent syntactic boundaries coincide with tone unit boundaries.

2 Try to make this observation in your own speech or in that of your colleagues.

3 What about the learners you teach? Try to observe their speech during the lesson. Is there any difference in the degree to which they do or don't use tone units to mark syntactic boundaries?

Intonation and discourse

This approach views the function of intonation as the speaker's way of organizing and relating together meanings throughout the discourse. Intonation reveals the information structure of the discourse, the relationship between utterances. The term discourse refers to the larger context of the whole conversational interaction between speakers, in which tone groups and sequences of tone groups occur in certain relationships to each other.

Since intonation is a way of indicating the relationship of parts of the discourse to other parts, and of indicating what goes with what in the discourse, it follows that you cannot isolate a tone unit from its discourse context and make valid statements about what the pitch pattern means. Intonational meaning cannot be separated from discoursal meaning.

The common ground

Since intonation is seen as being vitally linked, on a moment-by-moment basis, to the process of interaction between the participants, it follows that much significance is attached to the existence of *common ground* between speaker and listener. Common ground is the knowledge and experience that the participants think they share about the world, the topic and each other in terms of ideas, emotions, attitudes, viewpoints, etc at any given point in the interaction. Common ground is the overlap between speaker and listener, as experienced by each of them from their own point of view.

If we look at the difference between the interaction of friends and that of strangers we can see that between strangers there is a much greater degree of uncertainty about the boundaries of their common ground, about what each can take for granted about the other. Common ground is that which is somehow already negotiated, accepted, gone before, in some way known or implicitly agreed by the participants. That which is new, not yet known, not yet negotiated, not possible to assume or take for granted is outside the common ground. And of course one of the areas that is open to negotiation, manipulation and misunderstanding is what exactly constitutes the common ground between people.

The essence of this approach is that a speaker's intonation choices depend ultimately on his assessment of the state and extent of the common ground between himself and the listeners, or on how he wishes his assessment to appear to the listeners. The notion of common ground is exploitable by the speaker to his advantage, as we can easily observe in our own speech or that of others around us, or in the speech of advertisers and politicians who may use intonation to suggest that what they are saying is already negotiated and agreed by us, and part of our common ground, even when it isn't.

In the remainder of the discovery toolkit we will examine:

- *proclaiming* and *referring* tones: how the state of the common ground is manifested in terms of pitch choice;
- *oblique intonation*: used when the common ground is not being referred to;
- the notion of *key*: how tone groups are related to each other, how they are knitted into the fabric of the overall discourse.

Proclaiming and referring tones

The fundamental intonation choice is a binary one between information the speaker wishes to portray as additional to the common ground, and information the speaker wishes to portray as already part of the common ground between speaker and hearer.

Information which is additional to the common ground is marked by a pitch that finishes with a falling movement, and is given the name *proclaiming tone*. Information which is given as already shared and part of the common ground is marked by a pitch that finishes with a rising movement and is given the name *referring tone*, since it refers back to something already shared or negotiated.

The most frequently used proclaiming tone is the falling tone, and this can be transcribed with the sign ↘

The most frequently used referring tone is the falling–rising tone, which can be transcribed with the sign ＼／↗

If we contrast these two tones over the same sequence of words we can see how they convey different interpretations on the state of the common ground:

1 ＼ WHEN did she say she'd <u>COME</u>?

and

2 ＼／↗ WHEN did she say she'd <u>COME</u>?

When reading these symbols, remember that most of the pitch movement indicated by the arrow takes place on the tonic syllable (underlined).

In the first case the tonic and the main part of the falling tone are on COME. The question is proclaimed as new or additional to the common ground, in other words the speaker suggests that the specific timing of her arrival has not yet been clarified and shared between the speakers. Notice that WHEN is likely to be given some prominence (ie the onset syllable) and that the words leading up to COME already begin the fall.

In the second sentence the pitch is falling–rising, that is referring. The main part of the pitch movement is on COME, although the falling movement may begin earlier. The referring tone carries the suggestion that the timing of her arrival is not a new matter in the common understanding of the two speakers, so it refers back to clarify or restate something already negotiated.

Here is another example, this time consisting of two tone groups:

＼／↗ When we've VISited <u>HAST</u>ings ＼ we'll go to <u>CANT</u>erbury

Here the implication is that the visiting of Hastings is already shared information, while going to Canterbury is proclaimed as new. Notice that if you reverse the two tone units the meaning remains the same:

＼ We'll go to <u>CANT</u>erbury ＼／↗ when we've VISited <u>HAST</u>ings

Compare this with:

＼ When we've VISited <u>HAST</u>ings ＼／↗ we'll go to <u>CANT</u>erbury

Here the going to Canterbury is implied as being already known to the listener. It is the place to be visited before, namely Hastings, that is proclaimed as additional for the listener.

Again this is not changed by reversing the tone groups:

＼／↗ We'll go to <u>CANT</u>erbury ＼ when we've VISited <u>HAST</u>ings

Discovery activity 85

1 Sentences **a** and **b** each have two tone units here, but the first has referring tone followed by proclaiming tone, and the second has proclaiming tone followed by referring tone. Try to get the movement shown by the arrow onto the prominent syllable.

a | ⟋ The <u>TEA</u>'S | ↘ on the <u>TAB</u>le |

b | ↘ The <u>TEA</u>'S | ⟋ on the <u>TAB</u>le |

2 When you think you have made a significant distinction between them, see if you can match them to these alternative wordings:

a Well, as for the tea, it's on the table.

b Well, as for the table, it's got some tea on it.

More marked versions of proclaiming and referring tones

So far we have seen that the primary meaning distinction is between proclaiming and referring tones, and that proclaiming tone is most frequently conveyed by a falling intonation, and referring tone by a falling–rising intonation. In both cases, however, there is a more marked, more dominant pitch choice available denoted by rising–falling tone for proclaiming tone, and rising for referring tone. Generally speaking these two marked options are likely to occur less frequently than their unmarked counterparts, although this may depend on the discourse situation. The choices can be summarized as follows:

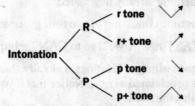

R = *referring tone*, which has two forms, the more usual r tone, and the marked, more dominant r+ tone.

P = *proclaiming tone*, which has two forms, the more usual p tone and the marked, more dominant p+ tone.

Here is an example of the contrast between the four tones (I first heard a similar story from David Brazil):

My two-year-old daughter Alice is poised, with obvious intent, to carry a bucket of mud and water (carefully mixed up by herself) through the back door from the garden into the house. Seeing the imminence of this undesirable event I first say:

1 ↘⟋ <u>AL</u>ice

The r tone attempts to call on our common understanding according to which *both you and I know that you shouldn't carry mud into the house*, or *WE know better than this don't we*. However, she continues, so I say:

2 ⟋ <u>AL</u>ice

Adopting the r+ tone, the marked and more dominating version of the referring tone, suggesting more strongly that there is common ground between us to appeal to, *Hey! Both you and I know this is not a good thing to do.*

However, she continues and I then say:

3 ⬂ ALice

Using the p tone I acknowledge that my appeal to the common ground has failed, and I therefore use a proclaiming tone to add to the common ground something that turns out to be missing. This is a warning or threat. *Look! In case you've forgotten I really must tell you this is not a good thing to do.*

She continues, so I say:

4 ⬈⬂ ALice

Using the p+ tone I not only add something new but I opt for a more marked and dominant version of it. *Look! If you don't stop I may have to stop you!*

At this point intervention rather than further intonation is called for.

Summary

We have looked at the communicative choices of tones. The primary binary choice is between proclaiming and referring, and the secondary choice is between the unmarked or the marked version of proclaiming and referring. This gives a total of four communicative tone choices. In the next section we look at tone choices that are not directly communicative, that is they are not based on assumptions about common ground.

Oblique intonation

This uses the falling tone ⬂ and may be used for:

- certain kinds of recitation, where the *language is being quoted* rather than any *meaning communicated*. Examples could include: rhymes and poems, multiplication tables, reading recipes and instructions aloud, saying prayers, repeating sentences after the teacher, etc;
- reading aloud from a text, where the reader sees her task as simply to say *what is on the page*, rather than to *communicate the meaning*.

In either case the speaker uses a proclaiming tone, not to add to the common ground, but to proclaim about what the language itself is. The speaker is saying to the hearer *I'm just telling you what the words are, make of it what you will.* Of course most often in reciting poetry or in reading a story aloud the speaker interprets and communicates a meaning through the full range of referring and proclaiming choices.

The following activity focuses on the distinction between recitation of the type *this is what the language says*, and recitation of the type *this is the meaning I am giving to this language.*

Discovery activity 86

1 Recite these letters first with each letter as a separate tone unit, like this:

⬂ A   ⬂ I   ⬂ F   ⬂ G   ⬂ S   ⬂ W   ⬂ R

and now with all of the letters making just one tone group, with the tonic on the last one, like this:

⬂ A   T   F   G   S   W   R

2 Say this sentence as a quotation, as the first line of the rhyme:

Humpty Dumpty sat on a wall

and now say it as if it were a piece of important communication. What is the difference?

3 Recite each of these numbers in such a way that you do not take account of the numbers that have gone before:

↘ 24 ↘ 37 ↘ 27 ↘ 23 ↘ 43

and now say them again, but this time as discourse (taking account of what has gone before).

4 Say this sentence as if it was being repeated in chorus by the class after the teacher:

That man on the bicycle is going very slowly

and now say it as a piece of communication.

Commentary ■ ■ ■

1 Here you made each letter a separate tone unit when you recited, and all of them one tone unit as communication.

2 When the rhyme is recited it has four prominences and one tonic syllable, *wall*, where the tone falls.

HUMPty DUMPty SAT on a <u>WALL</u>

A characteristic of recitation is that you increase the number of prominences in a tone unit. This can be done because it is not part of a discourse that relates to the common ground. When said as a piece of communication it would, if it were one tone unit, have no more than two prominences and only one tonic. Perhaps:

Humpty DUMPty sat on a <u>WALL</u>   (by the way, do you know what Humpty Dumpty did?)

If you can't get away from the recitation rhythm of the rhyme, then try:

Mrs SMITH sat on the <u>STAIRS</u>   (there was nowhere else to sit)

3 In the first reading you probably put the prominence on the second **digit** of each number. In the second reading you may have placed the prominence like this:

↘ 2<u>4</u> ↘ 3<u>7</u> ↘ <u>2</u>7 ↘ 2<u>3</u> ↘ <u>4</u>3 ...

showing that your choice of prominence, and therefore of tonic syllable, is influenced by what has gone before.

4 A characteristic of classroom drilling, chorusing, and repeating after the teacher is that more than two prominences are often placed in the tone unit. This makes it more like quoting intonation than communicative intonation. The intonation of the learners is saying *this is what the language is*, rather than *this is what I am saying to you*. Quoting uses the proclaiming tone.

In this classroom example prominence and pitch get chosen not out of communicative consideration between speaker and hearer but according to teaching technique. Much intonation is related to the methodology of classroom management, rather than to the language in genuine communicative use. This brings us on to the zero tone. ■

The zero tone

The zero tone is a level pitch, without significant pitch contrast. It can be indicated with a horizontal arrow: →

This tone is used when there is no reason for making communicative choices. For example, it may be used by native speakers during cognitive activity, while thinking aloud, during on-the-spot verbal encoding, for example:

→ er ...   → mmm ...

Likewise language learners may use zero tone while preoccupied with linguistic items, with cognitive formulation, with the form of the utterance rather than its meaning. And in that circumstance it is entirely appropriate.

The zero tone is also used during bored, aimless, non-interactive speech; and for example when reading a newspaper item aloud to someone else *until* you reach the section of focal interest when you drop into communicative pitch choices.

Discovery activity 87

Take any paragraph and read it aloud three times, the first time using only proclaiming tones, the second using only referring tones and the third time using level or zero tone. Notice what it feels like when you do this, and how the intonation choice affects your feeling of purpose.

Reading aloud and intonation

Reading aloud is an interactive process between reader and text. The reader is meshing information from the text with existing knowledge. The way the reader uses intonation to highlight the information structure of the text can provide you with a useful diagnosis of her understanding of the text. The reader can:

1 Leave words and chunks floating free, unconnected into sense groups or tone units, making it quite difficult for the hearer to follow. She is saying *This is what the disconnected words and phrases are*.

2 Quote the text. She is saying *This is what the connected text says* though she brings little outside knowledge to bear.

3 Enter the text, perform it, highlight syllables, words or phrases. She is saying *This is what the text means to me*. The reader is adding her own interpretation and orientation towards the hearer, making tone choices in the light of assumptions about the state of convergence of the common ground. This reading is interactive. There is a continuum of delivery from quoting the text: *This is what it says*, to entering the text and performing it: *Here is my version of it*. This is why many teachers have found reading aloud to be such a powerful instrument for diagnosing the reader's understanding of the text.

Key

Every speaker has a characteristic pitch range within which all their pitch contours take place. Some speakers have a narrow range, others have a wide range. According to the discourse approach to intonation every speaker distinguishes three significant pitch levels within her individual and characteristic pitch range. And every tone unit that is uttered is assigned to one of these three levels, or keys.

Key is determined by the first or only prominence in the tone unit, compared with the first or only prominence in the preceding tone unit. A tone unit is in high key if its first prominence is at a higher pitch than the first prominence in the preceding tone unit. It is in mid key if it is the same pitch, and it is in low key if lower. Thus all key choices are high, mid or low relative to the pitch choice of the previous tone unit.

The meaning of key

Each tone unit selects a new key choice and this adds a meaning independent of the rest of the pitch movement.

- High is *contrastive*. The tone group contains information that contrasts with what speaker or hearer might expect.
- Mid is *additive*. The matter is additional to what has gone before.
- Low is *equative*. The content follows naturally from the content of the previous tone unit. It has no new impact.

Mid key does not mean normal or average; it is the neutral or unmarked key against which the choice of high or low is significant.

Discovery activity 88

Make the following statement with two tone units, each with only one prominence (ie on the tonic syllable). The first tone unit is referring, and the second is proclaiming.

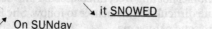 On SUNday ＼ it SNOWED

1 Try it like that.

2 Now try it first with high key.

＼ it SNOWED
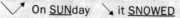 On SUNday

This means that regardless of the pitch movement on each tonic, the starting pitch of the second is higher than the starting pitch of the first. When you get this it should give the impression of *What a surprise! Who would have expected it to snow?*

3 Now try with mid key.

On SUNday ＼ it SNOWED

The starting pitch of the second tonic is the same as that of the first. This should give the impression of additional information, but no great surprise. *Oh by the way, another thing about Sunday is that it snowed.*

4 Now try with low key.

↘↗ On SUNday

 ↘ it SNOWED

The starting pitch of the second tonic is lower than that of the first. This can give the impression *It practically goes without saying that it should have snowed – what else would you expect?*

Summary: implications of intonation theory for the classroom

1 There is general agreement about the components of tone units, and the terminology used to refer to them, though learning them is not necessarily relevant to language learners.
2 There is less agreement on what intonation means, or on how to describe the meaning in a way that is systematic, learnable and generative.
3 However, the attitudinal, grammatical and discoursal approaches each have something to offer.
4 The discourse approach is attractive: its orientation is simple and workable enough to provide the basis for manageable and useful class learning activities, and a good foundation for the development of both learner and teacher sensitivity to intonation.
5 Another feature of the discourse approach is the emphasis on practising intonation in context, which suggests integrating intonation work with the natural life of the classroom, rather than importing special practice materials.
6 Mechanical practice of pitch patterns out of context may have only a limited role to play.
7 Authenticity in human relations could encourage more authentic uses of intonation.
8 The often unarticulated assumption that learners' problems with intonation stem largely from mother tongue interference needs to be questioned. Preoccupation with language means that learners lose touch with intonation. You can't use the intonation system if you don't yet know the language well enough, and if there is no communication going on.
9 Furthermore, preoccupation with the calculation of rules and formulation of sentences, rather than with a genuinely experienced need to communicate, means that lack of intonation is a natural and in fact quite authentic choice. While you can choose *words* 'as if' you are communicating, it may not be as easy to choose *intonation* 'as if' you are communicating, because intonation may not be an essentially cognitive choice.

Part 2
Classroom toolkit

Level 1 Sounds in isolation   96

Level 2 Words in isolation   145

Level 3 Connected speech   171

Introduction to the classroom toolkit

The classroom toolkit is designed to help you to develop trust and confidence in your creativity to turn classroom events into learning events, so that the learners become their own resource, and their performance provides their own syllabus.

Level 1　Sounds in isolation

1	General applications of the chart	96
2	Using the pointer	98
3	Introducing and integrating the chart	99
4	Seven modes of chart usage	100
5	A first lesson with the chart	107
6	Four ways of giving models	110
7	Developing your internal imaging of sounds	114
8	Developing your use of mime and gesture	115
9	Working with individual sounds	118
10	Working with mistakes	132

1　General applications of the chart

The chart has applications in many kinds of lessons and at any language level. Here are some of the applications:

Level 1: Individual sounds

- learning new sounds and sound sequences;
- shaping and fine-tuning sounds;
- using the visual cues in the chart layout to strengthen the link between aural perception and oral production;
- relating the visual arrangement of the chart to the internal muscular sensation of each sound;
- inviting learners to identify their own areas of difficulty on the chart;
- recognition and discrimination activities, eg minimal pairs, odd one out, same or different, etc;
- highlighting the pronunciation of word endings, past tenses, agreements, etc;
- prompting and correcting learners by touching the chart rather than by speaking yourself;
- inviting learners to collect their own key words for each sound.

Level 2: Words in isolation

- separating the sounds of a word, working on them, and then putting the word back together;
- giving feedback to learners on their word pronunciation;
- working on syllabification and word stress;
- highlighting and working on sound/spelling relationships;
- developing learners' ability to write down pronunciations of words using phonemic symbols;
- promoting self-help by relating use of the chart to use of dictionaries for checking and discovering pronunciations;
- presenting and recycling vocabulary;
- promoting better learning, retention and recall of vocabulary through precise and vivid attention to pronunciation and word stress.

Level 3: Connected speech

- examining small samples of connected speech for ear training, awareness raising, and practice;
- focusing on fluency by highlighting linking sounds that join words together;
- isolating important words and pronunciations from continuous speech on tape or video, and reassembling the fluency of connected speech;
- focusing on changes and modifications to consonants in the stream of speech;
- drawing attention to the effects of stress and unstress on vowel sounds;
- examining the reduction and simplification of structure words in connected speech;
- studying rhythm and the changes necessary in pronunciation to achieve a good rhythm;
- drawing attention to intonation contours and how they relate to the prominent syllables;
- practising structures without repetition by focusing on the fluency and connectedness of the students' utterance;
- as an alternative way of addressing the class (eg giving instructions, asking questions, setting homework) without speaking yourself.

General

- Use pronunciation work as an opportunity to change pace and re-focus attention during a lesson.
- Bring phonology alive as an active, creative, physical, joyful and integral part of all other language activities!

All of the kinds of activity outlined above can be worked on in seven different ways. These ways, or modes of work, are described in Section 4 below.

2   Using the pointer

The attention of the group is focused on a symbol on the chart by touching that symbol lightly and deliberately with the pointer, somewhere within its box. This has the effect of selecting that symbol and bringing it forward for attention. Touching a sequence of symbols in turn makes a sequence of sounds or a word.

When you are working at higher levels of discrimination you can point to the centre of the box to indicate that a learner's sound was the exact target sound you are after, and point closer to the edge of the box to indicate that the learner's sound was *acceptable but not quite right*. You can point to another box if it was closer to another sound, or to a mix of boxes if the sound seems to be a mixture of two or three sounds. You can point outside the chart if the sound given by the learner does not exist in standard English. Learners can be helped by this kind of precise feedback. But keep the work light, and with enough supportive humour to maintain both pleasure and curiosity.

Everyone is active in this, one person pointing, others watching, recognizing the sound, saying the sound internally, and retaining it until invited to say it aloud. The activity of pointing can evoke a high degree of attention from learners. In the spirit of this approach the pointer belongs to the whole class, not just to the teacher. After you, the teacher, have introduced something on the chart, you might offer the pointer to anyone who would like to come to the chart to test themselves, or test another, or get a response from another, or seek further guidance, or try something out to see if it's right or wrong. This helps the way the class manages itself in terms of turn taking and respect for the efforts of each other.

You can be very much in control by initiating tasks, by giving feedback to the learners on their efforts, and by deciding who is to have the pointer next. But the learners too can take this control once they see how to use the chart, and you can stand aside and leave them to take the initiative while you watch and listen, intervening when needed. Used with this attitude the action of pointing can help reveal learners' perceptions of problems and can encourage initiative-taking.

I use a telescopic pointer as used by speakers and presenters, but any thin stick or rod about 40–60 cm long would do just as well. A pen is a bit short, as then the wrist and forearm obscure part of the chart, and a ruler is a bit wide, also obscuring other symbols. But either can be used.

One final point, and perhaps the most important. The dynamic of pointing necessarily slows the speed and deepens the attention. When the chart is being used for pointing out words, learners will probably say the word slowly and with more care. As soon as they've done that I ask them to say it faster or 'in English', an invitation to retain the insight but bring the utterance up to natural spoken speed.

3   Introducing and integrating the chart

The aim is to use the chart not only to add impact to your normal pronunciation work, but to infuse all class work with an easy access to its pronunciation content. Before the chart can be helpful in these ways you will have to think about an initial introductory stage for the benefit of those (including yourself) who may not have used the chart before.

So, there are essentially two stages:

1   Introduction of the chart
2   Integration of the chart

Introducing the chart

Introducing the chart refers to the initial two or three sessions where the class are meeting the chart for the first time. Learners are beginning to identify individual sounds and gradually to recognize and distinguish them from each other. In doing this they are beginning to find out *what there is that they can pay attention to*. They are beginning to attach the aural and oral impressions and the physical sensations of individual sounds to the symbols on the chart, thereby investing the symbols with the capacity to evoke the same sounds again when the symbols are pointed out.

As learners become familiar with the workings of the chart and become able to use it, the chart increasingly becomes an instrument for all sorts of pronunciation work and for integrating that work with other language work.

Once you have read about the seven modes for using the chart outlined in Section 4 you will probably see how in the first few moments of this introduction stage mode 1 is likely to predominate, but that it should quickly be followed by work using modes 2, 3 and 4.

Integrating the chart

This is the main use of the chart. Both you and the learners are becoming able to use the chart as an instrument for refining awareness of what is involved in making isolated sounds and in running the sounds together to make words. The chart provides an immediate way to test hunches and take risks. Its most important attribute is that it enables objectification of inner processes that otherwise go unseen, and this in turn makes possible a more subtle level of feedback, initially from teacher to learner, but increasingly from learner to learner and from learner to teacher.

The chart is integrated into all areas of language work at all three levels using a wide range of the applications described in Section 4. Mode 1 will still be used from time to time, modes 2–5 will be in constant use, and modes 6 and 7 will increasingly be used as learners gain confidence.

4   Seven modes of chart usage

A vast repertoire of activities is possible. Many are specific to the chart, while others are conventional activities made more focused and precise through appropriate use of the chart. In this section I describe a way of ordering them so that they form a basis from which you can investigate the potential of the chart and adapt it to your style of teaching. It will enable you to create an unlimited range of games, exercises and techniques.

Each mode is characterized by its basic *transaction*. The transaction consists simply of a first move and a second move in response to it. For example, the transaction of mode 2 is 'teacher points' followed by 'learner speaks'. Fig. 37 shows the seven possible transactions in the second and third columns. Each mode includes all the activities that are possible using that basic transaction format.

As you become familiar with the modes you will soon find that you no longer need to think about the modes separately, but that you move naturally from one mode to another. For instance if you wanted to prompt a learner to add the past tense ending /ɪd/ you might use mode 2 ('teacher points' followed by 'learner speaks') and it would take two or three seconds. If you wanted to help a learner to distinguish more clearly between two vowels you might use mode 5 for a moment to diagnose and give feedback to the learner, then mode 4 to give her the opportunity to hear one or more models, then mode 3 to give her the chance to distinguish them aurally, mode 2 for you to hear how she is doing, and back to mode 5 or 6. This might take fifteen seconds or three minutes, and could involve some or all of the other learners in the group.

As you will see each mode offers its own distinctive way of approaching pronunciation problems, and in combination they make up a coherent and balanced set of options. I've put them here in an order in which you might use them, moving from more teacher control (mode 1) to more learner control (mode 7). The teacher is completely in control in mode 1. In modes 2 and 3 the teacher makes the first move. In modes 4 and 5 it is the learners who make the first move, and modes 6 and 7 are characterized by learner–learner interactions which the teacher observes (Fig. 37).

Mode	First move	Second move
1 Sounds are introduced and attached to the chart	Teacher gives model and learners try it	Teacher points
2 Teacher uses the chart to prompt learners to speak	Teacher points	Learner speaks
3 Learners use the chart to point to what teacher has said	Teacher speaks	Learner points
4 Learners use the chart to prompt teacher to speak	Learner points	Teacher speaks
5 Teacher uses the chart to point to what learners have said	Learner speaks	Teacher points
6 Learners use the chart to prompt other learners to speak	Learner points	Learner speaks
7 Learners use the chart to point to what other learners have said	Learner speaks	Learner points

Fig. 37: The seven modes of chart usage

Mode 1 Sounds are introduced and attached to the chart

This is the mode in which learners first meet the chart. In this mode you introduce new sounds, you invite learners to practise them, and you help them to shape the sounds. Once the sounds are provisionally acceptable you point to the symbol on the chart in order to 'attach' the sound to the chart, perhaps indicating those learner utterances that are closer or not closer to the target. Alternatively of course you can point out the symbol first and then give the model.

As soon as two or three sounds have been 'attached' to the chart in this way you can practise them further in modes 2 and 3, and then modes 4 and 5.

Although the first move in this mode is the teacher giving the model, there are many different ways of putting a model into circulation. Obviously you can say the sound (or word or sentence) aloud, but you can also use mime or gesture to evoke the sound from learners, or you can elicit the model from the learners or take it from an audio tape or from some other source. Four ways of giving models are described in Section 6.

Whichever type of model you use, the aim of mode 1 is to put new sounds into circulation, to work on them, and to attach them to the chart so that the symbols on the chart begin to take on some personal meaning for each learner. They do not have to be perfect when attached to the chart, just the best that the learners can manage at that moment.

Mode 2 Teacher uses the chart to prompt learners to speak

This is probably the most frequently used mode, and typically the starting point for many pronunciation, vocabulary and grammar activities. In this mode you silently point to the symbols on the chart, singly for individual sounds or in sequences for syllables and words, and you invite a vocal response from the learners (or some learners or just one learner). You help them to hear themselves critically, and to evaluate, reshape and improve what they are saying. Here are some typical activities for mode 2:

- Point out contrasting or confusing sounds for learners to practise.
- Use the pointer to initiate discovery of diphthongs by combining the relevant monophthongs.
- Combine consonants to practise typical clusters.
- Combine sounds to make syllables and words.
- Select a vowel and ask learners to suggest English words containing that sound – ie they say them or write them on the board or point them out on the chart.
- Present or recycle vocabulary items on the chart. (I find that the added dimension of working on and arriving at the best possible pronunciation of a word helps learners to fix it in their memories and to recall it later.)
- Practise words that will occur in a text or on tape.
- With multi-syllable words you work on word stress, linking this to the stress symbols on the chart and in dictionaries.
- Intonation can be usefully introduced at the level of single words, without necessarily worrying about meaning, to get learners accustomed to consciously controlling the pitch of their voice. You can relate this to the intonation symbols on the chart.
- While pointing out words you can either have learners say each sound as you touch it, or remain quiet until you have finished. Both ways are useful, though the first is probably better until learners are confident. In either case the word is said as a whole once you have finished pointing it out.
- You can use the chart for giving general class instructions and setting up activities that have nothing to do with pronunciation. This is an interesting way of using your authority without using your voice. It usually rivets attention.

When building up words or short connected speech utterances it's important at the end to get the learners to say it at least once with the focus on the right sounds in the right order, and a second time to say it up to speed and with an 'English flavour'.

In this way each symbol, and its position on the chart, gradually becomes a 'visual memory hook' capable of evoking for each learner their accumulating physical, oral and auditory experience of that sound. This experience is not static, but is constantly evolving as the sound is brought into play again and again, and refined, shaped, forgotten, rediscovered, and so on.

Though the most frequently used mode, and important in establishing the conventions of the chart, it becomes monotonous if overused. It invites extension and elaboration into modes 3, 4 and 5 to increase learner participation and activity, and back to mode 1 whenever new models are needed.

Mode 3 Learners use the chart to point to what teacher has said

In this mode you say a sound (or word or phrase) and the learners respond by silently pointing out the sound or sequence of sounds on the chart. This requires the learners to pay attention to their inner registration of your model, to listen to it again internally, and to identify the appropriate symbols on the chart.

Use of this mode could follow from work in mode 2 which has revealed (for example) that a learner is not able to distinguish between two vowels when she speaks.

- Say the sounds that a learner is confusing, and see whether she can point them out on the chart. This enables you to diagnose whether the problem is that she cannot hear the difference or cannot say the difference. If she can hear the difference you can swap roles and work on her ability to say the difference (mode 5).
- You can do the same thing to help learners discriminate between similar sounding words, and to become sensitive to the location of word stress.
- The model comes from a tape the class is studying. The learners try to reproduce a key phrase from the tape on the chart. This draws attention to a word or phrase (even where pronunciation is not the main focus of study). In this mode the challenge of trying to reproduce what is heard *other than by oral repetition* forces discrimination of what is heard and provides instant feedback for both you and your learners.
- You can change the activity by not looking at the chart yourself. You turn your back to the chart so that it is clear that you cannot see what symbols the learner is pointing out. Then the class has to decide whether the learner is pointing at the right symbol by saying *yes* or *no*. If they are unanimous then you accept their decision without looking. If they are not unanimous then the class need to say both your original sound, and the sound being pointed out, in order to savour the difference. By not watching the chart you shift responsibility for discrimination onto the class.
- Whatever learners point out on the chart gives you the opportunity to follow and gain insight into their inner processing. When they get stuck there are several options: to give the model again; or to ask them to say the sound they think they are looking for; or to say clearly the wrong sound that a learner has just pointed to so that everyone is clear about the difference; or pass the pointer to another learner to try while keeping the first learner at the chart ready to take over again.

Mode 3 provides a subtle way for learners to hear an oral model from you without immediately repeating it themselves. Instead they have to organize what they have heard onto the chart, while rehearsing and rehearing it internally.

Mode 4 Learners use the chart to prompt the teacher to speak

A learner indicates on the chart any sound or sequence of sounds (making a word or phrase) that he would like to hear you say. It may be that he is uncertain of a sound, or is confused about the difference between two or three sounds. You simply say whatever he points to, without adding any comment yourself, leaving him time to assimilate what he has heard and decide what to try next. The learner can continue to 'feed' himself sounds of his own choice in various combinations, and can stop when he has got what he wanted.

This leads easily into mode 5, where the learner speaks the sounds first, and you then point at what you have heard, thus giving feedback. Or it can lead into mode 2, where you point to the sounds and the learner tries to say them.

Mode 4 puts the responsibility for what happens entirely in the learners' hands. They tend to use this opportunity to focus on their own perceived areas of uncertainty, and to become clearer about what it is they are uncertain of. This gives you insight into a learner's own perception of what he is finding difficult. The rest of the class is also able to see the symbols he is requesting and to hear your response.

So in this mode learners have the opportunity to hear as many teacher-spoken models as they like, but entirely at their own discretion and their own request. This is quite interesting, in terms of the politics of the classroom, since the learner chooses what he wants to hear the teacher say (which makes a change!).

Mode 5 Teacher uses the chart to point to what learners have said

You make an offer to a learner that you will point out on the chart whatever sounds she says. The rationale for this is that learners can more quickly learn to distinguish English from non-English pronunciations if they are given feedback that is immediate and precise. The feedback should be given in a warm and supportive way, devoid of praise or blame or of 'anxious helpfulness'.

Suppose the student is aiming to make the sound /e/. These are some of the responses you can make with the pointer:

- If the sound is an acceptable /e/ you point to /e/ on the chart and she knows that her intended sound was heard as such.
- If you hear not /e/ but another quite clear English sound, eg /ɪ/, you point at /ɪ/. Now she knows she has unexpectedly made a different but also quite acceptable sound. She can use this as a basis for further attempts.
- If what she says is an ambiguous mixture of, say, /ɪ/ and /e/, you point at the border between the two sounds /e/ and /ɪ/ or indicate a mixture of the two by stirring the two boxes together with the pointer. She uses this feedback as a basis for further attempts.
- If the sound was too un-English to be able to give accurate feedback on, you can point outside the chart. Done with the right attitude this usually causes a chuckle, and can be illuminating for the learner.
- If you hear a mother tongue version of /e/ you can point near the perimeter of the /e/ box.
- This often reaches a point where a learner who is trying to disentangle the pronunciation of three different vowels by saying them and trying to make you point at them, finds that she can get you to point at two of them but every time she says the third you point somewhere else on the chart. She realizes that she is not making the right sound, and tries to change it. If she is not successful then you can help her to reshape the sound, or use mode 3 to find out how she is hearing that sound, or use mode 4 to enable her to request more models of the sound(s).
- The same game can be extended so that learners can test their ability to articulate correctly any sound on the chart while you offer immediate feedback on what they say.
- Games in this mode can be extended further to include words, word stress, phrases and intonation.

The immediate and precise (and non-verbal) feedback helps learners to become aware of the discrepancy between what they say and what they think they say. Learners soon stop saying the sounds they are sure of and begin to focus on ones that elude them, using your feedback as a basis for exploration.

Mode 6 Learners use the chart to prompt other learners to speak

As learners become familiar with the discipline of attention to sounds, you will find an increasing use for this mode. Once the transaction is in progress your job is to watch and wait, and to learn from all the evidence that surfaces about how the learners are learning. You are ready to intervene as soon as they need help which they can't provide for themselves.

This has similarities to modes 2 and 4, except that a learner takes the teacher's place. One of the learners is helping the other to solve a problem or to hear or produce a particular distinction.

- The first learner may point to symbols she is uncertain of, prompting the second learner to say them (similar to mode 4).
- The first learner may be testing and giving feedback to the second (similar to mode 2).
- Another family of activities work like this: Learners each prepare a word or sentence. Each comes to the chart to point out what she has prepared. The others try to say it aloud. Mistakes and problems come to light and provide a spontaneous syllabus for further work.
- As students' facility at this grows, you can invite two students to have a short dialogue with each other using the chart as the only medium of expression, and with the whole class following.
- Any appropriate mode 2 or 4 activities can be used in this mode.

Mode 7 Learners use the chart to point to what other learners have said

One learner is at the chart pointing out sounds or words spoken by other members of the class. You watch and wait, learning from this autonomously-run diagnostic process. You only intervene if unacceptable mistakes pass unnoticed by the class, or if there are difficulties that require you as resource.

This requires precision on the part of the learner who speaks, and careful listening by the one who is pointing out what has been said. There are three sources of mistake and each can be turned to advantage:

- The pronunciation of the speaker is unclear or not acceptable.
- The learner at the chart is thrown by what was said unclearly, or hears something other than what was said.
- The learner at the chart selects the wrong symbol for a correct sound that she heard correctly.

You need to be ready to intervene at any of these points, and in particular to distinguish between the second and the third type of mistake and to exploit them fully.

Diagrammatic summary of the seven modes

So far we have considered seven basic kinds of transaction, around which are
built all the activities of the seven modes. Each transaction has been seen in terms
of a first move and a second move. However in order to extend this you only have
to see the second move as being also the first move of a further transaction, and so
on. This is one way in which the modes can flow seamlessly into each other during
classroom work. Fig. 38 illustrates this.

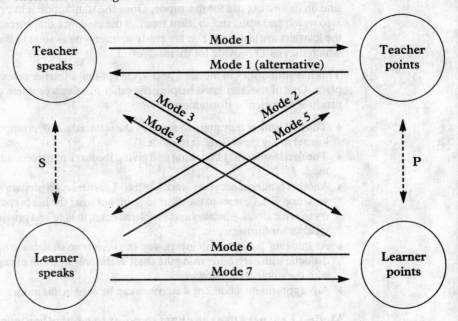

S = conventional spoken dialogue
P = pointer dialogue

Fig. 38: The seven modes for using the chart

All of the modes can be simplified down to two basic moves. The variables are:

● who points;
● who speaks;
● which happens first.

In Fig. 38 each arrow points from the first move to the second, and is labelled
with the corresponding mode. The second move can then become the first move
for any of the transactions proceeding from there so that by following the arrows a
single activity can be extended through several modes.

The dotted line S shows the transaction of normal dialogue, and dotted line P
shows the transaction of a dialogue that takes place entirely through the medium of
the chart.

5   A first lesson with the chart

Here is what I might do during a first lesson with the chart. In this case I devote a whole 45-minute lesson to it, though I could just as easily spread the same content over several lessons. This is an example rather than a recipe, and it may give you an insight into the spirit of this approach if you have not seen it used before. During this lesson I work with monophthongs, diphthongs, consonants, words, word stress, intonation and rhythm. But this is just to introduce the chart and get it into circulation. In subsequent lessons I would not normally cover so much ground because I would use the chart to work on pronunciation issues arising from normal course work, perhaps five seconds here for a prompt, or two minutes there to work on a specific problem.

The numbers in brackets refer to which of the seven modes has predominated in the previous activity, and is simply to help you study the modes in more depth.

The chart hangs permanently beside the board, for easy use during each lesson, but for this lesson it is in the middle of the board, as we are going to focus on it for a longer period, and also so that we can write on the board round the chart during the activities.

Introducing some monophthongs

To introduce the chart I usually start with a few vowel sounds. I put one sound into circulation at a time, eg /i:/ or /u:/, either by miming it (model type 4) or by saying the sound clearly once only (model type 2). Then I leave a couple of seconds of quiet, or 'hearing time', after which the learners try it themselves. I indicate those learner responses which seem closer to the target sound, and with a variety of techniques help them to tune or shape their articulations. I try not to correct them by just repeating the model at them, though if the model is needed again, I give it (1).

I encourage them to listen carefully to each other and to the variations between them by listening carefully myself. Although I value correctness, what I value more at this stage is their discovery that they can (re)gain conscious control of the muscles that make sounds, and that they can not only hear the difference between sounds but also feel the difference in their musculature, and even see the difference. My main aim is to help them discover that they can unlock themselves from the grip of the phonemic set of their mother tongue (1).

Once the new sound is reasonably well established (even though it may not be 'exact'), usually after a minute or two of the class saying and listening and changing and trying, I point to the relevant symbol on the chart, making the connection between the muscular and acoustic experience of what they have just done, and the symbol on the chart which will become a visual memory hook (1).

I repeat this for several other vowel sounds, eg /ɜ:, ɑ:, æ, e/, (1) frequently revising the sounds just studied by pointing at them in turn (2), helping them to make modifications, to rediscover ones they have 'lost', and to distinguish clearly between neighbouring sounds on the chart.

Practising sounds

Having done three or four vowels in this way I invite learners to take my place at the chart and to point to sounds we have done while the class responds (6). Then I invite learners to point at sounds they are not sure of, and I say them myself (4). They also test each other (6,7).

Then I might invite a learner who I think is not hearing the difference between a couple of the sounds to point at one or the other of them on the chart after I have said them (3). Once she has got the hang of this I deliberately turn away from the chart to face the class so that the feedback has to come from the rest of the class rather than from me (3). From the earliest stages I look for every opportunity to have learners take my place as judge, as this keeps them actively searching for the criteria of Englishness, and gives me feedback on the progress of their insight. All of this proceeds at a fairly fast pace, and every activity has the dual function of providing both practice and feedback.

Introducing diphthongs

I now introduce a diphthong, but instead of saying it I use the pointer to run together the component monophthongs which we have already worked on, thus guiding the learners to discover the diphthong for themselves. After shaping the diphthong so that it sounds English and practising it for a moment I point out the diphthong symbol on the chart which from then on acts as the visual memory hook on which to hang their growing experience of that sound (1).

I enjoy the fact that the mouth movements of diphthongs are quite visual, and so I mime the diphthong and some monophthongs and ask the class to watch closely, in order to discriminate between diphthong and monophthong, to say each and to point to the exact one on the chart (3).

The lesson may have been going on for about twenty minutes, and six or eight monophthongs and three or four diphthongs have been introduced and worked on. By now it is becoming clear to learners that the message is not *you must be perfect at this before we can move on to the next* but rather *do what you can on each of these at any given moment, and we can move forwards on many fronts at the same time. We will also come back to sounds as often as we need to.*

Introducing some consonants

Now I introduce a few consonants, again by saying them once and then giving hearing time, or by miming them. The ones to the left of the chart are generally easier to mime, though you can develop ways to mime all of them. I usually introduce both the voiced and unvoiced members of a pair at the same time so that we can focus on triggering the muscle that starts or stops the voicing (1). This means that we get 'two consonants for the price of one'.

Making words from sounds

Now after about half an hour they have worked with ten or fifteen sounds and have begun to put them together into different sequences, forming English words which they say and point out on the chart. Once again the learners are up at the chart, using the pointer and prompting and responding to each other as well as the teacher (2–7). Through paying attention to detail and through being alert the learners begin to discover that they can modify and control the target sounds more precisely, and that paying attention in this kind of way is engaging and enjoyable.

Words are put into circulation in different ways. I may say a word once, leave a couple of seconds' hearing time, and then invite someone to come to point it out on the chart (3). Or I might point a word out on the chart and invite them to say it (2). Or a learner could say the word and others try to point it out on the chart (7).

Word stress

We may need to work on word stress in words of two or more syllables. I ask them to listen to the word once, and then to listen to it again internally in their 'mind's ear' while counting how many syllables the word contains, and which one is stressed (3). We may use the Cuisenaire rods to indicate the syllables, and to work on stressing and unstressing different syllables, savouring the difference, learning to make the difference at will, and noting which version is actually English. White rods represent unstressed syllables, red rods represent stressed syllables.

This helps to develop a more conscious control over the articulation of stress. Then the pointer is offered to anyone who would like to come to verify the pronunciation and stress of the word on the chart (6). Turns are taken until it is correct. Then I may give another word, and the learners also offer words to work on.

Intonation

I introduce intonation, not by requiring specific patterns, but by inviting the learners to experiment with their voice pitch and to produce different effects. We do this on single vowels, diphthongs, words and connected speech. In this first lesson we take simple words or phrases like *hello*, and *nice to meet you*, and I ask them to 'sound happy!' or 'sound bored!' or 'be sad!' or 'be in love!' or even 'be English!' or 'be Spanish!'. Later on, as they gain confidence, we can begin to notice and talk about falling and rising pitch movements, and relate these to the intonation arrows on the chart, just as the sounds were hooked to the symbols.

Phrases and connected speech

In the last few minutes of the lesson I use the chart to point out short English phrases consisting of several words. These are practised for their sounds, word stress, rhythm and intonation (2). The object here is to arrive at short bits of English that the learners know they are saying in a very 'English' way. The lesson ends with the students learning a couple of lines of strongly metrical verse, for example a nursery rhyme (2).

Throughout the lesson mistakes provide starting points for further games and exercises. I view mistakes, or 'not quite right sounds', as opportunities that can guide and enrich the moment-by-moment emerging syllabus.

Commentary ■ ■ ■

The aims of such an introduction are:

1 To establish some of the conventions for working with the chart.
2 To foster a positive attitude towards phonology and a way of working which is engaging and enjoyable.
3 To work with all three levels of phonology (sounds, words, connected speech) at the same time, and to move elegantly between the three levels.
4 To help learners discover that they can relate to pronunciation not just intellectually, but also through the eyes, the voice, the ears, physically through muscular sensation, and through the feeling of being pleasurably challenged.

This introduction would have been essentially the same with only small modifications at elementary, intermediate, advanced and native-speaker level, though I would always demand the best the participants can do 'plus a bit'. What I am effectively saying to each learner is *do the best you can at this and then see if you can improve it*. My job is to provide both the activity and the psychological climate that will encourage them to do that. ■

6 Four ways of giving models

Here are four ways of giving pronunciation models, or of putting new sounds or words or phrases into circulation:

The repeated model

You give the model several times, and then the learners repeat it several times, both together and individually. This has become the conventional approach, and is certainly familiar to you.

The single model

You give the model once only, requiring your learners to derive as much as they can from a single exposure, and to do as much as they can with it. When they have made the most of the single exposure you can ask if they'd like the model again.

The internal imaging model

This approach introduces the idea of internal imaging, a natural human faculty which can usefully be exploited in the classroom. You give the model only once, and then leave a couple of seconds for the learners to listen to their own internal registration, that is to hear it again internally in their mind's ear. Only then do you invite them to say it aloud.

The non-verbal model

This is about evoking new sounds from your learners without giving a spoken model. Options here include using mime or gesture; lifting a 'new' sound from an already known word; lifting the sound from the learner's mother tongue; using a sound spoken by another learner; or reshaping an incorrect sound offered by a learner.

Each approach has its advantages, and each can be used for individual sounds, for words, or for whole sentences. Adapting them to suit your style could help you to extend your repertoire of choices. Here they are described in more detail.

Classroom activity 1 The repeated model

This is widely used, with many variations, but typically it goes like this:

1 You say the model (for example /əʊ/) two, three or four times.

2 The learners repeat that model several times, usually in chorus first, and then individually.

3 You indicate the responses that seem closer to your own model, perhaps inviting others to use those as new models.

4 Alternatively, you might give further repetitions of your model.

5 When several learners are close enough to the target sound you point to the symbol on the chart, to make the connection between the sound and the symbol which is now going to represent that sound.

Commentary on the repeated model ■ ■ ■

I think that both teacher's repetition and learners' repetition have great validity when the teacher conducts the process with sensitivity and interest, and in a non-competitive way. For example, you can enliven the learner responses by inviting repetitions with different intonation, voice tone, speed, volume, etc. You can keep learners on their toes by telling them as soon as their model wavers away from the target sound. Accurate sounds come and go, they don't suddenly arrive and stay.

The teacher's quality of listening can do much to convey an attitude of curiosity and engagement in even the simplest activity, and also an acceptance of the learners as people that allows each of them to take risks in what they try, without being held back by reluctance to make a mistake or by carelessness (sometimes just a way of coping with that fear).

Here are some thoughts about the dangers of repetition. I feel that over-repetition by the learners can encourage parroting at the expense of attention to the internal processing of what has just been heard. I feel there is a danger that the learner 'spits out' the response and with it the responsibility for doing anything further with it. I suggest one solution to this in 'The internal imaging model' below.

Over-repetition of a model could also undermine a learner's capacity to listen accurately to something the first time round, turning him into a lazy listener since he knows he will hear it several times. The problem is that repetition is by nature repetitious! And the helpfulness may backfire by reducing the need to be alert. It's the old problem of the teachers being so helpful that they underestimate the learner's ability, and so under-demand, and so the learner under-achieves, and so the teacher is 'proved right' in her under-estimation, and so on.

Does the teacher's repetition of the model also carry the hidden suggestion *you wouldn't be able to get this if I only said it once?* Maybe this is not significant. But the unspoken subtext of the teacher's behaviour, and the effect of this on the psychological learning atmosphere of a group, is something we need to take note of. I suggest one solution to this objection in 'The single model' on p 112. ■

Classroom activity 2 The single model

This is identical to the repeated model outlined above, except that the model is given once, not repeated.

1 Give the model once.
2 Invite learners to respond and if between them there is not a model that is sufficient to work from, then
3 Give the model again, once.
4 Or, when the learners have done what they can with the single model, ask them if they would like it again, and if they say yes, give it.
5 Once some learners are close enough to the model, indicate the symbol on the chart to make the connection.

Commentary on the single model ■ ■ ■

There is a different intention and different delivery involved in giving the model once only. The aim is to help learners to be as alert as possible, and to sharpen their capacity to listen accurately to something the first time. When they've heard it once, you invite them to do what they can with it, only giving the model a second or third time if needed.

I have found that when learners are encouraged to do the best they can after hearing the model once, they have a stronger wish to hear it a second time, and they listen to it with a fresh curiosity, since they have already invested their effort. I think this can help to reduce the repetitiveness, and it has a different underlying message (*see what you can do when you hear this only once, but if you need it again that's fine*). There is something more democratic about asking learners if they want it again, rather than assuming that they do or that they don't. ■

Review your own way of giving models

- Do you give models?
- If you don't, then how else do your learners focus on a new sound?
- If you do, then how do you do it?
- What is your intention when you do this?
- Why?
- Do you repeat the model? How many times?
- What is your tone and manner?
- Could you try giving just one model? Perhaps as a game at first?
- How much time do you give yourself and your learners?
- Would it be relevant to ask your learners what they think of the process?

Classroom activity 3 The internal imaging model

This makes use of our natural ability to retain an impression of a sound, and to continue to hear it internally for a few seconds.

1 Give the model once, clearly.

2 Leave a couple of seconds' silent 'hearing time' while maintaining a moving eye contact with the class. Encourage them to 'hear it again' internally.

3 Invite them to say it aloud, perhaps to themselves at first, and then to the group.

4 Indicate those utterances which are closer to the model, or ask the learners to indicate.

5 If another model is needed, give it.

6 When some responses are close enough, indicate the appropriate symbol on the chart.

Commentary on the internal imaging model ■ ■ ■

This approach combines the single model with an intentional silence which allows learners to attend to their own internal representation of the model they have just heard. It makes use of our capacity to 'record' something we hear, and to carry on hearing it internally for several seconds in our mind's ear. This also allows people to process it in their own different ways. Some people 'see' it, some 'hear' it, some 'feel' it, and so on. The experiments below in 'Developing your internal imaging of sounds' will help you to explore the potential of internal imaging. ■

Classroom activity 4 The non-verbal model

The aim here is to evoke sounds without giving a spoken model. One way of doing this is through mime and gesture. The rationale is to make use of the visual aspect of the articulation of sounds by drawing attention to what can be seen of the movement of lips, tongue, jaw, and throat. The visual impact is heightened by doing the mime silently.

1 Mime the sound using gesture to help.

2 Invite learners to rehearse it by saying it aloud to themselves.

3 Invite them to say it individually to the group.

4 Appreciate each attempt while also indicating those which seem closer to your target sound.

5 Help them to shape and reshape their sounds using other non-verbal means.

6 Mime again if required, or use the internal imaging model.

7 Indicate any learners whose sound is close enough to serve as a model for others.

8 Use the pointer to make the link between what they are saying and the symbol on the chart.

7   Developing your internal imaging of sounds

We have the ability to hear a sound externally and then to hear it again internally for several seconds. The aim of internal imaging is to use this ability intentionally for learning pronunciation.

Classroom activity 5   Internal imaging

Try these experiments:

- One person says a word; the others hear it internally for two or three seconds. Each person states how he or she internally represented the word. Some will have seen an image, others seen the spelling, others heard it in one way or another, and so on. The aim is to get insight into the different internal responses people have to the same external task.
- One person says a word once in a language unknown to the others, who allow themselves to hear it several times internally *in the voice of the speaker*. Then they say it aloud. The speaker indicates how close each is to the original. If required the model can be given a second or third time, but always with a couple of seconds for internal registration and hearing.
- Someone says a word in a language unknown to the others, who hear it internally, first in the voice of the speaker, and then *in their own voice*. They gradually connect this with their own vocal tract until it becomes audible, and they say it aloud.

Commentary on internal imaging ■ ■ ■

Only when we discover these latent learning faculties in ourselves do we have the possibility and the confidence to help our learners make use of them. I feel that our mainstream procedures tend to recognize and value only the external processes that can be directly perceived by the teacher. By being unaware of, and unresponsive to, the inner processes, we may lose an opportunity to interest learners in their own learning and in the discovery that they can rely on themselves more than they thought. ■

8 Developing your use of mime and gesture

By mime I mean a helpful exaggeration of the actual physical movements involved in producing a sound, eg rounding the lips for /ʊ/. By gesture I mean other non-verbal signals that help learners to shape and modify sounds, but which are not part of the muscular movement of the sound itself, eg using the fingers to 'draw out' or lengthen a vowel sound. Mime is based on the visual aspect of the sound. Gesture is a substitute for teacher instruction.

All forms of model-giving can be enriched by introducing a stronger visual element. Here are some ideas to help you develop a systematic use of mime and gesture in pronunciation work. For more detailed ideas on miming specific sounds, see Section 9, 'Working with individual sounds'.

Classroom activity 6 Developing your use of mime

When I mime a sound I say it silently. If it's a vowel then I say it on its own, and if it's a consonant then I may join it to a vowel. My aim is to draw attention to the essential muscular movements of the sound, so I may exaggerate the lip, tongue and jaw postures but I want to avoid distortion. The trick is to keep it simple, not to labour it anxiously, and to feel full of confidence that the class will know what to do! Here are some things you can try to get into this way of thinking:

- Imagine that you are trying to speak to someone through a thick plate glass window. They can see you but not hear you. You have to exaggerate the mouth movements without distorting them. Take a few simple phrases and try this with someone else. How much can you understand each other?
- Do the same while paying attention to your tongue, jaw and lip movements.
- Take a list of words (a copy for each person). Mime one word at a time to the other person, and see if they can guess which one you are saying.
- Now try miming isolated sounds. Start with those that are more visual, which includes most of the monophthongs, all of the diphthongs and the consonants nearer the front of the mouth (see Fig. 39).

iː	ʊ	uː	ɪə	eɪ
e	ɜː	ɔː	ʊə	ɔɪ	əʊ
æ	ɑː		eə	aɪ	aʊ
p	b	t	d	
f	v	θ	ð	
m	n			w	j

Fig. 39: Sounds whose key articulations are fairly visible with mime

- If you find difficulty in beginning to mime, I suggest you go back to speaking the sounds quietly while maintaining awareness of the muscular movement, and then progress to whispering the sounds, and then when you're comfortable with that try miming again.
- It helps if you can let go of anxiety about getting it right and at least look as if you are enjoying yourself!

Classroom activity 7 Developing your use of gesture

By gesture I mean other non-verbal signals that help learners to shape and modify the sounds they are making. I use gesture to organize and clarify who is doing what during an activity. I also use gesture to emphasize the visible movement in a mime, and to indicate articulations that are less visible and so less amenable to mime. Such gestures draw attention to some aspect of the place or manner of articulation of the sound.

ɪ		ɪə	eɪ	✕ː
ə		ʊə	ɔɪ	əʊ
ʌ		ɒ	eə	aɪ	aʊ
			tʃ	dʒ	k	g
			s	z	ʃ	ʒ
	ŋ	h	l	r	

Fig. 40: Sounds whose articulations can be suggested quite well by mime supported by gesture

Here are some things you can try if you want to develop your repertoire of gesture:

- When miming there is no sound, so in order to indicate that you are 'speaking' you can draw the sound out of your mouth with your hand, as if you are pulling a length of string out of your mouth.
- When you reverse this, you can use the same gesture to draw the sound from your learners.
- This gesture of pulling a sound can be used to lengthen and shorten sounds.
- You can indicate an increase or decrease in the energy put into a sound with a firmer or softer hand movement.
- You can draw attention to lip position by tracing the rounding or spreading of your lips with your finger.
- You can emphasize the degree of jaw opening with thumb and forefinger held vertically next to your jaw. Extend or reduce the gap between thumb and forefinger, while miming the same thing with your jaw.
- You can indicate tongue positions by pointing in or beside your mouth.
- You can indicate nasalization by pulling the sound out of your nose (!) (A magician once pulled a long string of coloured flags out of my nose!)
- You can use the gesture of switching your Adam's apple on and off (like a light switch) to indicate voicing and unvoicing.
- You can use the fingers of one hand held separately or together to indicate sounds spoken separately or run together into a word, or to indicate words spoken separately or run together into connected speech.
- You can also use fingers for syllables, and so for manipulating stress and unstress.
- The use of fingers in relation to silent correction and shaping of sounds, words and phrases is an elegant and powerful visual art form, and we'll go further into this in the Level 2 classroom toolkit on finger correction.

Commentary on mime and gesture exercises ■ ■ ■

These starting points for experimenting with mime and gesture are not intended as prescriptions but only as examples. Find and develop what works for you and what you feel comfortable with. Change and adapt these ideas and invent new ones. In any case gesture or mime on its own doesn't work; it's how you use it that counts.

Mime and gesture offer ways of extending our non-verbal interventions in a lesson, and give us the opportunity to reduce our verbal intervention. The speaking/listening channel is the one the learners need to explore, and the more I am able to vacate that channel and leave it free for them the more they are able and willing to use it. Imagine the conductor of an orchestra using words instead of gesture!

We'll investigate mime and gesture in relation to vowels and consonants in Section 9. ■

Classroom activity 8 Other sources of non-verbal models

Non-verbal models raise the learner investment, requiring more internal co-ordination than do spoken models. Here are some other non-verbal ways of putting a sound into circulation:

- Lift the sound from an English word already known and pronounced by the learner. If you want /æ/, for example, and the learners can say *cat*, guide them to lift out the middle sound by isolating it with the pointer. If in doing that they change the quality of /æ/, then it may help to ask how many sounds in *cat* (which requires them to internally image the sounds in order to count them). Invite them to write the sounds on the board in both letters and phonemes, and then rub off first /c/ and then /t/ while trying to maintain the quality of /æ/.
- If you want an example of a sound, the chances are that you can find it on almost any page of your coursebook or class reader.
- You may be able to lift an English sound from your learner's mother tongue, either directly or with a bit of shaping.
- You may be able to arrive at new sounds by making use of the layout of the chart, eg making diphthongs from monophthongs; by isolating monophthongs that occur between other monophthongs (eg /ɪ/ and /ʊ/ lying somewhere between /iː/ and /uː/); by using the front–back spectrum built into the visual display of the vowel and the consonant sections, etc. Some of these ideas will be followed up in the next section. The discovery toolkit in part 1 gives a good insight into how you can exploit the layout of the chart.
- You can also use a learner's guess or hunch as a starting point. For example, 'What sound do you think this is?' (pointing to a symbol). Or 'What sound do you find difficult in English – can you try to say it?' The learner may come up with something you can work on, by shaping or tuning. Or perhaps not, so you leave it.

Commentary on the non-verbal model ■ ■ ■

I am often astonished at how close learners can get to an intended sound without actually hearing a model, how attentive they become when invited to use their eyes, how the sound-producing musculature can be evoked by simply watching someone else do it, and how awareness is heightened when the teacher actually raises the stakes by giving the learners this kind of challenge. It also helps learners to listen to themselves. Finally, and most importantly, this focuses attention on pronunciation as a physical activity, rather than only a mental one, or simply a mechanical response.

Developing your own repertoire of non-verbal model-giving takes practice and curiosity, and the best place for that is in the classroom. Take pleasure in trying things out, and if possible involve your learners in discussing outcomes. If you can enjoy what doesn't work, as well as what does, you'll be able to learn from whatever happens. There is no need to get things 'right' first time. I think it helps the class atmosphere if you too are a learner. ■

Summary

I have outlined four ways of putting new sounds into circulation, and each has many variations. Each model has different strengths and different uses, and I suggest you experiment with all of them, and mix them up and develop them in your own personal way. Bear in mind that these basic forms of model are as applicable to giving whole sentences as they are to words and isolated sounds.

9 Working with individual sounds

Working with monophthongs

A sound syllabus?

There are various ways of sequencing and ordering the learning of grammatical structures and vocabulary. But I don't think it's helpful to construct an artificial teaching syllabus for sounds. Firstly there are only forty-four phonemes in English, and secondly all the sounds are needed from the beginning. I would rather deal with sounds as they come up and according to their difficulty or 'differentness'.

Having said that, I do find there are certain rules of thumb that can help you decide what to work on when you are introducing the chart to a class for the first time. For example, some sounds are easier to perceive for your particular learners, and can help establish reference points for other sounds. When introducing the chart I usually establish a few monophthongs first, then build a few diphthongs from those monophthongs, and then work with a few consonants, ending up by building up a few words. There is an example of this in the lesson in Section 5.

Vowels in most languages use the same mouth space and divide the space up to yield the number of different vowels required by that language. Few languages have as many discrete, significant vowel sounds as English, which means that most learners have to fit more vowels into the same mouth space. I find it helpful to have this picture in mind while I am working with learners.

Some generalizations about sequencing monophthongs

1 I sometimes find it helpful to establish long vowels before their neighbouring short vowels:

/iː/ before /ɪ/ and /e/
/uː/ before /ʊ/
/ɜː/ before /ə/
/ɑː/ before /ʌ/ and /æ/
/ɔː/ before /ɒ/

This is because the longer duration gives more visual and aural evidence to work on; there is more to get hold of. The longer sounds can act as 'anchors' or 'benchmarks' against which other sounds can be 'weighed' or 'measured'.

2 I find that the two sounds /iː/ and /uː/ provide a good starting point for introducing the chart and the monophthong section. Both sounds have a very visual mouth posture, and together they form two ends of a continuum which has at one end full lip rounding and tongue back, and at the other end full lip spread and tongue forward. Having learners glide slowly between /iː/ and /uː/ draws their attention to the inner muscular movements of both tongue and lip, and to the changing aural signal that results. Then, when the continuum from /iː/ to /uː/ has been established as a slow glide, the sounds approximating /ɪ/ and /ʊ/ can be 'discovered' by stopping at particular points along that continuum and making small adjustments. See 'A first lesson with the chart' and 'Monophthongs' in the discovery toolkit.

3 You may also decide to start with those mother tongue vowel sounds of your learners which approximate to English vowels. I help learners identify a few such sounds in the first couple of sessions. With a monolingual group these common L1/L2 sounds may be the same for the whole group. With a multilingual group I'll help individuals to identify the English sounds they can already do.

4 I think spontaneity is of great importance in learning and teaching pronunciation. What comes up naturally has energy in it, and if I can follow it and work with it I may encourage learners' initiatives rather than trying to ensure that my own initiatives prevail. The 'syllabus of spontaneity' is an interesting idea, similar to the idea that 'mistakes are the syllabus', and we'll follow this up in Section 10.

Introducing a monophthong

Of the four types of model described in Section 6 the first three are fairly straightforward. So I'll describe some approaches to the fourth type, the non-verbal model using mime and gesture.

Classroom activity 9 Presenting a monophthong using mime and gesture

1 Think and **say the sound to yourself** observing your lip, tongue and jaw position.
2 **Mime it** to the class very clearly, perhaps a bit slower, adding a little exaggeration to the tongue, lip and jaw position.
3 Use any **gestures** you feel appropriate to complete the picture.

4 Invite learners to **rehearse it** to themselves and aloud in the class.

5 Give **feedback** to indicate which are closer to the English sound. My own preference is to avoid congratulation and focus on supportive feedback such as 'That's closer,' 'Make it longer,' 'Try it like her,' 'You've changed it,' 'Listen to the difference.'

6 Offer to **repeat** the mime or to say it aloud if the class wishes.

7 When some are close enough to be acceptable for the moment, **touch the symbol** on the chart, which from now on can represent that sound, and in future work the sound will be refined further.

Commentary ■ ■ ■

As I've said, you can help your learners by encouraging them to use their eyes as well as their ears in pronunciation work, and to be attentive to the inner sensations of muscular coordination and movement. Your own helping curiosity is a good starting point.

Keep in mind the visual features of monophthongs:

• jaw position;
• lip rounding and lip spread;
• vowel length. ■

Specific mimes and gestures for monophthongs

Here are some descriptions of gestures relating to specific sounds. My aim is just to give you enough of an idea so that you feel inspired to look for the gestures that work for you.

/iː/ You have your lips clearly spread, and your jaws close together. You can focus attention on these two features with a gesture. Then you mime the sound and with your hand you gesture the sound coming out, as if pulling the sound firmly from your mouth. At first you can exaggerate the length. Then to get the class to say it you turn your 'pulling' gesture round and pull the sound from them, while still miming it yourself. Then you invite individuals to say it aloud, and so on.

/æ/ You have your jaws open, your tongue visible behind the lower front teeth, and your lips slightly spread. You can draw attention to this set-up with gesture. With your hand you pull the sound from your mouth with a fairly firm and short gesture. Then you reverse the gesture and pull the sound from the class. I find that it helps to indicate a slight tension of the muscle at the corners of the mouth and at the top of the throat. I gesture this as well.

/ɜː/ You relax your whole tongue, jaw and lips, and indicate by gesture that they are loose, and in neutral, and perhaps even show that your arms and body are floppy. Then you can pull a long and relaxed silent /ɜː/ from your mouth. Learners often put too much energy into this and distort the sound with muscular tension. Use gesture to indicate and evoke a 'letting go' of muscular tension.

/ə/ You can begin with /ɜː/, and while pulling the sound from them several times you gradually shorten its length with your hand gesture until you are left with a very short /ɜ/. Then you just have to remove the excess energy they are probably giving to it and you are left with /ə/. You can convey this by miming and gesturing the sound as an almost imperceptible movement, with minute energy.

/ɑː/ You open your mouth quite wide, as if the doctor is to look **down your throat**.

Your tongue is low and towards the back of your mouth. Your lips are well open but neither rounded nor spread. With your two hands open you can gesture that your throat is full, or open. You pull a long sound from your mouth. You can also indicate by gesture and mime the act of saying or sighing /ɑɑɑɑ/.

/uː/ You round the lips and push them forward. The jaws are close together, and the tongue is back though that is not visible. Draw attention to the lip position by appearing to pull your lips forward with your hands, and to your jaw position by appearing to close it with your hands. Then you can pull, or 'extrude' the sound from your mouth, and then from the class.

/ʊ/ You have your lips rounded but more relaxed than /uː/. It can be helpful to set the scene by miming the forward and tight rounding of /uː/, and then visibly relaxing the lip position to that required for /ʊ/. Then mime the sound with the gesture of a short tug from your mouth indicating a short sound, but don't imply too much energy in the tug. It can help to do this sound after doing /uː/, as the contrast can clarify.

The trick in all of this is to think the sound while you mime it. This helps to inform your body and your gestures. Gestures don't have to be logically related to the sound, they just have to help.

Introducing diphthongs

I'd like to suggest two non-verbal ways of helping learners to arrive at a new diphthong:

1 You can use mime and gesture, as we have already seen. Diphthongs are strong on visual information given by the movement of lips and jaw between the first and the second position.
2 You can build the diphthong from its two component monophthongs (eg /ə/ + /ʊ/ = /əʊ/), which means working on the monophthongs first, and then joining them together.

Here is a fuller description of these two ways:

Classroom activity 10 Using mime and gesture to model diphthongs

1 Think and say the diphthong to yourself. Notice the mouth posture of the first sound and of the second sound. Notice also the movement of the glide in between.
2 Mime the diphthong to the class, adding some legitimate exaggeration. Make sure the first and last position is clear, and slow down the glide in between.
3 Use any gestures that could help learners focus on the movement.
4 Invite learners to rehearse it to themselves and aloud in the class.
5 Give feedback to indicate which of your learners' attempts are closer to your target sound.
6 Offer to repeat the mime or to say it aloud if the class wishes.
7 When some are close enough to be acceptable for the moment, touch the symbol on the chart, which from now on can represent that sound. Later on the sound can be refined further.
8 Practise the diphthong in the context of other sounds and words.

Classroom activity 11 Building diphthongs from monophthongs

1 Think and say the diphthong to yourself, eg /eɪ/. Identify the first and second elements /e/ + /ɪ/. Locate those two elements on the monophthong side of the chart.

2 Point to the first element /e/ and have the class say it. Take a few seconds to focus attention on the quality of the sound and to fine-tune it. Do the same for the second element /ɪ/.

3 Now build the diphthong by sliding the pointer very slowly from /e/ to /ɪ/ on the monophthong section of the chart, inviting the class to say it as you do so.

4 Invite them to work on the glide, making it smooth rather than jerky. Again you can use gesture to convey this quality.

5 Once the glide is fairly smooth invite them to speed it up.

6 Give feedback to indicate which attempts are closer to the target sound.

7 When some are close enough to be acceptable for the moment, touch the appropriate diphthong symbol in the diphthong section of the chart, which now represents that sound, though in future work it will be refined further.

8 Practise the new diphthong with consonants and in words pointed out on the chart.

Commentary ■ ■ ■

The building and the miming approaches complement each other. I usually start with one and then bring in the other to reinforce it. ■

Specific mimes and gestures for diphthongs

/əʊ/ You can mime or say silently the move from the first to the second sound, the lips going from neutral to rounded, and the jaw closing slightly. Slow down and appreciate the movement of the glide. It may be necessary to isolate and work briefly on /ə/ and /ʊ/ first, before joining them together.

/aʊ/ I suggest you start with the monophthong /ʌ/ with jaw open, lips neutral, and then glide towards /ʊ/, with jaws close together and lips fairly rounded and forward. Appreciate the movement of the glide itself. Use a gesture to pull the sound out of your lips, and then reverse the gesture and draw the sound out of the class.

/eɪ/ Start with /e/, jaws half open, tongue at the front behind the lower front teeth, and lips fairly spread. Glide to /ɪ/, which is mainly just a closing of the jaw, the tongue staying in place but moving closer to the roof of the mouth. The lips remain fairly spread.

The same principles can be applied to the other diphthongs.

Classroom activity 12 Pronunciation of the alphabet

From the beginning learners need to be able to use the letters of the alphabet to ask for, talk about, and understand spellings of words. This is a good opportunity to practise English pronunciation, which only requires seven different vowel sounds for the twenty-six letters. You can work on the pronunciation of the letters using the chart. The following activity is a puzzle for your learners.

1 Draw this on the board:

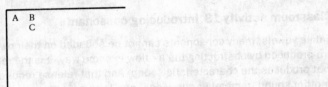

Fig. 41: Vowel sounds puzzle – starting point

Practise the pronunciation of the three letters. Don't tell the class why the letters are arranged like this. Explain that there is a single rule about where to place the rest of the letters, and that you will help them discover it by indicating which of their attempts follow the rule and which do not.

2 Now ask learners to come up to the board to place the next letter. If they put it in the right place leave it there, without saying anything. If they put it in the wrong place then rub it out, again without saying anything. Let them try other places.

3 When they write a letter in the correct place leave it there, and learners go on to the next. At first they will be guessing, then once there are a few in the correct place they will try to see the rule, and test it out.

4 Once learners have got the rule, ask them to stop participating and watch, but to join in again if they find they have not got it. Some have got the rule by halfway through the alphabet, others near the end, and others not at all.

So what is the rule? The letters are grouped into columns according to the vowel sound in each letter name. A new column is started when needed.

A	B	F	I	O	Q	R
H	C	L	Y		U	
J	D	M				W
K	E	N				
	G	S				
	P	X				
	T	Z				
	V					

Fig. 42: Vowel sounds puzzle – solution

5 Once they have correctly constructed this layout, you can point to the letters and ask the class to say them, both across and down columns, working on the pronunciation as necessary. Very soon everyone will understand the layout.

6 Then try the variations:

- Invite a learner to the board to prompt the class to speak by pointing out letters and deciding whether the class pronunciations are acceptable or not.
- Have learners call out a letter; you point to that letter if their pronunciation seems acceptable, and you point outside the diagram if it does not, thereby giving them instant feedback on the acceptability of their pronunciation.

Commentary ■ ■ ■

This is a good game for working on the pronunciation of letters. And it is good for you since you have to watch and listen while the learners work. ■

Working with consonants

Classroom activity 13 Introducing consonants

Unlike vowels, many consonants cannot be sounded on their own. As consonants are produced by obstructing the air flow in some way, it is the release of the block that produces the characteristic sound. And that release requires movement into another sound (remember *con* + *sonant* = 'with sound', or 'sounding with ...').

In fact, you can sustain the fricatives /f, v, θ, ð, s, z, ʃ, ʒ/ (second row of the chart) in isolation, but the plosives (top row) and the nasals and sundries (bottom row) need the addition of a vowel sound either before or after to complete the release stage of their articulation. Having decided which consonants you want to practise, here is one possible procedure you could follow:

1 Say the consonant to yourself to decide whether it needs a vowel to accompany it. If it needs a vowel, then choose one that will not divert the learner's attention away from the consonant.

2 Put the consonant into circulation using any of the four model types (see 'Four ways of giving models', Section 6).

3 Use the chart to practise the consonant by altering the vowel that goes with it, eg /he, heɪ, haɪ/.

4 Build words around the consonant, eg /hɑːt, hiːt, hɜːt, həʊtel/, using the kinds of activities suggested by any of the seven modes (see Section 4).

Making use of the chart layout

To work with exactness on a consonant you need to be constantly aware of the distinction between **how** and **where** each consonant is produced in the vocal tract. These are the two main variables that enable you to help learners to reshape an incorrect consonant. If you hold one variable constant and change the other significantly you will arrive at another consonant sound which may or may not be part of the English phonemic set. Through this learners can gain insight into the different ways they can control the sounds they make. Each variable is a muscular component manifested in sound. Put the muscular components together and you get the sound. This gives the learner something definite to focus attention on. These two variables are built into the layout of the chart:

- The **where** is built into the horizontal arrangement of consonants on the chart. (How visible a consonant is, in terms of miming or lip reading, is part of the **where** and therefore is also part of the horizontal arrangement on the chart.)
- The **how** is part of the vertical dimension of the consonant layout.

For a more detailed investigation of the link between the articulation of consonants and the layout of the chart, see the discovery toolkit section on consonants.

Here is a summary of how the layout can help you in practice.

'Where' or place of articulation

Consonants articulated at the front of the mouth, eg /p, m, v/ are on the left side of the chart, and those articulated at the back of the mouth, eg /k, g, ʃ/, are on the right side of the chart.

Using the horizontal consonant arrangement

Keep the manner of articulation the same, and change the place of articulation by moving the pointer horizontally along the consonant row.

Example: You decide to practise the fricative /θ/. Keep the fricative quality going while pointing in turn to the unvoiced fricative in front of it, ie /f/, and then sliding back to /θ/. Then slide the pointer back to the unvoiced fricative behind, ie /s/. The sequence produced is /θθθ ... fff ... θθθ ... sss ... θθθ/. In this simple set of moves the learner focuses on maintaining the fricative quality while changing the place where the friction is produced. At the same time she hears the sound change.

You could do the same thing with the voiced version, and work on the sequence /ððð ... vvv ... ððð ... zzz ... ððð/.

I have found this a useful approach to practice and correction.

'How' or manner of articulation

Plosives are in the top consonant row, fricatives in the second, and 'the others' are in the bottom row. (For more on this see the discovery toolkit on consonants.)

Using vertical groupings

The correspondence of manner of articulation up and down in any vertical column is not as neat as the correspondence of place of articulation along each row. However, the chart makes visible some interesting groupings of consonants according to their place of articulation. These groupings show how for each place of articulation (for each **where**), several different sounds can be produced by varying the manner of articulation (the **how**).

			where
Group 1	/m, p, b, w/		bilabial
Group 2	/n, s, z, t, d, l/		alveolar
Group 3	/ʃ, ʒ, tʃ, dʒ/	/r/ is close behind	palato-alveolar
Group 4	/ŋ, k, g/		velar

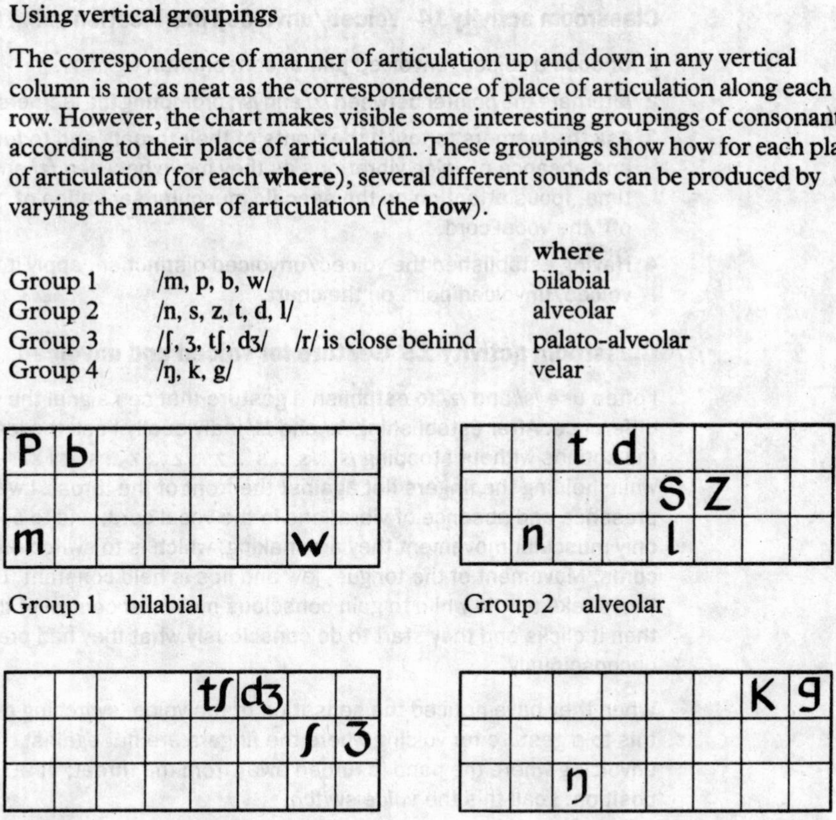

Group 1   bilabial

Group 2   alveolar

Group 3   palato-alveolar

Group 4   velar

Fig. 43

I find that making these vertical connections in the chart is useful for:

- discovering new sounds by moulding familiar sounds, for example helping learners to discover an unfamiliar place of articulation by drawing on their experience of other sounds that use the same place;
- helping learners to explore the different manners of articulation that can be applied to the same place in the mouth.

The voiced/unvoiced distinction

You can see from Fig. 44 that in the first two rows the first sound of each pair is unvoiced, while the second is voiced, eg /t, d/, /f, v/, /s, z/. The bottom row consists entirely of voiced sounds except for /h/.

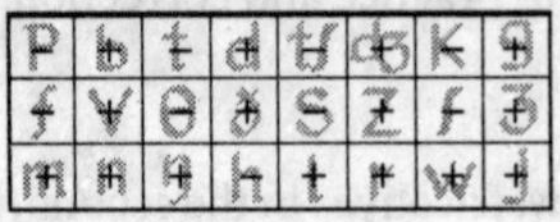

– unvoiced and *fortis*
+ voiced and *lenis*

Fig. 44

Classroom activity 14   Voiced/unvoiced clarification using the chart layout

1 Choose a voiced/unvoiced pair of consonants, eg /s, z/.

2 Alternate the pointer between /z/ and /s/, prompting the learners to say the sounds.

3 Ask the learners to touch the fronts of their throats and to feel the presence and absence of voice vibrations as they move between /z/ and /s/. At the same time, focus attention on the specific muscular sensation of 'switching on and off' the vocal cord.

4 Having established the voiced/unvoiced distinction, apply it to each of the eight voiced/unvoiced pairs on the chart.

Classroom activity 15   Gesture for voiced and unvoiced

I often use /s/ and /z/ to establish a gesture that can signal the voicing/unvoicing difference. After establishing /z/ and /s/ individually I ask the learners to alternate the sounds without stopping /s ... s ... s ... z ... z ... z ... s ... s ... s ... z ... z ... z ... /, while holding the fingers flat against the front of the throat. I want them to feel the presence and absence of vibrations in the vocal cord, and to connect that with the only muscular movement they are making, which is to switch on or off the vocal cords. Movement of the tongue, jaw and lips is held constant. Learners some-times take a little while to gain conscious muscular control of this distinction. But then it clicks and they start to do consciously what they had previously done unconsciously.

When they have noticed the sensation of the voice 'switching on and off', we link this to a gesture for voicing where the fingers are flat against the throat, and for unvoicing where the hand is turned away from the throat, at 90 degrees to the first position. I call this the *voice switch*.

Commentary ■ ■ ■

The contrast is most marked with the eight fricatives (second row), since they can flow into each other without the intervention of a vowel sound. An agreed gesture for voiced and unvoiced can be useful, but more important is what it stands for: awareness of the muscular movement necessary to switch the voice on or off. ■

Fortis/lenis clarification

The unvoiced sound of each pair is produced with a stronger *fortis* exhalation, while its counterpart is produced with a relatively weaker *lenis* force. This distinction is especially clear with plosive consonants: If you remove the voiced/unvoiced distinction from the pairs by whispering them, you may still be able to tell the consonants apart because the unvoiced are given more breath force, or aspiration.

Classroom activity 16 Practice of *fortis* and *lenis*

1 Ask learners to hold a sheet of paper 2–3 cm in front of the mouth and say the pair of consonants /piː/ and /biː/.
2 The voiced and *lenis* sound /biː/ should hardly move the paper, while the aspiration of the unvoiced and *fortis* sound /piː/ should move the paper noticeably.
3 When your learners have found a distinction, invite them to experiment with controlling the degree of aspiration at will.
4 Apply what they have found to other voiced/unvoiced pairs of consonants. The distinction is most clear with /p, b/, /t, d/, /k, g/, /f, v/ and /θ, ð/.

Commentary ■ ■ ■

You can try the same thing but whispering. The sheet of paper should still move in the same way, and though the voice difference has been removed you should still be able to distinguish aurally between the two sounds due to the difference in their aspiration. Whispering game: one whispers pairs of consonants, another listens carefully and tries to point them out on the chart.

I think it is important and helpful to give guidance in varying the amount of muscular energy and breath force they use in speaking English. It is a subtle and significant part of sounding English and of hearing English accurately. This seems to apply both to individual sounds and to connected speech. ■

Using mime and gesture

The aim of miming a sound is to encourage learners to become sensitive to the visual impact of the articulation of sounds, that is to the discernible movement of lips, tongue, jaw, throat and muscles generally. Mime may contain a degree of exaggeration; it may also be a little slower than speech, and it is always silent. It is not the same thing as whispering.

Gesture refers to other movements, usually of the hand, but also of face, arms and body, which aim to clarify or amplify or draw attention to a particular aspect of the **how** or the **where** of the articulation.

Classroom activity 17 Using mime and gesture for consonants

This is essentially the same as for vowels. Adapt it to suit yourself and your learners.

1 Think and say the consonant to yourself. Think of both the manner and the place of the articulation.

2 Mime the consonant to the class, adding a little exaggeration, and using gesture to indicate exactly when the mime begins and ends.

3 Use any other gestures that could help the articulation to be more vivid.

4 Invite learners to rehearse it to themselves and aloud in the class.

5 Give feedback to indicate which of your learners' attempts are closer to your target sound, and which may serve as temporary models to the others.

6 Offer to repeat the mime or to say it aloud if the class wishes.

7 Help them to shape and reshape their sounds using other non-verbal means.

8 When some are close enough to be acceptable for the moment, touch the symbol on the chart, which from now on can represent that sound. In future work the sound will be refined further.

9 Practise the consonant in the context of other sounds and words.

Commentary ■ ■ ■

Remember only to use mime as long as it is helpful, and to use spoken models wherever they are more helpful. One of my aims is to encourage self-sufficiency by devolving responsibility for the model onto the learners, so that instead of remaining dependent on me for the 'perfect' model each time, they can see that I am approving one or several of the learners' attempts as temporary models for the others. ■

Mimes and gestures for specific consonants

Here is a summary of mime and gesture that I find useful for consonants. I'm not sure that mime can be accurately described in words, but the most important thing is to experiment and see what works for you. Remember that the more aware you are of the **how** and **where** of the movements in your own mouth, the clearer and more evocative your mime will be. Where consonants need to move to a vowel I am assuming the neutral /ə/.

Mime and gesture for sounds in Fig. 45

p	b	t	d			
f	v	θ	ð			
m	n				w	ʃ

Fig. 45: Consonants with fairly visible articulatory clues

/p, b/
Mime: The two lips part to let out a puff of air, which is less energetic for /b/ than for /p/.

Gesture: Both forefingers, just below the chin, make a definite forward movement of about 5 cm as the air is released. This indicates the direction of air and the precise beginning and end of the mime. Act as if the puff of air is visible. Touch the front of the throat to indicate voicing for /b/.

/t, d/

Mime: Clear movement of the tongue away from the alveolar ridge to let out a puff of air, which is less energetic for /d/ than for /t/.

Gesture: Locate the tooth ridge by pointing behind the top front teeth just before the mime. Then a small but definite jerk forwards of the fingers below the chin as the 'sound' is released.

/f, v/

Mime: Lower lip and teeth contact, exaggerated slightly.

Gesture: Indicate the contact between lip and teeth, and then move fingers slowly forward for the length of the mime. This is a fricative sound and can be prolonged. Use the voicing/unvoicing gesture to distinguish /f/ from /v/.

/θ, ð/

Mime: The tip of the tongue just protrudes between upper and lower front teeth. Initially I may exaggerate this by having the tongue clearly visible. Later I may show a more natural and less visible version with the tongue at the back of the teeth.

Gesture: Point to the position of the tongue between the teeth. Indicate the duration of the mime with hands moving slowly forward a few centimetres.

/m/

Mime: Perhaps a slightly exaggerated 'sealing together' of the lips, showing that the air flow is blocked.

Gesture: Indicate the closed lips with the forefingers, take a breath and exhale rather obviously. As you do so 'pull' the air flow from your nose! This one is vivid, amusing, and usually quite successful.

/w/

Mime: This sound is visually quite clear, especially if you exaggerate the movement of the two lips slightly.

Gesture: Just indicate the beginning and end of the mime with the fingers.

/j/

Mime: This is visually less clear. Nevertheless if you do it confidently and slowly most people will get it.

Gesture: Indicate the beginning and end of the mime with the fingers.

Mime and gesture for sounds in Fig. 46

			tʃ	dʒ	k	g
			s	z	ʃ	ʒ
		ŋ	h	l	r	

Fig. 46: Consonants with less visible clues, needing gestures in support of mime

These movements are less visible, but gesture can help the mime. Use the 'voice switch' gesture (classroom activity 15) to clarify the voiced/unvoiced distinction.

/tʃ, dʒ/

Mime: Clear movement of the tongue, but slower than /t, d/ as affricates are released more gradually than plosives.
Gesture: Locate the position just behind the tooth ridge by pointing, just before the mime. Then a small but definite slide forwards of the fingers as the sound is released.

/k, g/

Mime: Mime the sound slowly and clearly, perhaps with the mouth a little more open than usual.
Gesture: Indicate the velar location by touching the back of the lower jaw bone just below the ears. Then use the gesture of drawing the sound from the mouth with the hands while miming the sound. Use the voicing/unvoicing gesture to distinguish /k/ from /g/.

/s, z/

Mime: The visual clues are less obvious here. However the front teeth are so close as to be almost touching, and if initially you exaggerate the appearance by spreading your lips, there will be evidence for the learners to build on.
Gesture: This is necessary to indicate the duration of the mime, and to distinguish voicing from unvoicing. For /s/ I sometimes gesture the hissing sound that snakes are supposed to make while making a snaky, wiggling movement with my hand. For /z/ I sometimes mime the buzzing of a bee while making a hand gesture to indicate its unpredictable flight. Simple but essential.

/ʃ, ʒ/

Mime: I usually mime /ʃ/ first, by rounding my lips while holding my forefinger to my lips to indicate 'hush'. Then with a gesture I invite the learners to say it. Then since /ʃ/ + voice = /ʒ/, I can derive /ʒ/ from /ʃ/ by using the voice switch.

/n/

Indicate the ridge behind the top teeth and conspicuously place your tongue there to indicate that that is where the air flow is blocked (approximately the same place as for /t/ or /d/). As you exhale, 'pull' the air flow from your nose.

/ŋ/

As with the other three nasals, you need to show where the air flow is blocked and diverted through the nose. With the flat of my hand I indicate the block to the air flow at the velum by pressing the side of my hand against the angle between my throat and chin. At the same time my mouth is open and my tongue visibly back. Then once again I 'pull the sound' from my nose.

/l/

This sound is all to do with tongue movement, there are no strong external clues. But if you observe yourself in a mirror saying *la la la* there is quite a definite tongue movement. I hold the initial position of tongue against tooth ridge, and as my tongue breaks contact with the alveolar ridge I make a corresponding downward flick with the palm of my hand in imitation of the tongue.

/r/

Again not a visual sound. I mime it slowly, which sometimes helps. To get the right place I may start the learners from /ʒ/, and help them to move the tip of the tongue slightly further back. I also find it helpful to sustain the initial sound of /r/ while asking them to move the tongue up, down, forward or back.

/h/

Mime: A sigh, followed by the vowel, or take the vowel and put a sigh in front of it.

Commentary ■ ■ ■

I've gone to some length to describe possible mimes/gestures for the consonants. I think this is a good way to focus attention on the muscular movements involved. It can also help you to develop spoken models that have a more visual element. There are, of course, many options besides the ones I have described here. ■

Classroom activity 18 Further activities for practising consonants

Here are some activity types using the chart for further practice of consonants. These activities are short and are quite elegant, since all you have to do is to prompt the learners by silently pointing on the chart. As soon as you have initiated an activity you can hand the pointer to a learner, who can continue the activity. You don't say anything; you are free to watch and help.

- Keep the consonant the same but change the vowel occurring with it.
- Change the consonant to compare and contrast it with other consonants on the chart, horizontally, vertically and diagonally. Keep the vowel the same.
- Continue the first three exercises but building typical consonant clusters.
- Build words around the consonants. I prefer to keep the practice of isolated consonants short, and as soon as possible to practice them in the context of words (Level 2).
- Where a mother tongue consonant interferes, I would include it as an intentional part of the practice. You can do this by assigning a symbol – perhaps invented by the learner in question – to the mother tongue sound and writing that symbol in its own box beside the chart or on the board. Include that sound/symbol in the exercises described above and use it to identify, recognize and discriminate.
- You can develop each exercise by inviting learners to explore the sounds themselves. Remember that the pointer can be used not just to initiate a response, but also as a response to a spoken sound or word. The various combinations of activity possible with the pointer and chart are described in 'Seven modes of chart usage' (see Section 4).

10 Working with mistakes

Ear and mouth training for teachers

Awareness of what you – the teacher – do with your own speech organs to make and alter sounds, stress and intonation is the basis of your insight and creativity. It is much easier to 'do' things to your learners that you have already 'done' to yourself. If you are not aware of and not able to control consciously your own articulation of sounds, then you will not have a very rich experience to draw on to diagnose or work on learner problems. This does not mean that you have to be highly correct yourself.

It is not enough merely to read descriptions of articulations and as a result to 'know' from the outside how it all works. It must be experienced from inside the various sound production mechanisms, and linked with what your ear hears. Ear training and mouth training therefore must be developed together in the teacher. That is what the discovery toolkit of this book is for.

Being 'with' the learner

Correction is not simply the eradication of mistakes, but an opportunity to engage learners in their learning, and to assist them to develop the inner criteria that can help them to drive their own self-correction. I see 'mistakes' as an instrument that enables learners to experiment, to see what happens, and to get feedback that can guide their own investigation. It is not a mistake I am working with, it is a person. Through recognizing the validity of mistakes I create opportunities to nurture the learners' learning processes, to encourage experimentation, to encourage them to be curious about their own performance, and to develop a positive and robust concept of their own learning abilities. In a sense mistakes are the most precise syllabus. They show me exactly where the learner is and what they need to do next.

Mistakes as opportunities

Mistakes are:

- evidence that a particular item is not yet ready to be delegated to the more automatic functionings that produce our speech;
- an opportunity to pay attention to something that the learner is doing, and to something the learner isn't doing, and to the difference between them;
- a window of opportunity for you, the teacher, to watch and to be with the learner, and to look for the exact point at which you can make the most economical intervention with the most effect.

Learners' attitudes to mistakes

A healthy attitude on the part of learners towards their own mistakes is important. Problems arise when the main way for learners to feed their self-esteem is to be correct in the eyes of the teacher, their peers or themselves. The more afraid they are of being wrong the less they are likely to be able to take the risks that might lead to discovery. And the more they focus only on trying to be correct, the more they may feel constrained to play safe by resorting to intellect or calculation at the expense of other intuitive and creative faculties.

The teacher's attitude to mistakes

This attitude of the learners towards their own mistakes seems to be influenced by the teacher's attitude. There are three areas where your outlook on mistakes can affect the psychological learning climate of your class:

- Your attitude towards your own mistakes. If you are particularly intolerant or anxious about your own mistakes you may project this anxiety onto the class, perpetuating a discomfort, an embarrassment or a sense of failing in making mistakes.
- Your attitude towards your learners' mistakes. You may think that learner mistakes are evidence that they are learning, but are you really interested, and do you inspire curiosity? Are you patient in front of your learners' mistakes, or do you pretend you are while busily wishing your learners would be correct? Do you take the opportunity to work with mistakes, or do you exercise such a strong preference for correctness that there is little space left for hunch, intuition and inspired guessing?
- Your view of how the learners themselves feel about their own mistakes. Do you assume that they are not interested in them, and that at best they only want to get it right and move on? Do you confirm them in their own attitude towards their mistakes by your own attitude? How can your attitude help them to use their own mistakes to advantage?

Some definitions: *slips* and *errors*

I use the term *mistake* to refer to something that at that moment is not acceptable. It could turn out to be either a *slip* or an *error*.

The mistake is a *slip* when the learner already has the inner criteria for self-correction but isn't applying them at the moment, perhaps because her attention is elsewhere, or perhaps at the moment she is not recalling the criteria, though she might recognize them. At some level she already knows what is required for correctness.

By *error* I mean that the learner does not yet have the criteria for correctness. This is something new that she cannot work out for herself.

In practice the distinction is sometimes not as clear as I've just implied.

Three kinds of correction

I am using the word *correction* to cover three types of event:

Correction type 1. The learner changes the mistake to something acceptable, but without insight or knowing why. An outer change without a corresponding inner move.

Correction type 2. The learner gains some insight into what is acceptable in the target language, but is not immediately able to get her mouth round it. There is an inner movement of insight not yet manifested through the speech organs, though that will follow.

Correction type 3. Both one and two occur – the learner changes the mistake and gains insight. An outer and an inner movement take place together.

Various forms of telling or giving the correction – including of course learner-learner correction – can achieve the first without the second. On the other hand, the second can occur without the first when a degree of insight is gained without the learner yet being able to change a muscular habit of the mother tongue.

Self-correction

For self-correction to occur the learner has to hear herself. She has to hear what she said in order to be 'jarred' by it, in order to discover that what she has done offends her own budding criteria. She has to be creatively dissatisfied with what she has said. Otherwise self-correction can't proceed. I have often seen teachers (including myself) enthusiastically drawing self-correction from a learner in a way that is no more than thinly veiled teacher coercion.

Self-correction can happen where the mistake is a slip, though you may need to help it along. In the case of an error an attempt at self-correction, or enforced self-correction, can lead to guesswork which may or may not be helpful. The appearance of self-correction can take place with an error, but in this case some of the prompting that the learner is given forms sufficient new information to trigger a new learning.

Just guessing in itself – though a useful activity – is not self-correction if there is no recognition by the learner of the right version when she accidentally hits on it.

Two strategies

A slip requires one strategy. The learner needs the least help that is sufficient to activate her existing criteria for correctness. An error requires another strategy. The learner has to be given something new, as she cannot derive correctness from what she knows so far.

Both strategies can be carried out in hundreds of different ways; both are valid when used in the right context. Both can become invalid when the teacher is out of touch with what the learner can do at that moment and uses one strategy instead of the other. For example, the second strategy is often used by teachers instead of the first, particularly when they want to go quickly. Typically the teacher or another class member tell the learner the correction. But something is lost when the learner is given a correction which she could have arrived at for herself. Teachers also use the first strategy in place of the second. When this happens the learner is encouraged to self-correct although she does not have the criteria or experience or information to do so.

Eliciting and telling

These two strategies roughly correspond to *eliciting* and *telling*. This is also the difference between *I tell you* and *I help you to tell yourself*. Sometimes you may hear people equating telling with more traditional approaches, and eliciting with more progressive approaches. I think this is misleading. Perhaps it is true that many traditional approaches adopted telling too often, and perhaps it is also true that more recently eliciting has sometimes been over-used. There is nothing wrong with either strategy when it is used to do the job to which it is suited, and broadly speaking eliciting may be appropriate to working with slips, and telling to working with errors.

A third strategy: *the least that is sufficient*

The rather gross distinction between telling and eliciting disappears if we adopt a more subtle rule of thumb, which is, whatever the cause of the mistake, to give the learner *the least that is sufficient.* According to this principle you vary the help you give from the smallest clues that may trigger a learner's not-quite-active knowledge, to wholesale corrections if that is what they need. Thus over the period of working with the mistake – say a few seconds or a couple of minutes – you continually adjust the density of your intervention until you reach the point where the learner can make something from it.

This is in contrast to a more rigid kind of correction where one level of intervention or help is given, and possibly repeated, even though the learner can't respond to the intervention. An example is when eliciting is overdone and the learner is given too much time to give an answer that she hasn't got.

Multisensory dimensions to sounds and to changing them

Working with sounds need not – and should not – be confined to the aural sense. I have already referred to the importance of the visual and muscular/tactile sensation in pronunciation work, and appealing to the different senses is particularly important in helping to make pronunciation work as vivid and engaging as possible. When helping learners to get free of the grip of their mother tongue pronunciation, you could try some less usual types of instructions.

Appealing to the tactile sense

Sounds are plastic, tactile, malleable and can be moulded and shaped. Instructions could include exhortations such as 'Make it longer!' 'Stretch it!' 'Make it shorter!' 'Smoother!' 'More sudden!'

Appealing to the visual sense

When we talk of 'clarity' of speech we already hint at a visual quality of sound. We can also 'see' sounds just as lip readers do when they observe the muscular movements that make the sounds. Instructions could include 'Watch my lips' (while I mime). 'Move the tongue back like this!' 'Shape your lips like this.' 'Does he look relaxed?' 'Try to look like this while you say it!'

Appealing to the aural/musical sense

Sounds can be made harmonious. When we try to change a phoneme we are simply modifying some of the harmonics. Instructions could include 'Listen to the others while you say it yourself!' 'What is the song of this sound?' 'Say it with more music.' 'Make it sing!'

Appealing to the sense of taste

I may ask learners to 'taste' the pronunciation of a word or phrase we are working on. It is just an invitation to receive the impact of that word through sensation in the mouth. Instructions could include 'Say it slowly as if it tastes very good!' 'Taste that sound!' 'Compare the flavour of these two words!' 'Which tastes better?'

Internal sensation

Learners can feel their own speech by touching their throats at the front. Instructions could include 'Put your hand on your throat!' 'Where in your mouth does that sound vibrate?'

Appealing to feeling

'Feel it!' 'Say it as if you enjoy it!' 'Say it with sadness!' 'Say it with boredom!' 'Which sound do you prefer?'

Awareness and attention

Instructions can include 'Notice exactly what you do!' 'Now do it differently!' 'Now make that sound in your own language!' 'And now in English!' 'Notice the difference!' 'Notice how you can change it!' or, 'Notice how at the moment you can't change it!' (though you changed that other one yesterday and you'll probably change this one tomorrow!).

Classroom activity 19 One approach to correcting sounds

This basic procedure has many variations and many applications. The application here is for pronunciation slips and errors. (In Level 2 there is a version that incorporates finger correction, and that can be used for pronunciation, grammatical and semantic corrections.) Here is a basic procedure:

The learner makes a mistake (a slip or an error) at a point when you are working on individual sounds in isolation.

1 Pause the learner with a gesture. (The unspoken message is *Are you sure about that?*) This may help her to hear it again internally, and may be sufficient to trigger her internal knowledge of what is correct. If she tries to change in the right direction, or even corrects herself, then it was a slip. If she cannot help herself then you have to make your intervention one degree more dense.

2 Without referring to the chart you invite her to say her mistake again, perhaps slowly. This may help her sense more exactly what she is doing with her speech muscles and how that relates to the sound she hears herself making. This awareness could be enough to trigger her self-correction, and if so it was a slip, and the lesson proceeds. If not then your intervention needs to be yet more focused.

3 At this point you could offer her some intervention such as pointing to the chart, or miming, or gesturing, or referring to another learner, or referring back to a previous time when she said it well, or referring to another word containing the required sound, etc. Once again the aim is to offer a definite piece of help which triggers her self-direction rather than undermining it. This intervention could enable her to self-correct if it was a slip, and if it was an error the interventions may offer sufficient clues of new information for her to realize what has to be done.

If this does not help her it seems likely that this is an error that she cannot at the moment fix by herself, and at this point she needs to be given some piece of data that she does not have. Your intervention now becomes not just catalytic but informative and instructive.

4 You use one of the four types of model, or some other prompt. This may be given by another learner, or by yourself, or taken from the tape, etc. (See 'Four ways of giving models', Section 6.)

Commentary ■ ■ ■

The issue here is how to honour and promote the learner's capacity to self-direct and self-correct, while not trying to elicit something that isn't there. This is why I favour interventions that are open-ended to start with, and that gradually become more closed, more dense, more informative. The question is *What is the least intervention that is sufficient?* Overdo the intervention and you direct the learner, who would have been better off directing herself. Underdo the intervention and you leave the learner without a framework within which to correct herself, or without a piece of information she needs.

Throughout a correction sequence it is important to involve everyone, even if only one person is overtly active. You can involve other learners not by asking them to demonstrate or give help, but by inviting them to upgrade their own pronunciation of the sound. Thus all participants are investigating the sound/word at their own level of proficiency. From this variety the learner in question may well 'catch' what to do. ■

Techniques for working with mistakes

The next few pages outline a variety of ways of working with mistakes, and of upgrading and polishing learner pronunciation. Each of the approaches outlined here can give rise to many specific techniques.

Initial questions

1 What exactly am I going to focus on? There may be a single isolated mistake, a series of different but more or less isolatable mistakes, or a general unacceptability which makes it difficult to unravel specific mistakes.
2 Have any of these been consciously worked on before?
3 How long shall we give it? Do I want to work further with this at the moment? Do I at the moment just want to eradicate the mistake in the simplest way possible (probably by instruction), or shall we take a moment to gain more insight into it?
4 What kind of mistake – is it a slip or an error?
5 Shall we do something now or later?
6 Is this wrong pronunciation in fact a good pronunciation of another sound? If so can I indicate that on the chart, so that the learner can see where she is?

Plotting the learner's correction route

When trying to help a learner with a not-quite-right sound, first I find the sound the learner is making in my own mouth and throat. Then I find the sound I am helping her to make. By saying these two sounds one after the other I highlight the difference between the two, and I make clear to myself the route that the learner has got to take. This helps me see what has to be done. I can do this silently to myself or aloud, in which case the learner may benefit from overhearing me. I can even ask the learner to teach me her mistake, which may give her insight into it.

Minimal response

Another minimal convention that I find effective is that if I make no response apart from my continued attention, then whatever is being done is at an acceptable standard for the time being. In other words I will intervene when the learners need something from me and not when they don't. This reduces the impulse to keep approving the learners' right actions, often by showing transparently artificial pleasure.

Teacher gives correction

Choose from the four types of model and their variations. Experiment with the whole range. Adapt them to make them yours. Take risks and experiment with gesture and mime. It doesn't matter *what* you do, the question is *how does it help?*

Gesture

Gestures when used consistently and economically can convey with surprising directness a range of crucial articulatory features. With a little practice, you can build up your own repertoire of gestures to convey such things as jaw position and degree of opening of mouth; tongue position; lip rounding and spread; nasal; voiced and unvoiced sounds; more or less energy in articulation; stopping sounds suddenly or gradually; glide in diphthongs; deletion or addition of sounds; adjustments to stress, rhythm and intonation; etc.

Mime

When miming sounds, words or phrases, you are drawing attention to certain visual features of articulation and energy distribution simply by going through the motions silently but in a slightly exaggerated way. This can often be useful when learners have got a bit tied up with the sounds themselves and need a different starting point.

Instructions leading to insight

Try to extend your range of instructions and interventions. I have found the most potent instructions to be: 'Say it very slowly!' 'Change it!' 'Say it in English!' The following paragraphs deal with these three instructions.

'Say it very slowly!'

When intervening to change the sound a learner is making I find it helpful to ask them to slow the sound right down. This enables me to see and hear what is going on in much more detail, and it strengthens the speaker's internal sensation of what he is doing with his muscles and how that relates to the sound he is making.

On this basis, and still with the sound slowed down, I can indicate changes for the learner to make. When he has made a change in the right direction I ask him to speed it up again as much as he is able while retaining the change. It's like putting the sound under a microscope in order to perceive the detail and alter some parts without changing others.

'Change it!'

This seems to be a very useful instruction, especially when a learner has got stuck in an articulatory rut from which he can only seem to offer the same wrong sound again and again. My aim is to help him to change one variable, whatever it is (perhaps simply to make it longer or shorter), so as to keep him in contact with the muscles that are shaping the sound.

To help him to do this I may say 'Change it!' or 'Make it different!' and if he does so then I may repeat the instruction to yield another change, and so on several times, all the time giving him feedback on any changes that bring him significantly nearer the target sound.

Once the learner has released himself from the constraints of his mother tongue he sometimes arrives quickly at the target sound. And if not he can still learn two things: that I am patient and that it's OK by me if he doesn't reach the target sound; and that I am glad to see him explore what he can do with his mouth and sharpen what he can perceive with his ear.

'Say it in English!'

Ask the learner to say the sound as it might be in his own language (Spanish, Arabic, etc). Recognize the learner's own language, recognize the difference, recognize that he can make some kind of change from one to the other even if it is not exactly right. It is interest in the process that we want to inspire at the moment. Correctness will be a product of that. This instruction also challenges learners to build their own criteria of Englishness.

I make particular use of this question after learners have focused on some aspect of accuracy (of a sound, a grammar point, a sequence of words, etc) and though they now have the 'correct things in the correct order' it no longer sounds like English as it has lost life and fluency. So with this instruction I challenge them to bring it back to fluency with some speed, energy and precision.

Questions leading to insight

The aim of these questions is to direct the learner's attention to what he is doing so that he can become more self-directing. Questions that can induce awareness include 'noticing questions' such as 'Which one sounds more English?' 'How many sounds?' and at Level 2, 'How many stresses?' 'How many letters/words/syllables?'

'Which sounds more English?'

This is a simple and interesting technique. Whenever two or more pronunciations or stress patterns are offered by the class, of which only one is correct, ask 'Which is more English?' and then have them give the differing versions or say it the different ways yourself. This calls on learners' own knowledge of 'Englishness', and I am sometimes surprised by how often the class as a whole chooses the right version. But if they don't it doesn't matter; what's important is the invitation to test their own criteria of Englishness followed by immediate feedback from you.

'How many sounds?'

When I can see that one or more learners are confused by the sequence of sounds in a word, or are omitting or adding sounds, or are unable to point out a word on the chart, I may ask 'How many sounds?' In order to count them they have to play the word slowly through in their mind's ear, trying to separate the sounds and to hear where one sound ends and the next one begins. They usually come up with a range of different answers, which tells me something about each individual's perception of sounds, and we go through it together, me counting on my fingers while they say what they think each sound is. Then we join the sounds together to say the word fluently, and we find that some of the problems of perception and articulation have been ironed out. Someone then comes up to point it out on the chart.

Using the chart in the language laboratory

Have the chart on display at the front of the language laboratory when you are working on pronunciation exercises. Use it to give guidance to the whole class on the aims of the exercises they are doing, and also use it to clarify the help you give to individual learners.

Using pocket mirrors

Mirrors can be useful in helping learners to become more aware of their own lip, tongue and jaw movements and so perhaps more aware that these are things which can be changed. This in turn may incline them to be more observant of these variables when they watch you model sounds or words, and perhaps to study native speakers more closely. Encourage your learners to 'look English' and 'feel English' when they speak. If possible, arrange for them to watch themselves speaking English on video.

Using diagrams

A simplified mouth diagram such as the one below can be a useful instrument to help learners become more conscious of their speech organs and can be used to illustrate some key features of vowels and consonants.

Fig. 47a: Draw this mouth outline on the board. You can draw the tongue with a dotted line, or indicate the tongue with a finger or pen held against the diagram to show its movement in relation to other parts of the mouth.

Fig. 47 b–e: These four diagrams show how you can indicate points of contact for consonants.

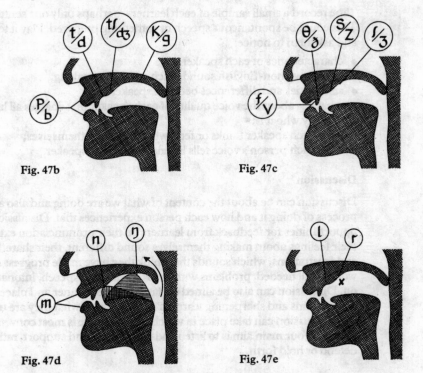

Fig. 47b

Fig. 47c

Fig. 47d

Fig. 47e

Grouping the learners by their mistakes

You can group together those learners making the same mistake and see if they can sort it out. Or ask them to group themselves. Or pair those that can do it with those that can't and see if peer help is useful. Make sure you challenge those who can say it correctly so that everyone knows they have room for improvement.

Exploiting the chart layout

Use the logic of the layout of the chart to relate sounds to each other, and to improve one sound by contrasting it with the one next to it on the chart, etc. Once you have studied the reasons behind the layout of the chart (see discovery toolkit Level 1), you will find that many ways of correcting sounds and arriving at new ones are suggested by the arrangement.

Here are some examples:

You can get a learner to change a sound by 'colouring' it with another neighbouring one; you can make use of the front–back spectrum in both the consonant and monophthong section; you can approach difficult sounds through other sounds. For example, if someone seems unable to discriminate /ʌ/ from /ɑː/, try approaching /ʌ/ from /æ/, which is further forward. If there is trouble making the sound /æ/, then try approaching it from above by going through /iː/ and then /e/, and then extending to /æ/, all of them front vowels with the jaw gradually opening.

Tape recording the group

Tape record a small sample of each learner – perhaps only one sentence each. This could be spontaneous speech or something prepared. Play it to the group and ask them to notice:

- characteristics of each speaker;
- one or two non-English sounds each speaker is making;
- similarities and differences between speakers;
- what it is about the voice quality of each speaker that enables all listeners to identify who it is;
- what each speaker thinks or feels when they hear themselves;
- what each person's voice tells listeners about the speaker.

Discussion

Discussion can be about the content of what we are doing and also about the process of doing it and how each person experiences that. Discussion can provide opportunities for feedback from learners on their pronunciation experiences, their feelings about making themselves sound different, their shared difficulties and frustrations, which sounds they think they have made progress on and where work is still needed, problems with stress, connected speech, intonation and so on. Discussion can also be aimed at clarifying the manner and place of specific articulations and sharpening learners' perception of what they are trying to do. The discussion can take place in whichever language is most convenient to those present. Your main aim is to listen and understand and support, rather than defend or hold forth.

Amount of energy

Over-exertion is a typical feature of the pronunciation learning process and one that we need to watch and understand. Sometimes it can indicate the summoning of the learner's attention and energy to break into a new and unfamiliar articulation, and at other times it can prevent just such a discovery from taking place. So getting the learner to put more or less energy into his articulation is another variable at your disposal. What we are aiming for is maximum clarity of articulation with minimum energy. Instructions include 'Let go more!' 'Relax a bit!' 'Mumble like this!' or 'Attack the sound!'

Using the discovery activities

The awareness-raising activities in the discovery toolkit section of this book are a source of activities for your learners, especially if you adapt them to suit your teaching and their learning style.

Involving the whole class in one person's mistake

I find that there is more time and less sense of pressure if I involve everyone in one person's mistake. It might go like this:

1 Work as usual with the mistake of one learner.
2 Invite the attention of the others with a gesture, as if to say 'Watch carefully, this is interesting.'

3 While still working with the first learner, invite the others to practise the sound individually, and to make it as 'English' as they can.

4 When the first learner has finished, invite the others to try their version, but with the clear intention of seeing what their own best effort is, rather than simply as an example to the first learner. On hearing the various suggestions from the class the original learner may show recognition of his mistake or of the correction. You can also ask him to choose which of the offerings sounds most English.

This helps to find out where the others stand on the issue raised by this mistake. To what extent do any of them share the same problem? How many have the knowledge to correct it?

In this way every mistake offers an occasion for diagnosis, feedback and insight into your learners' learning styles. It can be an event for the whole class.

Commentary on the approaches offered above ■ ■ ■

The techniques described above are not specific recipes, but general procedures which can be adopted and adapted in different ways to broaden and enrich your existing repertoire. Each one can give rise to a whole range of techniques.

The emphasis here has been on helping the learner to improve either without the aid of an oral model from the teacher, or at least with the minimum amount of verbal noise from the teacher. This does not mean the teacher is silent, just that the teacher takes care to offer the least that is sufficient to do the job, and does not solve for the learner what he could solve for himself. It has to do with the teacher not getting in the way of the learning.

If you decide to build up a range of more silent teaching and correcting techniques you could begin with some of the suggestions given here and experiment and adapt. You will notice how when you talk less in class, even a little less, you somehow create for yourself more space in which to think about what you are doing and observe its effect on your learners. You may also find that you feel more relaxed and more in touch with what's going on.

When I am working with learners I have the view that they are all capable of any pronunciation as long as they have throats, mouths, tongues and breath. If a learner can't make a certain pronunciation change then it's for a good reason. And if I want to get behind that reason, then I have to be very watchful. I see myself as searching for an 'invisible thread'; when I help the learner to pull it, it will somehow precipitate the new sound in that learner. If I pay close attention to that person's learning process and take opportunities as they arise I increase the chances of finding the invisible thread and tricking the two guardians of the mother tongue pronunciation, namely the habits of the mouth and the habits of the ears.

If English is not your first language, it may be that you are uncertain of your own pronunciation. Well, don't worry! You may have an advantage over native teachers because most of them do not consciously know how they produce their pronunciation, whereas you have had to work for your English and have actually done what you are asking your learners to do. *But*, you say, *surely my learners are going to imitate my accent*? Well, yes and no. Because when you use silent correction techniques your learners cannot rely on your spoken model but are required to search for their own criteria. On the basis of that they make their best effort and it is your ear that judges their efforts. In other words, your receptive criteria rather than your productive ability sets the standard. At the same time these techniques ask you to listen very carefully, to demand the best from everyone, to experiment and explore, and you are likely to find that your own pronunciation loosens and changes at the same time. In my view a mark of the very best teaching is that the teacher is learning along with the students. ■

Level 2   Words in isolation

1 Establishing the sound flow   145

2 Working with the spelling-pronunciation link   146

3 Word stress: working with words of two or more syllables   151

4 Word stress and Cuisenaire rods   154

5 Finger correction   160

6 Integrating the learner's dictionary with pronunciation work   166

7 Lip reading, ventriloquism, pronunciation and vocabulary   169

Introduction

At Level 1 we focused on the recognition and articulation of the individual sounds of the English phonemic set. The classroom toolkit of Level 1 aimed to develop an attentive ear and a more conscious control of the speech organs.

At Level 2 we focus on the way individual sounds are strung together into a flow to make up individual words. A spoken word has its own characteristic sound flow, which is more than the sum of its separate sounds because each sound influences or overlaps with the articulation of its neighbour. This is referred to as *co-articulation*. The aim of the Level 2 classroom toolkit is to work with techniques that develop learners' capacity to receive, process and produce these English sound flows.

The way in which the sounds of a word flow together, and the way in which word stress affects the distribution of energy across the syllables, combine to yield the identity of words spoken in isolation. Sound flow and word stress cannot be separated entirely from each other.

The actual selection of words to be studied at Level 2 depends on what you select from your course materials and on what your learners bring. In your general vigilance over pronunciation quality you will find all sorts of opportunities to refer to the chart to upgrade or draw attention to particular pronunciations during any classroom activity. Every time you do this you not only attend to the specific difficulty but you also help to strengthen your learners' capacity for watchfulness.

1   Establishing the sound flow

Classroom activity 20

1 Visually dictate words from the phonemic chart by touching each sound in turn with the pointer.

2 Learners either say each sound as it is pointed out and then join the sounds together, or they remain silent while watching the pointing, retaining the sounds internally, and then saying the connected word aloud.

3 Listen and see how well the learners are managing to say the word.

4 Your options at this point are:

- to leave it at that and continue the lesson;
- to isolate problem sounds and work with them (Level 1 focus);
- to help improve the flow of sounds/fluency (Level 2 focus);
- to focus on the stress pattern (Level 2 focus).

Commentary ■ ■ ■

You can extend and vary this work using any of the seven modes described in the classroom toolkit (Level 1 Section 4). The chart is an instrument which allows you to focus learners' attention on any individual sound or group of sounds in the word. For example, you can focus on vowel quality and vowel length, and help mould them as required. Or you can pay attention to consonant clusters, practising the sounds separately and together. You can check that vowels are not intruding where they shouldn't, and you can practise the same cluster in different contexts simply by pointing on the chart without speaking yourself.

You can take the opportunity to work on the typical intonation pattern for single-syllable words spoken in isolation, perhaps a falling tune from mid to low. This intonation has no meaning in that it is not chosen by the speaker to emphasize part of a message. But by keeping several variables in play at the same time (eg varying pitch while practising stress or sound flow) it is possible to engage learners' attention and to encourage practice without repetition.

As at Level 1, attention to detail need not be primarily aimed at getting learners to be correct, but at helping them to be more perceptive, to notice what they are saying, and so to be able to change it at will. Correctness is a by-product of noticing. ■

2 Working with the spelling–pronunciation link

You can use the phonemic chart to highlight the links between the alphabetical spelling of a word and its pronunciation. I sometimes think that teachers too easily project the negative suggestion that English spelling is hard because there are as many exceptions as there are rules. A few centuries ago English spelling closely reflected the pronunciation of the writer, so that individual and regional variations in spelling were both permissible and natural. However, with the invention of the printing press, spelling gradually became standardized and fixed while pronunciation continued to evolve. The result today is that most phonemes can be represented by a number of different spellings in different words.

Instead of worrying about the consequent lack of clear spelling rules, and so inducing doubt in our learners' minds, we can create conditions in which they can face the facts of English spelling boldly and playfully, and can internalize spelling–pronunciation relationships in their own way. Here are some suggestions for developing sensitivity to these links, an alternative (or a supplement) to the process of handing down lists of spelling rules and exceptions.

Classroom activity 21 Inferring spelling from pronunciation

Encourage your learners to try to infer spelling from pronunciation and vice versa, without necessarily feeling obliged to account for or explain the links. Here is a toolkit of four questions that I have found simple and subtle for doing this job.

Awareness question 1: 'How do you think this is said?'

- A learner puts the written form of a word on the board and you ask 'How do you think this is said?'
- The learners try their versions aloud, and you invite everyone to listen to each, attending to the differences and trying to decide which they think is most likely to be the English version.
- Then, if they haven't spotted it, you can point out the English pronunciation on the chart, or say it yourself, or invite them to check in the dictionary.

Awareness question 2: 'How many sounds does it have?'

- When faced with a doubtful word, ask 'How many sounds does it have?' Perhaps the learners have the spelling in front of them, or perhaps they hear you or another person say the word.
- When they have counted, ask them each to give their estimate and then go through it together aloud saying the sounds one at a time, perhaps using the chart at the same time to clarify.
- When you have the right sounds in the right order, say 'Now in English, please!' in order to link the sounds together into a smooth flow, and bring it from a Level 1 utterance to a Level 2 utterance.

Awareness question 3: 'How do you think this is spelled?'

- Say the word aloud and ask 'How do you think this is spelled?'
- Invite learners to come to the board, several at a time, to write up their suggestions.
- Invite them to study each other's suggestions, and perhaps to improve on them.
- Ask them to use a dictionary to check hypotheses and to discuss what they find.

Awareness question 4: 'How many letters does it have?'

This question can be useful if learners have got stuck on question 3. It calls for a different internal response:

- If they have heard the word and are having trouble spelling it I may ask 'How many letters does it have?' This requires them to separate out the letters in their mind's eye.
- When they have counted, ask them each to give their estimate and go through it on the board.

Commentary ■ ■ ■

There is nothing new about these four questions. What is important is the way they are asked and the reason for asking them. The aims are:

- For learners to become aware of their own perceptions (eg of pronunciations and spellings) by getting them first to identify their perceptions, and then to commit themselves to them.
- For learners to notice how their perception differs from that of other class members, and how it might differ from their own perception of a moment ago. I want to enable them to 'see their own learning'.
- For learners to draw conclusions from all the discrepancies in the class and to use discrepancies as a resource.
- For learners to develop their own internal criteria of 'Englishness', and to learn to trust their hunches.
- To invite learners to test out their own hypotheses. This requires that they be invited to have hypotheses in the first place. It is vital that these are not just 'teacher's questions', but opportunities to show and share your own genuine curiosity.
- To make contact with each learner's inner world of perception. A learner's answer to the question 'How many sounds are there?' can help to reveal the cause of mispronunciation. ■

Classroom activity 22 Vocabulary and phonemic spelling

Let it become quite natural to write phonemic and alphabetic spellings alongside each other on the board. When the alphabetic spelling has been written up, ask a volunteer to come up and write the phonemic spelling beside it, or vice versa. Encourage your learners to do the same when they record vocabulary in their notebooks. Wherever possible, let learners do the writing at the board.

Classroom activity 23 Transforming spelling into pronunciation

1 Learners select and write on the board about ten recently learned words. They can be of various syllable lengths.

2 Divide the class into two teams. Each team takes it in turn to send a member up to the board who selects one of the words by underlining it, and then tries to point out its pronunciation on the chart.

3 If the person at the board makes a mistake you 'pause' the pointer at the place where the mistake is, and then pass the pointer to a member of the other team, who tries the same word again.

4 This continues until the word is correctly pointed out, which earns a point. The word is then crossed off the list. The game finishes when all the words have been used up.

Variations

You can also play the game the other way round, that is going from sound to spelling. In this case, the exact phonemic spelling is pointed out on the chart without speaking. The other team have to say the word and try to infer its spelling using their experience of what is possible in English, and using the dictionary to check. Members of the team come up to the board and write the spelling. You 'pause' them where a mistake is made, and the chalk or board pen passes to the other team.

It helps if you give learners a couple of minutes to investigate the words in their dictionaries before the game.

This works well as a team game, but you could have people working simply for themselves, or with a large class you could use several teams.

Commentary ■ ■ ■

The fact that you 'pause' the pointer or chalk, and then hand it to the other team as soon as a mistake is made, is a convention that encourages watchfulness on the part of all the other learners because they are having their own knowledge put to the test at the same time as the one who is at the chart. When their turn comes they know that everything up to the point of the mistake is acceptable.

The relationship between sound and spelling can become significant just through being observed. There may be no need to explain or give rules. Intuition is a powerful instrument and has to be used at the point where cognitive explanation is not possible or is too complex. ■

Classroom activity 24 Exploiting the origins of spelling mistakes

There are several good reasons for making intelligent spelling mistakes. The interference can be from simple lack of knowledge, but it can also be from mother tongue spelling forms, from individuals' own associations, and from pronunciation. A mistake can tell a story which contains its own insight and you can use this as an opportunity to investigate and practise pronunciation. Here is a procedure:

1 Ask a learner to say aloud a word she has misspelled.

2 Help her to focus precisely on the articulation of the sounds by slowing her speech down. You may now see that the spelling mistake is a reflection of the way she is pronouncing the word.

3 Help her to make changes to individual sounds (Level 1) if necessary.

4 Join the sounds together again and bring the pronunciation up to speed (Level 2).

5 Now ask her if she wants to change the spelling. Let her try her hunch and help her if necessary.

Variation

After a piece of written work has been corrected (by the author, by peers or by you), ask the authors:

1 To select their own most interesting mistake and to prepare the story of this mistake. (By story I mean a one-sentence account of its origin.)

2 To come to the front of the class and write the mistake and the correction on the board, and then to tell the story of the mistake (eg 'It was a guess,' or 'I said it to myself with this sound in it so that is how I spelled it,' or 'I was thinking of this word XXXXX in my language,' or 'The first time I heard it I thought it had this sound in it and now I keep thinking that,' or 'I always confuse it with ...,' etc.

Commentary ■ ■ ■

Mistakes can teach us a lot if we can meet them with creative curiosity rather than fear. If we teachers could apply that to our own mistakes it might begin to rub off on our learners. ■

Classroom activity 25 Finding words with a given sound

This game and its variations focus on two important fields of awareness: the similarities and differences in quality between a phoneme in isolation and the same phoneme embedded in a variety of words, and beyond that the relationship between spelling and pronunciation.

1 Point to a vowel sound on the chart and ask your learners to search their memories and write down words containing that sound. Give them a short but sufficient time. Walking round and glancing at individuals' lists will give you insight into each person's own perceptions.

2 Suggestions may be discussed in groups and put in two columns on the board, one column thought to contain the given vowel, the other column for any rejects. (Variation: put them all in one column initially and then discuss each in turn.)

3 The correct column can be practised aloud to trace the same sound through a variety of words and spellings. The words in the other column should also be pointed out on the chart to clarify which sounds they do in fact contain, and to locate the point of the original confusion.

Variations

When learners have developed a certain accuracy at this, you can make it more challenging by pointing out two or even three sounds, asking learners to make two or three lists simultaneously.

Another variation is for learners themselves to come to the chart and choose the sound(s). You can ask them to select vowel sounds they are unsure of or that they confuse.

A third variation is to give them a mixed group of single-syllable words and ask them to sort them into groups according to the vowel sound.

The chart is an instrument that enables you and your learners to illuminate confusions and to defuse confusions. This is also an opportunity to have them refer to dictionaries to check pronunciations.

Commentary ■ ■ ■

I find this a powerful game for diagnosing which phonemes are unclear for a learner. It also gives me access to learners' own inner perceptions of the pronunciation of English sounds and words. The next activity is like this but the other way round. ■

Classroom activity 26 Minimal pairs and triplets

1 Whenever you find two or three sounds that are being confused with each other, you can put on the board a short list of words containing those sounds, perhaps with different spellings of each sound. For example, if /ɑ:/, /ʌ/ and /ɒ/ are causing problems you might choose *cut, cart, cot, rough, cough, heart, love, dance*, etc.

2 Learners then group the words according to the vowel sound they contain, first by referring to their inner pronunciation criteria, then by negotiating with each other, and then with reference to dictionaries.

3 The game can finish with learners pointing the words out on the chart, saying them aloud, and identifying those spellings which seem surprising.

Commentary ■ ■ ■

This shows your class a way of disentangling their own confusions when they arise. And more than that, it gives them a way of recognizing such confusions in the first place. Step 1 can carry more weight when one or several learners put up on the board their own list of confusing words. ■

3 Word stress: working with words of two or more syllables

Word stress is a characteristic and integral part of the phonemic identity of a word, so learning to stress the right syllable may also help to lay a sound foundation for the perception and production of rhythm in the stream of speech.

Here are some activities that work on awareness of syllable stress. (These are extended in the following section, which introduces the use of Cuisenaire rods.) The placing of this stress is marked in learners' dictionaries.

Classroom activity 27 Another set of awareness questions

Awareness question 5: 'How many syllables are there?'

To study syllable stress learners need to be able to identify syllables. A way of sharpening this awareness is to ask 'How many syllables?' with reference to any word isolated from a text, tape or spoken by a class member. Apart from giving rise to group discussion, the different answers to your question will tell you about each learner's aural perception of that word, and also about their own perception of what a syllable is.

Awareness question 6: 'Which syllable is stressed?'

Having established how many syllables there are in a chosen word, you can ask 'Which one is stressed?' (or if the concept is new, you might prefer 'Which one is strongest?') with reference either to a spoken model or to a word from a text. This requires learners to say the word internally or aloud and to identify the point of greater energy. Once again, class discussion and differing perceptions can be a resource.

Awareness question 7: 'Do you notice a difference?'

If the word has not been heard before, a revealing exercise is for you to say the word aloud several times, shifting the stress to a different syllable each time. For example: <u>un</u>derstand; un<u>der</u>stand; under<u>stand</u>. You can then ask 'Do you notice a difference?' which they almost certainly will, even if they can't explain or reproduce it.

Awareness question 8: 'Which sounds most English?'

If in response to question 7 the learners can hear the difference, then you can ask 'Which sounds most English?' It is surprising how often learners can discern the correct English stress pattern of words they have not met before. Finally, you can highlight the correct version by saying it, by drawing attention to one of the learners who has got it, or by asking them to check in their dictionaries.

Practising the stress pattern

Having isolated and drawn attention to the stressed syllable, the word can be practised aloud using any of your usual techniques. I think it is helpful to encourage learners to pay attention not only to the stressed syllable itself but to the neighbouring unstressed syllables with which it is contrasted. If the word still doesn't sound correctly stressed, then look at both the quality of the learners' unstress, and at the manner in which they are stressing the main syllable. Invite them to play around with the length, pitch and volume of the stressed syllable.

If your learners are having difficulty with word stress, it may be useful to draw attention to the three variables that can signal a stressed syllable. These are pitch change, vowel length and volume (see discovery toolkit level 2).

Classroom activity 28 Different ways of stressing a syllable

1 Take a multi-syllable word, eg *different*, as an example, and ask learners 'How many syllables?' and 'Which one is stressed?'
2 Tell them you are going to try to stress the first syllable in three different ways, but that you are not sure if you will be successful.
3 Put the words *longer, higher, louder* on the board.
4 Say the word *different* three times, stressing the first syllable by exaggerating each variable in turn. Try to keep the other variables unchanged, so that you have the syllable longer but not louder or higher, or louder but not higher or longer, etc. You won't sound very 'English' when you do this!
5 Ask the class to guess which variable you are trying for.

6 It's probably just as well if you *don't* do this too well! It's more important to do it with humour and playfulness. The aim is to raise awareness rather than to be right, and to put into circulation the idea that stress can be manifested in these three ways.

7 With the class, select a few multi-syllable words, and ask them to experiment with the three variables and to give each other feedback.

Commentary ■ ■ ■

The aim is to plant an awareness rather than to demand immediate capability. It is a way of finding out what they do with their voice, and also what else can be done. This enables you to focus on whichever of the three variables seems to bring about the maximum improvement in their pronunciation in any given situation. Different mother tongue speakers may require emphasis on one or the other of the variables. I find the length variable to be the most accessible. Of course you can also stress with lower pitch providing there is also length or volume. You could offer this option. ■

Making word stress visible

Word stress and symbols

Once you have started to work on the perception and production of word stress, you will need to introduce a visual symbol to represent stress that can act as a memory hook and as a trigger for its production, in the same way as the phonemic symbols represent the sounds.

You can use the symbol /'/ to indicate that the syllable immediately following is stressed. You can use this with both phonemic and alphabetic spellings:

> 'dictionary   dic'tation
> /'dɪkʃənrɪ/   /dɪk'teɪʃən/

The symbol is located in the top right-hand corner of the chart.

When you want to use the chart to indicate word stress, you touch the stress symbol with the pointer at the appropriate place in the sound sequence.

When marking word stress on the board, you can either follow the dictionary convention, or underline the stressed syllable, or put a circle or square over the syllable.

> 'dictionary   dic'tation   <u>dic</u>tionary   dic<u>ta</u>tion   dictionary   dictation

Once we have started to mark stress, I encourage learners to do so whenever they are noting down new vocabulary in their books or on the board.

4   Word stress and Cuisenaire rods

Cuisenaire rods are one of the most powerful tools for language teaching that I have discovered. The particular use that I have made in *Sound Foundations* draws on a small fraction of their potential while maintaining their clarity, effectiveness, and ease of use.

Here is a series of simple and engaging games which promote a conscious appreciation of both appropriate and inappropriate placement of stress. Since red rods are twice the size of white ones you will be able to tell the difference in the illustrations.

Basic rules for Cuisenaire rods and word stress

- Only white and red rods are used.
- Any rod placed on the table represents one syllable.
- An unstressed syllable is represented by a white rod.
- A stressed syllable is represented by a red rod.

You need a small table in clear view of the class. As far as possible, the manipulation of the rods is done by individual learners invited to come to the table, though for some exercises it may be easier to divide learners into groups, each with a supply of rods.

Classroom activity 29 Using Cuisenaire rods

1 Isolate the word you want to focus on and say it using the single model plus hearing time. Or listen to it on a tape, or simply focus on its spelling form in a printed text.

2 The group then decides how many syllables the word contains and one learner comes to the table to place one white rod for each syllable. The rest of the class says each syllable aloud as she places each rod.

If the word were *excellent* she would place the rods like this:

3 The next question is, where is the stress? Any learner can come to the table and put a red rod in place of a white one to give a profile for the word 'excellent'. They could do this in one of three ways:

(correct)   (incorrect)   (incorrect)

4 The others agree or disagree and come up to change the arrangement accordingly. Each version is tested by saying it aloud and perhaps the dictionary is consulted.

Commentary ■ ■ ■

This draws attention to the stress pattern as an integral part of the identity of the spoken word in a way that is visible, tactile and instantly changeable. It is also under the control of the learners. This awareness can now be taken further to strengthen their ability to articulate different stress patterns at will.

I and many other teachers have found that Cuisenaire rods can be used with classes of fifty or more. But if you find class size is a problem, you can:

- divide the class into groups, each with a supply of rods;
- place rods directly on an OHP transparency - they show up well on the screen;
- make or obtain a few larger blocks to use in the same way. ■

Classroom activity 30 Manipulating the word stress

Suppose some of your learners are finding the stress pattern of *engineer* difficult to produce:

1 Ask how many syllables the word has.
2 Lay out three white rods, one for each syllable.
3 Now, in a deliberate manner, put a red rod in the place of the first white rod, like this:

and ask them to say the word like this (ie incorrectly, with the stress on the first syllable) in this case.

4 Then immediately move the red rod to the second syllable ...

... and ask them to say the word this way (and again incorrectly).

5 And then immediately move the red rod to the third syllable ...

... and ask them to say the word this way (this time correctly).

6 Now ask 'Which sounds most English?' Discuss their different answers to this question and go back to the rods if necessary.

Commentary ■ ■ ■

Do the moves with the rods swiftly so the learners can appreciate the shift of energy between the stress placements. They should be aware of the contrast both aurally and through internal sensation. Don't interrupt verbally while doing this. Try to let the rods and their configuration give the instruction.

This exercise can help learners to arrive at an elusive stress pattern, and to become more aware of how a small change in the distribution of energy can make a big difference to native speakers of the language. Regarding the question 'Which sounds most English?' the fact that learners are often able to spot the correct stress pattern, even with words that they seem not to have heard before, suggests that they have already begun to internalize intuitive criteria of 'what to expect' in English, based on what has been met so far. ■

Classroom activity 31 Using rod profiles to give feedback to learners

This is an extension of the last game. It quite often happens that a learner 'knows' the correct stress pattern but is unable to make a sufficient contrast between the stressed and unstressed syllables. Suppose, for example, the word is *hotel*:

1 Ask the learner to say the word aloud.

2 Give immediate visual feedback on her stress pattern using a rod profile, without saying anything yourself, to give her a basis on which to try something different. For example:

If she puts the stress on the wrong syllable (the first), place the rods like this:

If her stress seems acceptable, do this:

If both syllables sound to you rather strong, do this:

If both sound too weak, do this:

3 On the basis of this immediate visual feedback the learner can try to change her pronunciation, and the rest of the class can be invited to join in.

Variations

- You say a multi-syllable word and the class use the rods to show the stressed syllable.
- A learner says a word and then lays out the rods according to what she thinks she has said. This gives you insight into how she perceives what she is doing.
- A learner places the rods and you say the word with the stress she indicates. She keeps changing the arrangement while listening to what she is prompting you to say.

Commentary ■ ■ ■

Having established the rules of this game you can then have learners working in smaller groups from a selection of multi-syllable words, giving each other visual feedback with the rods in the same way. This is good practice for both the listener and the speaker. ■

Distinguishing primary and secondary stress

Some longer words when spoken in isolation have a secondary stress as well as a primary stress. Secondary stress is also part of the aural identity of the word and must be taken into account when learning vocabulary. Most learners' dictionaries indicate secondary stress with the symbol /ˌ/ placed immediately before the relevant syllable to indicate the presence of secondary stress:

ˌciviliˈzation /ˌsɪvɪlaɪˈzeɪʃən/

In the phonemic chart the secondary stress symbol is below the primary stress symbol in the top right-hand corner.

You can integrate the primary/secondary/unstress distinction into the use of rods by using three different colours, green for primary stress, red for secondary and white for unstress. These are also of three different sizes, so typical word profiles look like this:

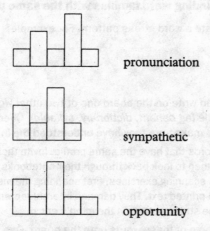

pronunciation

sympathetic

opportunity

This means you can adapt class activities 29, 30 and 31 to include attention to secondary stress.

Of course it is not always helpful to distinguish too closely between primary and secondary stress. It may be sufficient to accept a more or less equal value for either, as long as they are both in contrast to unstressed syllables.

When you do want your learners to discover and appreciate the difference for themselves, Classroom activity 32 (p158) gives one approach you can try.

Classroom activity 32 Primary and secondary stress

1 Establish the number of syllables and stresses in the word. Do not distinguish primary and secondary stress, but make sure all other syllables are unstressed:

   fasci<u>na</u>tion

2 Now ask if either of the stresses seems to be stronger. Give learners a chance to locate the secondary stress intuitively, and to listen to you saying it.

3 Using the rods as prompts try the primary stress in both positions:

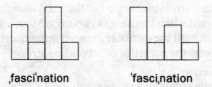

ˌfasciˈnation   ˈfasciˌnation

Invite the class to say it both ways, to make a clear difference, and to identify which seems 'more English', or is closer to the model you gave, or closer to a model on tape.

4 A class member can check the stress pattern in the dictionary.

Classroom activity 33 Finding word families with the same profile

1 Lay out the rods to indicate a word stress pattern. For example:

2 Ask the class to come and write on the board one or two other words that have the same pattern or profile (eg *benefit, dictionary, syllable*). Check their suggestions with them to make sure they have understood the instruction.

3 Ask them to write down words that have the same profile. Invite them first to recall words from memory, and then to look back through their notebooks, or through their textbook. (These are scanning exercises, first scanning the memory, and then scanning handwritten and printed text. They demand internal representation of the words in order to check the stress pattern in the mind's ear.)

4 The next step is to get some of these words onto the board. One way is to invite each person to put two or three of their words *that they are sure of* on the board. Another is to ask each person to put on the board only words *they are not sure of*. An alternative is for them to check their lists with a neighbour, and then put two or three certainties and two or three doubtfuls on the board.

5 You now have on the board a list of words chosen by the class on the basis of their perceptions of word stress, some of which belong to the profile and some of which do not. Now go through the words with the class, noticing and clarifying the stress pattern, and using the opportunity to work with the sounds where necessary. Encourage learners to listen to each other, and in cases of doubt (both yours and theirs) refer them to the dictionary. (As an alternative, you could begin step 5 by asking learners individually to identify the odd ones out on the board, and to come to the board and mark them.)

Variations

- Omit step 3, the individual writing stage, and ask learners to write their suggested words directly on the board. This is quicker.
- Present two rod profiles to work with at the same time. For example:

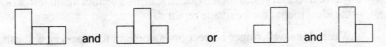

Commentary ■ ■ ■

A very simple exercise like this can engage learners at any level. But that on its own is not enough. A good exercise or game should also give us feedback on how each learner is meeting the challenge, how each is viewing and processing the task. This enables us to stay in touch with their efforts and so have a better idea what to do next. And that requires us to be watchful. Just as an illustration, here are some of the things we might learn about the learners while they are doing this activity:

- that as the exercise proceeds many of them become more able to discern and to reproduce stress patterns;
- that when writing their list they may confuse patterns that they can tell apart if they say them aloud;
- that the stress profile of a word is a useful heading under which the memory can be searched. ■

Classroom activity 34 Six word stress profiles

The majority of English words fall into one of the six categories below:

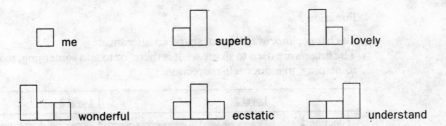

As a development of activity 33 you could present all of these rod profiles together and the class could spend a few minutes finding words for each one, perhaps by looking at a dialogue in the coursebook and categorizing some of the words.

Commentary ■ ■ ■

The outcome of this kind of activity can be to open up awareness of and sensitivity to the stress profile of a word, so that it is more easily registered when words are met in the future. It is another tool for the recognition and retention of words. ■

5 Finger correction

Finger correction is a technique in which you assign either the single sounds of a word, or the individual words of a sentence, one to each finger. The aim is to separate the flow of sounds or words for closer inspection, to carry out repairs where necessary, and then to join the units together again into a fluent whole. It is the ideal toolkit for 'roadside repairs'.

When done well, finger correction is a delight to experience. It can be quick, specific, and supportive of the learner's capacities. It is also striking because the teacher is silent, and therefore does not interfere on the learner's airwaves. It is the most elegant oral correction system that I know for enabling you to facilitate self-direction where it is possible, for giving direction when it is not, and for moving elegantly between the two. It is correction 'type three', that is inner and outer correction at the same time (see classroom toolkit Level 1).

But of course finger correction will only be as good as the intention behind it, and the skill with which that intention is carried out. I find it helpful to divide finger correction into two complementary functions:

Function 1

The fingers are used to separate and slow down the flow of speech into the component parts, to examine or identify the parts, and to put the parts back into a seamless flow.

In other words the fingers are used to move down a level from a flow to the components of that flow, ie from connected speech down to individual words (Level 3 down to Level 2), or from individual words down to individual sounds (Level 2 down to Level 1).

Function 2

To change, improve, correct, shape an utterance.
The fingers are used to shape what is there, or to add something, to remove something, to induce self-correction.

	Level 2	**Level 3**
Function 1	Fingers are used to break words down into their component sounds and to build the sounds back into words.	Fingers are used to break connected speech down into its component words and to build the words back into connected speech.
Function 2	Fingers are used to shape and correct words and the individual sounds they contain.	Fingers are used to shape and correct connected speech.

Fig. 48: Finger correction

A typical correction sequence would be: locate the problem (function 1), fix it (function 2), and bring it back to fluency again (function 1).

Function 1 Level 2 - dividing words into sounds

For finger correction you hold up one hand (the left hand if you are right-handed), palm towards you, fingers outstretched and vertical, so that the back of the hand and fingers are in clear view of the class. There are two basic hand positions here: either the fingers are apart, Fig. 49a, or they are together, Fig. 49b. For example, if we are working on the word *sleep*, then the fingers apart would represent the sounds spoken separately, /s ... l ... iː ... p/, and the fingers together would represent the sounds spoken as one flow, /sliːp/.

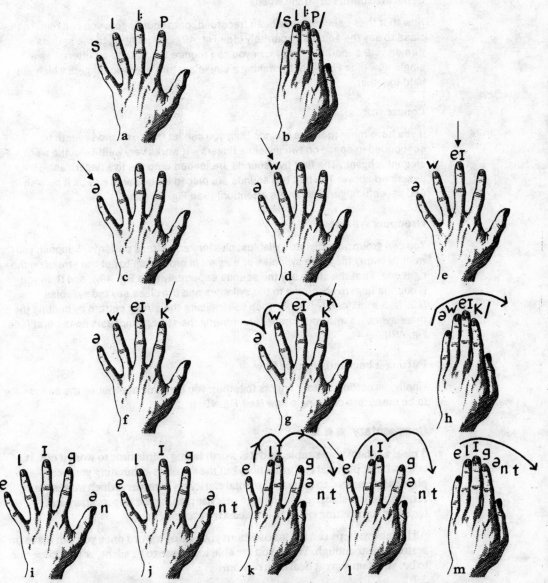

Fig. 49: You are looking at the teacher's left hand from the students' view. The first letter or word is placed on the little finger. The arrow indicates the movement of the forefinger of the right hand, to point out, to elicit, to phrase, to group the sounds, etc.

Classroom activity 35 Loading sounds onto fingers

Hold your hand up ready to load, and ask learners for the individual sounds of the word, which you assign to each finger in turn using the forefinger of your right hand. Take for example the word *awake* /əweɪk/. /ə/ is assigned to the little finger of the left hand, /w/ to the next, /eɪ/ to the middle finger and /k/ to the forefinger. (Fig. 49 c–f.)

Separate sounds or single words

Now that these sounds have been 'recorded' onto your fingers you can require the class to say the sounds separately (see Fig. 49g), by pointing to the sounds in turn on your separated fingers, or you can require the word to be uttered as a single flow (see Fig. 49h) by making a single gesture over your fingers which are held together.

Longer words

If you have more than five sounds then you can let the sixth and seventh be suspended in space on two invisible fingers – it works very well! Take the word elegant /elɪgənt/. The first five sounds are loaded onto the five fingers as described above. The last two sounds are placed in the same way as if on a sixth and seventh finger. This rivets attention! (See Fig. 49 i and j.)

Grouping syllables

You can group sounds into syllables, clusters and stress patterns. Suppose you want to clarify the three syllables of *elegant* in order then to get the stress on the right one. First the class say the sounds separately (see Fig. 49j), and then you group the fingers according to the syllables and the class say the syllables /e ... lɪ ... gənt/ (see Fig. 49k). Then you indicate the stress pattern by beating the three syllables with your forefinger, showing the strong emphasis on the first (see Fig. 49l).

Putting it back into a single flow

Finally, by putting all your fingers together, you can indicate that all the sounds are to be made into one single flow (see Fig. 49m).

Commentary ■ ■ ■

This is actually very simple, and it is worth taking a little time to work it out. It takes a bit of physical co-ordination, but the act of co-ordinating yourself physically can lead to increased mental clarity on your part which makes your responsiveness sharper. You have to practise putting the fingers apart and together, and getting rid of all unnecessary movements.

All the above steps can be done without you saying a word once you can make the gestures clear enough. When you are able to choose to be silent, or to choose not to be, you gain a great deal of precision.

If you want to carry out repairs to the pronunciation of the word, you need function 2. ■

Function 2 Level 2

Classroom activity 36 Connecting sounds in words

1 Load the mistake onto your fingers (function 1)

Load the word with its mistake onto your fingers as described above. If you are working with an individual then just that person provides you with each sound in turn while you feed them onto your fingers. The very act of loading them one at a time onto your fingers is already part of the correction process since it provides the learner with the opportunity to break down the word into individual sounds, and to hear himself saying them slowly. As a result he may correct himself at this stage. If not, then go on to step 2.

2 Pause at the mistake (function 2)

Simply take him through the sounds again and pause at the point of the mistake. Do not make any other indication. He knows that there is something wrong here since you have taken him here and stopped. Wait and see what he does. Does he look blank, does he guess, can you see a look of recognition or an inward *aha!* He may correct himself, but if not, go to the next step.

3 Correct the mistake (function 2)

Do so by giving the least that is sufficient. Finger correction enables you to shape a sound, add a sound, delete a sound, work on the stress. Each of these is outlined below.

- Shaping a sound. Take the learner to the wrong sound by pointing at the appropriate finger. If he does not self-correct but you know that he is able to say that sound, then point to it on the chart (or point to it in another word already on the board, or mime the sound, or ask other learners to say the sound).
- Adding a sound. Point to the chart and with a gesture insert the new sound between your fingers in the right place.
- Removing a sound. Bend that finger back at the first joint to take the sound out of circulation, then invite the learner to join up the remaining sounds.
- Work on stress. Group the word into syllables by grouping the fingers. Using gesture, indicate which syllables have more or less energy. Try different patterns and ask which pattern sounds best.

4 Regain the flow (function 1)

When the repair is carried out, put your fingers together so that the individual sounds flow together (function 1).

Commentary ■ ■ ■

Your fingers are being used to objectify and amplify certain mental processes. Your job is to operate this amplifying system smoothly, but to have most of your attention on what is happening in the learners, and to assist accordingly.

The fingers are used in much the same way for work at Level 3. It is more logical to present Level 3 finger correction here rather than in the next section. So here are the similarities and differences. ■

Function 1 Level 3

Classroom activity 37 Dividing connected speech into words

When apart the fingers represent words spoken separately, eg 'Hold ... up ... your ... left ... hand.' When together they represent the words spoken as one flow: 'Hold up your left hand.'

Loading words onto fingers

Ask learners for the individual words of the utterance which you assign to each finger in turn using the forefinger of your right hand. In 'Hold up your hand,' 'Hold' would be assigned to the little finger of the left hand, 'up' to the next, 'your' to the middle finger and 'hand' to the forefinger.

Separate words or stream of speech

You can require the class to say words separately by pointing to the words in turn on your separated fingers, or you can require the word to be uttered as a single flow by putting your fingers together and making a single gesture.

Longer phrases

If you have more than five words then you can let the sixth and seventh be suspended in space on two invisible fingers.

Grouping words

You can also group words into phrases and sense groups. Suppose you want to clarify the phrasing of 'See you in the morning'. First load the words onto your fingers (see Fig. 50a), then group the fingers according to the phrasing (see Fig. 50b). Then indicate the stress pattern by beating the two stressed syllables with your forefinger (see Fig. 50c).

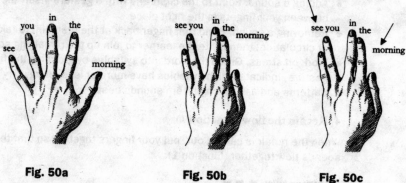

| **Fig. 50a** | **Fig. 50b** | **Fig. 50c** |

Working on linking

You can take any consecutive pair of words from a phrase (eg 'See you ...') and indicate them first singly with the fingers apart (Fig. 50d), and then linked with a short flowing gesture and the two fingers together (see Fig. 50e).

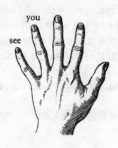

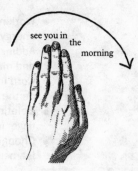

Fig. 50d **Fig. 50e** **Fig. 50f**

Putting it back into a single flow

Finally, by putting all your fingers together, you can indicate that all the sounds are to be made into one single flow (see Fig. 50f).

Commentary ■ ■ ■

When done well this technique can be clear and economical. It also has great potential for raising the level of attentiveness and expectation. Finger correction is particularly valuable for moving effortlessly between stream of speech and words in isolation. ■

Function 2 Level 3

Classroom activity 38 Shaping connected speech

1 Load the mistake onto your fingers (function 1).

Just doing this may enable the speaker to notice where her mistake is. If not, go to step 2.

2 Pause at the mistake (function 2)

Simply take the learner through the words again and pause her at the point of the mistake. She knows that there is something 'not quite right' since you have paused. Watch carefully to see whether she can take the next self-correcting step on her own or whether she needs information from you.

3 Correct the mistake (function 2)

Give the least that is sufficient while doing so. You can add a word, delete a word, add an ending, delete an ending, work on the stress, change the word order.

- Adding a word. Indicate the space where the word is missing and let the learner try to supply the word. Failing that the word can be spoken or pointed out by someone else.
- Deleting a word. Take the finger carrying the word and bend it towards you, taking that word out of circulation. Then invite the learner to join up the remaining words.

- Working on stress. Using gesture, indicate which syllables have more or less energy. Try different patterns and ask which suits the context best.
- Adding an ending. Take the finger representing the word that needs an ending and make the gesture of lengthening it a little to indicate the need to make the word longer. If the learner needs more help, then mime the ending or indicate it on the chart.
- Deleting an ending. Mime the gesture of 'snapping off' the sounds on the end of the finger in question.
- Changing the word order. Simply indicate the fingers in the order required, while the learner(s) say each word as you indicate them.

4 Regain the flow (function 1)

When the necessary changes have been carried out the words need to be linked together so that they flow into one another, and then the phrase needs to be brought up to speed.

6 Integrating the learner's dictionary with pronunciation work

You can help your learners to cultivate the habit of finding pronunciation and word-stress information from the dictionary for themselves. Whenever queries arise over pronunciation or stress, ask them to look them up. Perhaps the whole class searches, while you give guidance as necessary. Alternatively, one or two can refer to the dictionary on behalf of the rest of the class while the lesson continues.

Apart from using the dictionary to check information, you can set other challenges which involve using the dictionary and phonemic transcription.

Careful attention to the sounds and stress pattern (the energy profile) of a word can help learners retain and recall it by giving the brain opportunities to make associations of word form with word meaning and syntax. The right kind of attention to pronunciation provides the memory with another hook, a more vivid possibility for association.

Classroom activity 39 Vocabulary, the dictionary and phonemic spelling

The following activities illustrate some ways of bringing together pronunciation, stress, spelling and meaning:

1 Point out a new word on the chart including stress placement.
2 Learners say it and you help them to shape their pronunciation.
3 They write down the phonemic spelling based on their experience of saying the word.
4 Working individually or with others they try to work out or guess its alphabetic spelling.
5 They check alphabetic spelling and pronunciation in the dictionary.
6 The dictionary definition of the meaning is discussed, perhaps written on the board, and applied to the context in which the word has occurred.

Variation 1

1 Write the word on the board in alphabetic spelling.

2 Learners guess its pronunciation and stress, discussing among themselves and then checking in the dictionary.

3 A learner comes to the chart and points out the word without looking at the dictionary.

4 The meaning is studied, perhaps with reference to the dictionary definition.

Variation 2

1 Say the word aloud, once only (single model plus hearing time).

2 Learners savour the pronunciation for themselves.

3 They guess its alphabetic spelling.

4 They check both spelling and pronunciation in the dictionary.

5 One of them comes to the chart and points it out.

6 Another writes both phonemic and alphabetic spellings on the board side by side.

7 The focus enlarges to include the meaning of the word.

Variation 3

1 Each learner chooses one or two words that they have learned recently.

2 Each privately investigates and practises the pronunciation and stress using the dictionary if necessary.

3 When ready, each in turn dictates his word to the others by saying it aloud once only, and repeating it if requested. The others try to write it down in alphabetic spelling.

4 All the learners write their answers on the board and the causes of differences are investigated with reference to the speaker's original pronunciation, and to the dictionary and to the phonemic chart.

Commentary ■ ■ ■

As you can see, these games can integrate and practise a wide variety of language skills, and offer scope for team games if that is helpful. You will see that there are many other variations possible. Once again the aim is not just to be correct, but to become more discriminating, more confident, more self-evaluating and self-directing. ■

Specific exercises for using the dictionary

If your learners need a little familiarization with the dictionary, and with using phonemic symbols and stress marks to make use of information in the dictionary entry, then you can make up exercises such as the ones on p 168 using words from class texts.

Classroom activity 40 Using the dictionary for pronunciation

Find these words in the dictionary, and group them in columns according to their vowel sounds.

eg *door*	*dot*	*who*

board   two   bored
call   what   moth
cough   do   through

Put these words into three rhyming columns.

eg *me*	*may*	*my*

see   dye   say   hay
sky   key   sigh   eye
they   neigh ski   quay

Find these words in the dictionary and notice the different pronunciations of the letter 's'. Write each word under the appropriate phonetic symbol.

s = /ʃ/	s = /s/	s = /z/	s = /ʒ/

measure   is   his   sugar   us   closure   sure   list

Put these words into five columns according to their stress pattern. Use your dictionary to help.

eg *'palace*	*po'lice*	*'photograph*	*com'puter*	*under'stand*

eighty   eighteen   fantastic   cigarette   advertise   guitar   music   princes
princess   engineer   kangaroo   policy   important   refusal   dictionary

Fig. 51: These exercises are adapted from *Use Your Dictionary* by Adrian Underhill (OUP 1980)

7   Lip reading, ventriloquism, pronunciation and vocabulary

Lip reading involves visible movement without sound, while ventriloquism involves audible sound without movement. Both can be useful in studying pronunciation. At Level 1 we looked at the use of mime for cueing and prompting individual sounds. At Level 2 we can use the same idea for working with words. The 'speaker' has to convey the chosen word to the 'listener' purely by mouthing or miming the word silently. Naturally the speaker will slow down and exaggerate in an effort to be clear. The listener is simply lip reading, and automatically converting the visible muscle movements of the other person into sounds - a very sophisticated process.

Classroom activity 41   Miming and lip reading vocabulary

1   Learners collect some recently studied words on the board. Five or ten will do the first time. Or you can provide the words if, for example, they are key words from a text the class is about to study.

2   Invite the class to practise the words briefly using the chart.

3   Mouth one of the words silently and the others watch and try to recognize it.

4   A few learners come up and do the same thing with other words.

5   Once they are familiar with the procedure, learners can carry on in pairs or small groups.

Commentary ■ ■ ■

I think this activity is valuable in the way it forces participants to be more aware of the internal contact with the muscles that make the articulators move. It heightens awareness of which muscles make which sounds. While paying attention to sounds and articulation, vocabulary is being practised with the freshness of engagement, not the dullness of mechanical repetition.

The trick is to make sure that the words to be used are drawn from a limited set, just five or ten words to start with, on a list on the board or in the book. This is a good way of practising vocabulary sets.

Here is an interesting point: when I watch learners mouthing words I find I pick up pronunciation problems with my eyes that my ears may have missed. ■

Ventriloquism, pronunciation and vocabulary

Ventriloquism follows naturally from lip reading. With lip reading you have visible movement without sound, and with ventriloquism you have sound without visible movement. This can provide learners of language with another engaging challenge that again forces us to focus on the co-ordination between muscles, articulators, breath and voice, and their aural and visible manifestations.

The basic trick of the ventriloquist is to approximate all the sounds needed in speech while not making any visible movements. Essentially this means keeping the lips and the jaw still, while allowing the tongue to move unnoticed behind the neutral lips and the nearly closed jaw. So the ventriloquist can keep all the sounds that do not have a visible articulation, and has to find alternative ways of making, or seeming to make, those sounds that do have visible movements.

If you refer back to Figs. 39 and 40 on pp 115-6 you'll see that we have already distinguished these two groups of sounds. Going through the sounds in Fig. 39 you'll find that in fact some of them, /e, ɜː, t, d, θ, ð, n/ can be produced without external movement, though there is a loss in the clarity of the sound.

Classroom activity 42   Making sounds invisible

1 Introduce the idea of ventriloquism and see who knows about it or can give examples in their own language or in English.

2 Establish the distinction between visible and invisible sounds with a few examples of each from the chart.

3 Ask the class to work through the chart in small groups putting all of the sounds into one category or the other.

4 Bring the class together and look at their findings.

5 Ask them to find invisible sounds that could be used instead of the visible ones. In the case of consonants this means moving towards the right of the chart along the same row.

6 Taking any vocabulary list, ask learners in pairs or small groups to experiment with 'invisible speaking' and to give each other feedback.

Commentary ■ ■ ■

Admittedly this may not be a mainstream activity, but provided you feel comfortable with it, I think it has value because it heightens awareness, it is challenging, it is different, it is fun and it is relevant. ■

Level 3   Connected speech

1 Overview   171

2 Simplification and reduction of sounds in connected speech   173

3 Stress, prominence and rhythm in connected speech   176

4 Intonation   194

5 Some integrative activities and suggestions   202

1 Overview

At Level 1 we focused on sounds spoken in isolation, aiming to develop in teachers and learners a deep internally experienced awareness of what happens in the vocal tract, and how this relates to what is heard through the ears. This awareness was seen as the foundation on which to build an enhanced capacity to choose, change and modify how the musculature produces sounds and how the hearing apparatus perceives sounds.

At Level 2 we focused on individual words spoken in isolation. We studied how individual words consist of a 'flow of sound' which is different from the sum of the individual phonemes. We found that at the level of the word the distribution of energy across the syllables creates an energy profile, called word stress, that is typical and characteristic of a particular word.

At Level 3 in the discovery toolkit we focused on connected speech and on the way that words flow together to make a stream of speech that is different from the sum of the individual words. We studied the way sounds are simplified and reduced, and the way that the energy profile is extended from individual words to groups of words, that is from word stress that is fairly fixed to prominence that is chosen by the speaker. This energy package, called a tone unit, is held together by a pattern of pitch.

Class work at Level 3 does not mean the end of work at Levels 1 and 2. It is not a linear syllabus in that sense. Work at Level 3 means that there are now three levels of access available at the same time. Each level represents a different focus, each is tuned to do a different aspect of the job, and each level can be called on separately or in combination as required at any moment in any lesson.

In this classroom toolkit for Level 3 we are going to work on practical exercises for developing awareness and skill with connected speech.

Before we begin this journey into the territory of Level 3 it would be useful to refresh our sense of direction. What is the pronunciation target we are helping our learners to work towards?

Pronunciation targets in connected speech

My aim when working with pronunciation is to enable learners to achieve 'comfortable intelligibility'. This means that they can be understood comfortably, without undue effort by the listener, and that they can understand comfortably the speech of native and other speakers without undue effort on their own part.

This target of comfortable intelligibility gives us a realistic and achievable aim since it implies that learners' productive pronunciation need not be as sophisticated as their 'receptive pronunciation'.

I suggest that careful colloquial speech (eg BBC World Service newsreaders and announcers) is a realistic speaking target as it is clear and is likely to be understood in many parts of the world.

I suggest that rapid colloquial speech (eg native speakers interacting informally) is the ideal target for the listening skill in order to be able to understand in the widest possible circles. I call this target 'receptive pronunciation'. (See Level 3 of the discovery toolkit for a full discussion on pronunciation targets.)

Those learners who wish to achieve a near-native productive pronunciation will have rapid colloquial speech as both their speaking and listening target.

Implications of pronunciation targets on class work

A learner's listening menu should contain a wider range of phonological variants than his speaking menu. However, these targets do not imply any limit on our expectation of what learners may be able to achieve. Comfortable intelligibility is a minimum, not a ceiling. Through our attitude and the learning atmosphere we create we encourage learners to do the best they can manage at any moment. Anything less makes learning less challenging, less fun and less effective.

Since what the mouth can say and what the ear can hear exert a reciprocal influence on each other, it follows that there cannot be a purely listening or purely speaking lesson. Because of this interdependence we will often practise orally features of connected speech which we wish to incorporate in the learners' 'receptive pronunciation', even if we don't necessarily expect those features to become a part of their productive pronunciation.

All the activities in this section can challenge and engage learners at all levels from elementary through intermediate, advanced and proficient, including native speakers, with only minor modifications. What has to vary is the point at which any given learner can find his or her own level of challenge and engagement.

External and internal targets

We have been thinking about external targets because it is important to be explicit and objective about goals. It is also important for goals to be realistic and attainable so that the teacher does not get carried away by his own enthusiasm for perfection. Don't get excited by good accent, or carried away with complex and clever remedial activities.

External goals are fine for syllabuses, but in the work you do in the classroom, the target should be the best that each individual can do at that moment.

Materials needed

At Level 3, as throughout the book, no special pronunciation materials are needed. This approach makes use of already existing resources for all activities, especially current coursebooks, practice activities designed for any of the four skills, learners' own responses and spontaneous utterances.

2   Simplification and reduction of sounds in connected speech

The simplifications of connected speech, that is assimilation, elision, juncture, linking and vowel reduction, all affect rhythm, fluency and comprehensibility. The aim of the following exercises is to help learners become aware of these stream of speech simplifications, to practise instances of them in order to discern them better and to discover that incorporating them in their own speech can make it sound more English.

The approach of these exercises is to give learners the opportunity to experience directly the contrast between the Level 2 dictionary pronunciation of words and the Level 3 connected speech pronunciation of words. The exercises can be varied in many ways.

Classroom activity 43   Simplifications in the stream of speech

You need a short taped extract of authentic or semi-authentic English containing naturally occurring simplifications. The coursebook recorded dialogues will probably do. First use the tape for your normal activities such as comprehension, vocabulary, structure, etc. Having done this, you can add on the following exercise to focus in depth on a single short sentence.

1 Play the taped sentence. Learners write it on the board in alphabetic spelling. Give help if required, eg by referring them to dictionaries to check. Let them play the tape as many times as they need. (See Fig. 52 on p 174, step 1.)

2 Ask them to mark in the stressed syllables, listening again if necessary. (See Fig. 52, step 1.)

3 Ask them to write up the dictionary pronunciation of each word in phonemic symbols, without reference to the tape. Encourage them to use their dictionaries if they are not certain. (See Fig. 52, step 2.)

4 They now practise saying the sentence just a few times in dictionary pronunciation (Level 2), so it will sound somewhat stilted and unsimplified.

5 Refer them back to the tape to compare what they have just been practising with what they can actually hear on the tape. You can help by guiding their attention to any simplifications they don't seem to be noticing.

6 Invite them to use the chart to point out in phonemes what they hear on the tape, as nearly as they can. When they agree they write it on the board below the dictionary pronunciation. (See Fig. 52, step 3.)

7 If there are any remaining discrepancies between the transcription and the tape pronunciation you can guide the learners to notice them. Improvise other marks or symbols to indicate anything that you can't put in phonemic script.

8 Using the board transcription as a guide, invite learners to practise the fluent articulation of the taped sentence, ending by speaking the sentence while the tape plays.

9 Invite them to discuss the differences between the Level 2 and Level 3 transcriptions, making observations about assimilation, elision, vowel reduction and linking, but without necessarily using the technical names. (*See footnote on p 174.) Practise alternating step 2 and step 3. Ask them to find parallels in their mother tongue.

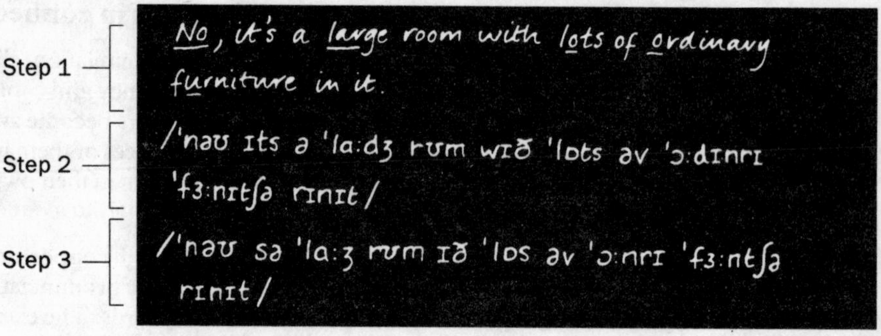

Step 1 — No, it's a large room with lots of ordinary furniture in it.

Step 2 — /ˈnaʊ ɪts ə ˈlaːdʒ rʊm wɪð ˈlɒts əv ˈɔːdɪnrɪ ˈfɜːntʃə rɪnɪt/

Step 3 — /ˈnaʊ sə ˈlaːʒ rʊm ɪð ˈlɒs əv ˈɔːnrɪ ˈfɜːntʃə rɪnɪt/

Step 2 = Level 2   Step 3 = Level 3

Fig. 52

Commentary ■ ■ ■

You are not 'telling them about simplifications' and you don't have to take the role of 'one who knows everything'. You simply structure the activity so that the learners can make observations and draw conclusions from experience. You don't even need to look for instant results. As long as they are engaged by the experience results will come.

Given your experience you can probably think of several variations on this activity. What steps would you use to highlight the same awarenesses?

Sometimes I structure the activity so that learners investigate the Level 3 stream of speech version before they analyze the Level 2 dictionary version.

Sometimes I try this: I do not play the tape at the beginning but write the sentence myself on the board in alphabetic spelling and give the learners the task of arriving at their own stream of speech version. Only then do I play the tape excerpt, not as a right answer, but so they can notice the differences between what they have been saying and what they now hear. ■

---

*In general I do not use the technical terms for simplifications with learners unless they show a particular interest in ordering and grouping and defining the different kinds. So with most groups of learners I use the following terms:

- *linking* or *joining* to cover liaison and juncture;
- *losing* or *disappearing sounds* for elision;
- *changing sounds* for assimilation and vowel reduction;
- *adding* or *extra sounds* for intrusion;
- *stress* to cover word stress, prominence and rhythm.

Of course this is a minimal glossary and you will judge when to introduce more specific terms.

Classroom activity 44 Observing and practising linking

1 When a sentence comes up in the class that could be made more fluent with better linking you can ask someone to write it on the board. For example: *I often go out in the afternoon.*

2 Ask the class to say each word definitely and separately.

3 Ask them to join the words together using the chart to identify linking sounds if there are any, and putting the stresses where they think appropriate.

4 Now ask them to write up the fully linked sentence in phonemic script. For example:

/aɪ j ɒfən gəʊ w aʊt ɪn ðɪ j ɑːftənuːn/

or   /a ɒfən gɜː aʊt ɪn ðɑːftənuːn/

Help them to work on the fluency.

Classroom activity 45 Working with degrees of simplification

The aim is to build up a board display as in Fig. 53.

1 Tell the class you are going to say something once, and to see what they can make of it.

2 Say the question /wɒstaɪm/ and leave a short silence.

3 Ask them to write what they hear on the board in phonemic script. Invite them to put up several different guesses or hunches. They will put up a variety of things.

4 Do the same again but this time saying /wɒsətaɪm/. Again invite some responses on the board.

5 And again, each time giving a fuller version: /wɒtsətaɪm/ /wɒtsðətaɪm/ /wɒtɪzðətaɪm/.

6 Point to different versions on the board asking learners to say them. Select those that agree with what you've said. Say again any which are missing.

7 Make sure that these five versions are on the board (see Fig. 53 on p 176) and rehearse each of them.

8 Say the versions at random and ask the class to identify by number which you are saying.

9 Invite individuals to say one at random for the rest of the class to identify.

10 They practise saying and identifying them in small groups.

11 Point at the most simplified and ask 'What is the most usual way of writing this in English?' They write on the board What is the time? or What's the time?

Ask the same question for the other versions. We find that these five ways of speaking only have one way of writing (two if you count *'s* as different).

12 Label the two ends rapid and careful, or simplified and complete.

Point out that almost any English utterance can be simplified more or less, and that they can look out for this kind of thing in taped speech and in their own speech in class.

The complete board display can look like this:

Most simplified, rapid

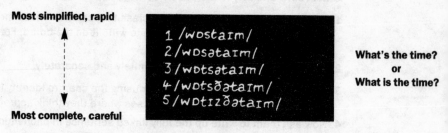

Most complete, careful

What's the time?
or
What is the time?

Fig. 53: One sentence with five degrees of simplification

Commentary ■ ■ ■

I find that this kind of exercise quickly raises awareness of and sensitivity to simplifications in the stream of speech. It is also an engaging and exact activity which can be carried out only by using phonemic script and it involves both receptive and productive discrimination.

It is interesting to observe the ways in which learners respond to step 3. They often 'hear into the utterance' more than I actually said. That is, they recognize /wɒstaɪm/ as meaning *What is the time?* but it is not until they hear the less simplified versions that they realize that they have been hearing more than was there.

Variations

Once again, you will find many. For example:

- Start with the most careful version and move towards the most rapid and simplified version.

- Ask learners to point out what they think they hear on the chart rather than write it on the board.

- Look out for other phrases which can yield two or three degrees of simplification, and then ask learners to work them out themselves. ■

3 Stress, prominence and rhythm in connected speech

Rhythm refers to the perception of some kind of underlying regularity of occurrence of prominences and word stresses. This may be more or less evident, and usually lasts for no more than a few beats at a time before disappearing and re-emerging again. This is a particular feature of stress-timed languages such as English, and learners need to pay attention to it not only in order to become comfortably intelligible in their own speech, but in order to tune in their own listening to the cues and signposts of spoken English.

The following sequence of classroom activities is one that I have found very helpful. It makes up a sort of 'rhythm syllabus'.

1 *Sensitization.* Simple activities to awaken an awareness of stress, prominence and rhythm.
2 *Strictly metrical material.* Material which exaggerates and emphasizes the rhythmic qualities of English.

3 *Less metrical material.* Extending awareness to more subtle and hidden rhythms, using sense groups.

4 *Rhythm in learner-originated utterances.* Extending awareness into learners' own spontaneous speech.

Commentary on the rhythm syllabus ■ ■ ■

- All four phases can occur within a single lesson as well as over weeks or months.
- The aim is to 'find' stress-timing and then gradually 'lose' it again into learners' spontaneous speech.
- Practice of stress-timing gives learners an organized way of working on the weakening of unstressed syllables, especially vowel reduction and word linking. ■

Sensitization to stress, prominence and rhythm

Classroom activity 46

This activity consists of three steps in one sequence requiring you only to read aloud to your class an excerpt of no more than two or three sentences. Prepare learners by asking them to listen to the *way* you speak rather than to the meaning.

1 Read a couple of sentences to the class without any stress at all, so that each syllable is given the same length, volume and pitch. Now ask them for their observations. This may provide a basis for the class to identify stress and rhythm.

2 Read the same sentences, this time placing the stress wherever seems natural to you. Exaggerate the stress a little if you like. Ask them what they noticed about your manner of speaking. Did some words stand out? Would they like to hear it again and spot which ones?

3 Read the same sentences again, this time with random and non-sensical stress placement. Ask them what they noticed this time. What are their conclusions from this?

Commentary ■ ■ ■

The first step immediately brings smiles to the faces of my learners, even at an elementary level, because their inner criteria already recognize English as innately stressed and rhythmical, and by reading like this I am offending those criteria.

It is most striking if you take material that is already familiar, perhaps from the coursebook or the reader or from an activity you have just been doing.

Since you provide the model you can control the speed of delivery and the degree of emphasis on the stressed syllables to suit the level of your listeners. Your mouth and other facial movements will also give useful clues.

Here is a useful addition: invite the class to have a go at these three steps themselves in groups of three or four. The threefold activity of deleting stress, putting it in the right place, and putting it in the wrong place is insightful, engaging and demanding. If the groups enjoy this perhaps they could perform their versions as 'nonsense theatre' to the rest of the class. ■

Classroom activity 47 A stress-timing chant

The more unstressed syllables there are, the quicker you have to say them in order to fit them into the beat. This is based on discovery activity 73 in the discovery toolkit.

1 Say the first sentence (a) aloud and rather slowly, with emphasis on each of the four words. Invite the class to join in, perhaps clapping quietly.

a <u>You</u>		<u>me</u>		<u>him</u>		<u>her</u>
b <u>You</u>	and	<u>me</u>	and	<u>him</u>	and	<u>her</u>
c <u>You</u>	and then	<u>me</u>	and then	<u>him</u>	and then	<u>her</u>
d <u>You</u>	and then it's	<u>me</u>	and then it's	<u>him</u>	and then it's	<u>her</u>

2 Say sentence **b** at the same speed, so that it occupies the same amount of time. Insert an unstressed *and* – pronounced /ən/ – between each of the four beats. Invite the class to join in.

3 Say sentence **c**, this time inserting unstressed *and then*, pronounced /ən ðen/, or once you get it up to speed /ən en/, between the four main beats. Invite the class to join in.

4 Say sentence **d** with the three unstressed syllables between each main word pronounced: /ən ðen ɪts/ or /ən en ɪts/. Invite the class to join in.

5 The next step is to divide the class into four groups, each saying a different line at the same time.

6 You can point to different lines at random while the basic rhythm continues unchanged. Learners can take the pointer and conduct the class.

Commentary ■ ■ ■

This is a very short activity but lively, instructive and memorable. Once you have tried it you may find you often refer back to it.

Only the pronouns are stressed, and each cycle occupies the same time. This simulates for your learners the experience of rhythmical patterns containing different numbers of syllables. ■

Classroom activity 48

You can make the rhythms from the previous activity visual using the Cuisenaire rods, following the convention where a red rod represents a stress and a white one an unstress.

1 Invite participants to come to the front and lay out red and white rods to correspond to the rhythms of the four lines of the chant. It would look something like Fig. 54.

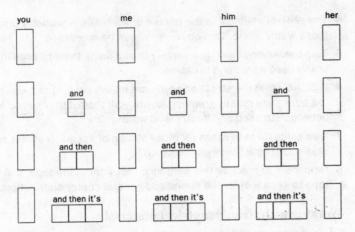

Fig. 54: Rods give a visual dimension to the rhythm

2 Ask a learner to arrange some rods to represent a mixture of these rhythms, while the others have to find the particular permutation of words that fits, and say them rhythmically. For example:

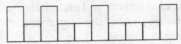

You and me and then him and then it's her

Fig. 55

3 Ask class members to find other quite different sentences that could have this rhythm. For example: *This is mine but the other one is yours.*

Classroom activity 49 Playing with loudness and stress

This requires a sentence of taped material. You can do it during or after any listening activity using an excerpt of the same material. Radio news bulletins can be very suitable, and the activity is based on the fact that loudness is often a correlate of stress.

1 Play the selected sentence, which could be a news headline, several times in succession, instructing your learners to focus attention on the loudest syllables, or loudest sounds.

2 Each time you play the sentence, turn down the volume of the tape recorder a little until the volume is so low that some of the syllables are hardly audible. You can usually find a point at which the stressed syllables are still audible while the unstressed ones seem to have disappeared.

These two steps are a useful way of showing that only some syllables are stressed and that one factor that makes them stressed is loudness. You may already notice that the stresses in some phrases form a regular or nearly regular rhythm. One way of continuing this activity is:

3 Learners identify the stressed syllables and write them on the board in the right order, leaving space between. You can help and prompt where necessary by simply pointing (silently) at the chart to indicate sounds they are missing or finding unclear.

4 The general meaning of the phrase or sentence is probably discernible from these words alone. This observation can be discussed.

5 Turn the volume back up as required and invite them to write in the rest of the unstressed words and syllables.

6 It is likely that the stressed words are mainly content or meaning words while the others are mostly grammar words. Ask them if they notice any distinction between stressed and unstressed words.

7 Now guide them to listen for other stream of speech features such as word linking and note these on the board.

8 Help them to practise this sentence first without the tape, and then with the tape to get a feel for the speed and general energy distribution.

Working with strictly metrical material

I find the most useful source of this is metrical verse, and good examples of this are nursery rhymes and limericks. In just a few minutes learners find they can recite an authentic English rhyme with a definitely English feel. When the stress is both regular and fixed learners find it easier to attend to the different energy distribution between stressed and unstressed syllables. Of course the intonation that naturally goes with this kind of activity and material is the intonation of recitation (*this is what the words say*), rather than communication (*this is what I say*). But that, too, is something to observe.

Here are a few ways of using nursery rhymes to introduce stress-timing and to work on rhythm.

Classroom activity 50 Learning a rhyme from the chart

The aim here is for the learners to arrive at an acceptable rendering of the rhyme without hearing it from you. This requires you to provide them with the minimum that is sufficient and for them to provide the rest according to their own developing criteria of 'Englishness'.

1 You build up each line from the chart, and add the stress. Make use of the chart, your fingers and sequences of rods to shape the sounds, rhythm and phrasing while remaining quiet yourself.

2 Learners write the rhyme on the board in alphabetic spelling, underlining the stressed syllables.

3 Learners can clap or tap to emphasize the regularity of the beat regardless of the number of intervening syllables. You can help them to emphasize the rhythm by working on volume, length and pitch of the stressed syllables and also by reducing the energy on unstressed syllables.

4 Use rods to make the rhythm of each line visible, and also to make any wrong placements of stress visible.

Commentary ■ ■ ■

My aim is to have the class saying the rhyme with the words joined together, with clear difference between stressed and unstressed syllables, at a good speed and with a feeling of lightness.

After they have worked on the rhyme for a few moments I might say it aloud myself, just once, if I felt the rhythm needed lifting, but I would not overdo this as my aim is to help them to discover the rhyme for themselves rather than to learn it parrot fashion. For the same reason I would usually (ie not always!) avoid reciting it to them at the beginning because I want to see what they can do with it themselves, and also because when learners have struggled with something for a bit they become more receptive to its subtleties when eventually they do hear it from me. ■

Classroom activity 51 Learning a rhyme from recitation

Here is another approach with the same aim.

1 Tell the class you are going to recite a short rhyme once only and invite them to be alert.

2 After reciting it naturally but with clearly emphasized rhythm, recite each line again, leaving the last stressed word for the learners to provide. Usually there are several learners able to provide the word. (No visual prompts yet.)

3 Do the same for the remaining lines.

4 Repeat the rhyme yourself leaving two stressed words per line for the class to fill in orally.

5 Continue this process until the class have provided all of the stressed words. Maybe they can write them on the board at this point. Now do the same with the unstressed words. Each time you provide less yourself.

6 If they get stuck at any point just provide the word yourself, perhaps by pointing it out on the chart.

7 Pay attention to rhythm, speed, smooth linking, length of stressed syllables and reduction of unstressed syllables.

8 In a very short time they will have learned the rhyme as a whole, not through repetition as such, but through the alertness required in sharp listening and attention to all the facets of making it 'sound English'.

Commentary ■ ■ ■

In this version you provide more of the input yourself, but the emphasis is on sensitivity + alertness rather than on model + repetition. ■

Classroom activity 52 Parallel speaking

1 If you have access to a language laboratory, then using your voice as the source you can record the rhyme on the learner tapes.

2 Learners transcribe it, marking the stresses, listening as many times as needed.

3 Then they can try parallel speaking, in which they attempt to merge their speech with your master track, by capturing your sounds, stress, speed, linking, intonation and timing. Give them the opportunity to do this several times, listening to their own attempts and working on their own improvements.

4 Finally let them work with a blank tape, recording and listening to their own unaided efforts, inviting from each their own personal best.

Commentary ■ ■ ■

You are probably thinking of variations of your own using rhymes. For example, once the class has worked with a rhyme you can simply write another rhyme on the board without saying it. Invite the class to mark the stressed words, linking sounds, simplifications, etc, and practise it. ■

Classroom activity 53 Mime the rhyme

Once the class have learned a rhyme by whichever means you can use it for a 'fluency lip-reading activity':

One learner silently mouths any of the lines to the others, and they have to say which line it is by observing closely the mouth movements and distribution of energy visible in the silent speaker. Once you have established the activity they can do it in pairs. This activity should be very short – just long enough to try each of the lines a couple of times.

Commentary ■ ■ ■

In all of this work the overt focus of attention is on the inherent rhythm which results from the contrast of energy placed on stressed and unstressed syllables and from the easy flowing together of the stream of words. All of this only comes to fruition, however, if you yourself remain in touch with the challenge the learners are facing, and enjoy the efforts of your learners in a simple and authentic way. ■

Some metrical rhymes and a limerick

Fig. 56 shows a selection of rhymes which I have found useful, together with their stress pattern, syllable count, schwa /ə/ frequency and Cuisenaire rod pattern.

It is interesting to note the high frequency of schwa, and I may do this calculation with the class after they have learned a rhyme. This information is relevant, and doing the calculation with the class is itself an excellent awareness-raiser as it involves distinguishing syllables, distinguishing stress and unstress, recognizing schwa and distinguishing it from other unstressed vowels.

Twinkle, twinkle, little star

How I wonder what you are

Up above the world so high

Like a diamond in the sky

syllables 28   stressed 16   unstressed 12   of which /ə/ 8

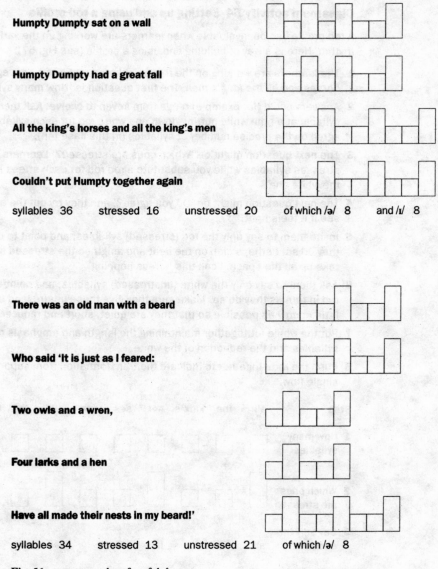

Humpty Dumpty sat on a wall

Humpty Dumpty had a great fall

All the king's horses and all the king's men

Couldn't put Humpty together again

syllables 36   stressed 16   unstressed 20   of which /ə/ 8   and /ɪ/ 8

There was an old man with a beard

Who said 'It is just as I feared:

Two owls and a wren,

Four larks and a hen

Have all made their nests in my beard!'

syllables 34   stressed 13   unstressed 21   of which /ə/ 8

Fig. 56: some examples of useful rhymes

Classroom activity 54 Setting up and using a rod profile

A rod profile can be invaluable when learners are working on the variables of rhythm. Here is a way of building and using a profile (see Fig. 57).

1 The learners are working on the rhythmical production of a line, eg *All the king's horses and all the king's men*. The first question is 'How many syllables?'

2 Answers could (for example) range from seven to twelve. Ask them to say one syllable at a time while putting down one white rod for each syllable. Check and agree on the precise number of syllables (in this case ten).

3 The next question might be 'Which ones are stressed?' Learners call out the stressed syllables while you substitute a red rod for each stress in the place of the white one.

4 The next question might be 'Do you agree?' and they try out the arrangement to see if it feels right.

5 Invite them to say only the red (stressed) syllables, and point to each in turn as they do so. Perhaps clap on the beat and lengthen the stressed syllables to take up all the space. I call this 'stress-hopping'.

6 Ask them to say only the white (unstressed) syllables, and point to each white rod in turn as they do so. Make sure they give these unstressed syllables as little energy as possible so that they are quiet, short and reduced.

7 Put the whole lot together maintaining the length and emphasis of the red syllables and the reduction of the white.

8 Push the rods together to indicate the transformation from separate bits to a single flow.

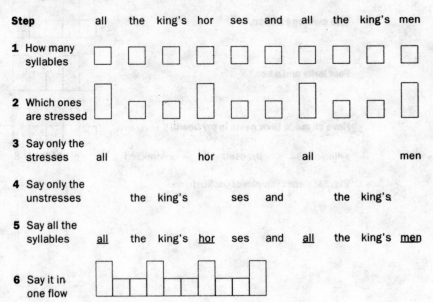

Fig. 57: Rod profile for classroom activity 54

Commentary ■ ■ ■

The culmination of this activity is to contrast steps 5 and 8. In step 5 learners say only the stressed syllables and in step 8 they say all the syllables but in the same amount of time. This activity makes the rhythm visible and tangible (because you can literally see and manipulate the rods). It is a powerful and rapid way of working on the fluency of any piece of connected speech.

One of the conventions you can establish, and one that I use a lot, concerns the spaces between the rods when they are laid out for a sentence. When the rods are apart, they signify a sequence of unconnected words, equivalent to Level 2. Then when you push them together (step 8) they signify the flow of connected words at Level 3.

Once you have established a rod profile you can ask the class to find other English sentences or phrases that fit the same pattern. This establishes a link between a fixed pattern in the rhyme and that same pattern as a viable rhythmic unit in the language at large. ■

Stress-time in non-metrical English

Once learners have developed an awareness of the way stress and rhythm work in metrical material, a next step can be to bring that awareness to bear on ordinary connected speech. In activities 55 to 60 the language is given, by text or tape, while the learners focus on creating the rhythm. In activity 61 the learners both create the language and structure it with their own prominence and rhythm.

Classroom activity 55 Providing rhythm for a given text

Use a few sentences of text taken from the coursebook or the class reader, preferably an excerpt that has not yet been intensively studied.

1 Take the first one or two sentences and ask the class to identify the sense groups, dividing them with a vertical line. (The idea and use of sense groups is explored further below.) For example:

There was a table / set out under a tree / in front of the house, / and the March Hare and the Hatter / were having tea at it; /a Dormouse / was sitting between them, / fast asleep, / and the other two / were resting their elbows on it, / and talking over its head./

2 Ask learners to choose where to place the stresses within each sense group, and to underline the syllables. For example:

There was a t<u>a</u>ble / set <u>out</u> under a tr<u>ee</u> / in fr<u>o</u>nt of the h<u>ou</u>se, / and the M<u>a</u>rch H<u>are</u> and the H<u>a</u>tter / were having t<u>ea</u> at it; / a D<u>o</u>rmouse / was s<u>i</u>tting betw<u>ee</u>n them, / f<u>a</u>st asl<u>ee</u>p, / and the <u>o</u>ther two / were r<u>e</u>sting their <u>e</u>lbows on it, / and t<u>a</u>lking <u>o</u>ver its h<u>ea</u>d./

3 Ask them to examine each sense group for any sounds that might impede the rhythmic flow, and to notice reduced vowels, consonant clusters, linking, etc. They mark these on the text. They can also mark any significant pauses between the sense groups with a double vertical line. For example:

//There was a table / set out under a tree // in front of the house, //and the March Hare and the Hatter / were having tea at it; //a Dormouse / was sitting between them, // fast asleep, / /and the other two / were resting their elbows on it, // and talking over its head.//

4 The next step is for them to rehearse the first few sense groups internally and aloud, by themselves, trying to get a smooth flow. You go round and listen to them individually, giving feedback on what they need to attend to.

5 Let them listen to each other's efforts in small groups, and encourage them to notice and enjoy all the differences they can hear.

6 Now ask them to apply steps 1 to 3 to the rest of the chosen text, with the aim of arriving at a spoken delivery of the text that reflects each person's meaning through the rhythm, the stress and the phrasing. It should sound as if the speaker understands what he is reading, and is even interpreting the text on behalf of the listener, rather than just reading the words at face value.

7 An optional step is that you now read the text aloud yourself, giving it your own interpretation while they just listen. The learners' prior investment will increase their sensitivity to your rendering.

Commentary ■ ■ ■

This activity follows on well from activity 54 and together they give a structured approach to phonological fluency that is not based on repetition, and that leaves room for self-investment and creativity. Activity 54 develops awareness using a single sentence. Activity 55 applies that to a longer stretch of several sentences. ■

Classroom activity 56 If you have a language laboratory ...

I think this activity in various forms is one of the most interesting and alive uses of a language laboratory that I have found.

1 Select a text and prepare it in the classroom by doing steps 1–6 of the previous activity. In the language laboratory you read the text yourself directly onto the learner tapes one or two sense groups at a time, leaving enough space for learners to say it in their own way. While you are recording they just listen.

2 Give them time to study your recording, and to try speaking each phrase in the space you have left on the tape. The aim is for them to work on stresses, pausing and linking.

3 After a few minutes on that exercise you rewind the tapes and record again, but this time reading whole sentences at a time, leaving enough space after each for the learner to say it.

4 Once again they have a go on their own at speaking each sentence in the space you have left on the tape.

5 After a few more minutes you rewind the tapes and record it again, this time reading the whole text quite naturally and at normal speed without spaces for them to speak in.

6 Now learners try parallel reading by merging their voices with yours in terms of speed, phrasing, stress and rhythm. If they record their voices doing this then they can replay and listen to the points of similarity between their speech and yours. Their aim here is quite definitely to try to do the same as you, not because you are right, but as an exercise in attention and noticing, and to gain insight from the experience.

7 After a further few minutes give them some time to work on a blank piece of tape, to experiment with creating and recording their own versions of the text without any model.

8 If possible let them circulate to listen to each other's final recorded version, again with the encouragement to appreciate the differences.

Commentary ■ ■ ■

Inevitably your rendering will vary each time, which adds to the interest and integrity of the exercise.

Teachers usually study a text for comprehension before studying it for pronunciation, but you can do it the other way round. If you do this activity first you could find that when you come to study the meaning in depth:

- learners already have a fairly clear idea of the semantic organization and direction of the passage;
- they understand specifically much of the meaning;
- they know which are the key words and which would be the most useful words to look up in a dictionary.

I find that this approach to the discourse structure of a passage forms a useful and enjoyable introduction to the more usual text comprehension activities, and that the overall result is an integration of phonology, syntax and meaning. ■

Sense groups – a way into connected speech

I have found the notion of the *sense group* to be a useful instrument for learners to work with when studying the features of connected speech. The advantage of the sense group is that it is not a fixed unit. It is the learner's subjective impression about 'which words go together to make up one bit of meaning'. Here are two examples of how a passage has been divided into sense groups by learners. Both seem valid, though the first is clearly more fluent, and each gives insight into the learners' view of the passage.

1 There was a table / set out under a tree / in front of the house, / and the March Hare and the Hatter / were having tea at it; / a Dormouse / was sitting between them, / fast asleep, / and the other two / were resting their elbows on it, / and talking over its head./

2 There was / a table / set out / under a tree / in front / of the house, / and the March Hare / and the Hatter / were having tea / at it; / a Dormouse / was sitting / between them, / fast asleep, / and the other two / were resting / their elbows / on it, / and talking / over its head./

Nevertheless I am often surprised by how easily learners take to the use of this type of division and what a large measure of agreement there is between them.

Classroom activity 57 Introduction to sense groups – three readings

Tell the class you are going to read them something in three different ways and ask them to notice carefully the differences.

1 Read two or three sentences to the class with no expression, no stress, no phrasing, no sense groups, no intonation.

2 Read the same piece of text divided into nonsense groups. For example:

There was a / table set / out under a / tree in / front of the / house, and the March / Hare and the / Hatter were having / tea at / it; a Dormouse was / sitting between / them, fast / asleep, and the / other two were / resting their / elbows on / it, and / talking over its / head. /

3 Read the same piece of text; this time making use of appropriate sense groupings, with short pauses between the groups.

4 Ask the class what differences they notice and what conclusion they draw.

Commentary ■ ■ ■

This is an economical way to put into circulation and give a label to the idea of the sense group. ■

Classroom activity 58 Sense and nonsense groups

There are many activities that follow straight on once the awareness has been seeded, as in activity 57. You are probably thinking of some right now. Here are three follow-ups that I have found useful.

Follow-up 1

Ask learners in small groups to follow the same steps as activity 57, reading to each other in the three different ways, and discussing the differences. This requires them to prepare the sentences first.

Follow-up 2

Each learner prepares one line of text by deliberately grouping the words into nonsense groups, that is by disguising the sense groups. Then they each read their sentence aloud to the rest, incorporating their chosen nonsense groups, and followed immediately by the same sentence again but with sense groups. The rest of the class comment on the differences between the two renderings.

Follow-up 3

As for follow-up 2, but this time the rest of the class, on hearing a sentence containing nonsense groups, have to hold it in their short-term memory, reprocess it, and give it back so that it makes sense.

Commentary ■ ■ ■

Consciously emphasizing and disguising the particular phenomenon under scrutiny is a feature of many successful awareness exercises. This represents the fundamental difference between mechanical exercises which depend on unaware repetition of correctness, and awareness exercises which depend on conscious discrimination between two or more choices, both of which are knowingly experienced. ■

Classroom activity 59 Creative use of sense groups

Choose a paragraph of printed text from the coursebook, the reader or something written by class members. Ask the class to prepare the text as follows:

1 Mark the sense groups with a single vertical line.

2 Underline the stresses or prominent syllables.

3 Indicate unstressed syllables with U.

4 Decide on occurrences of schwa /ə/, and mark them.

5 Mark in pauses with a double vertical line.

6 Mark in linking between words with a connecting line.

(See classroom activity 55 for example of fully prepared text.)

Now use this preparation to:

7 Rehearse the text both silently and aloud. You can circulate and offer help or coaching where needed.

8 Perform the text in small groups or as whole class, depending on size. Perhaps record it. Invite the class to notice the differences between versions.

Commentary ■ ■ ■

There is, of course, some leeway regarding which syllables are selected to be stressed, where the sense groups are divided, and so on. But leave the decisions to the learners, and even if they choose a quite unlikely stress you can leave it to see whether they want to change it once they start to say it aloud.

The majority of unstressed syllables are likely to contain the schwa /ə/ or a significantly reduced vowel, and this is one of the most important factors affecting rhythm. Fluency will also be affected by various linking devices, and you may decide to intervene in the process and practise some things out of context first. ■

Some observations about the use of sense groups

- It is a subjective and intuitive division which can be applied by each learner at his own level of awareness, and which he can change as his perception of the text changes.
- There is usually a high degree of agreement on where to divide sense groups, even where learners of different mother tongues are studying a text which they may not fully understand.
- It often works out that the sense group is in fact a viable tone unit, so that work with sense groups is a helpful step towards working with tone units and intonation, a step under the learners' control.

Classroom activity 60 Rhythm and sense grouping in a taped discourse

For this you need a short taped dialogue or monologue, perhaps one which is part of your current course materials, but the more authentic it sounds the better. News headlines or equivalent provide an ideal source of short, topical, careful colloquial English. The following detailed analysis need only be applied to the first one or two sentences, which is sufficient to put the necessary awareness into circulation.

1 Play the chosen section once or twice inviting learners to write any stressed words or syllables they can hear anywhere on the board. Let mistakes stand for the moment to allow them to re-hear and repair. The dictionary can be used to check spellings.

2 Rewrite the stressed words in the correct order leaving enough space between them for the unstressed words to be written in. At this point the gist of the message may well be apparent and the class can discuss it.

3 Play and replay small sections at a time while learners try to identify the unstressed words or syllables and write them in the spaces. They can write up fragments of words if that is all they can hear, perhaps using phonemic symbols. If necessary you can help by indicating with dashes the number of missing words or syllables, perhaps even giving the first letter of each word. Gradually the phonemic outline of the unstressed words emerges.

4 Once the sentence is complete you can ask 'Why are these words stressed and not the other ones?'

5 Referring to the tape again you can mark on the board other features of connected speech such as linking, assimilating and elision. You can also draw attention to any sections where the rhythm on the tape is particularly regular, that is, displaying a stress-time quality.

6 The learners practise aloud the stressed syllables only, 'stress-hopping' at roughly the speed of the tape. You can conduct the class by pointing at each stress in turn with the appropriate timing. It is as though the stresses form the stepping stones of the passage and the class are practising stepping from one stress to the next.

7 Do the same again, but play the tape quietly at the same time, so that the class are matching their timing and speed with the tape.

8 Still reading from the board, and without the tape, learners now say all the intervening unstressed syllables as well, trying to keep the stressed stepping stones the right distance apart.

9 Repeat step 8 but playing the tape at the same time. Now their challenge is to say all the syllables and stresses with the tape. Let them work with the speed, not worrying too much about the sounds, even gabbling the sounds, just to taste the speed. Over several repeats of the tape invite them to clarify their pronunciation, maintaining the rhythm and the contrast between stress and unstress.

10 Once the performance is as good as they can make it, ask them to read the passage several more times maintaining speed, and after each reading erase about twenty per cent of the words from the board. After the fifth reading they will be reading fluently off an empty board!

Commentary ■ ■ ■

This may seem rather a detailed activity, but I encourage you to understand, adapt and personalize it to suit your teaching style. I have found this activity of great help in many kinds of lesson, and an excellent way for learners to gain insight into what happens in the instant of hearing. I would not apply this level of detailed activity to an utterance of more than about twenty to forty words.

After this investment of attention you can rewrite the same words in a jumble on the board, and see what other sentences the class can make from them.

You can use the same tape as the source for language laboratory work as described in activity 56. ■

Rhythm in learner-originated utterances

Classroom activity 61 Rhythm in learners' own utterances

1 Invite a learner to make up an utterance of any number of words and to say it to the class with the rhythm they feel appropriate. When the learner has said it, someone else lays out a string of white and red rods to represent the utterance in terms of number of syllables and placement of stresses and unstresses.

2 The rod profile is tried out and discussed by everyone. Writing the sentence on the board may also help.

3 Once a rod pattern is agreed, invite someone to move a red rod to a different position, and then everyone has to re-stress the sentence accordingly.

4 Ask the class to compose other sentences to fit the same rod pattern. For example, this pattern:

could yield *Why did you close the door?* or *I really ought to go.*

This pattern (which is unlikely in normal spoken English):

could yield *Well! Well! Well!* or *Love! Love! Love!* or *Three blind mice.*

Variation 1

Foster creativity by restriction. Limit the number of rods available to ten (Perhaps seven white and three red). Ask people to make sentences of a maximum of ten syllables and to come up to the table and lay out the rods without saying what their own sentence is. Ask learners to make sentences that fit the rod profile and try them out. Then ask the learners to say them. In how many different ways can each ten-syllable utterance be stressed? How does that alter the shade of meaning?

Variation 2

An extra dimension to any of these exercises is to incorporate sense grouping on the rod pattern so that gaps between rods indicate the division into sense groups. This provides an extra challenge when learners try to compose sentences to fit, since both sense groups and stress patterns have to coincide with the arrangement of the rods. For example:

I left my house   in a hur ry   this mor ning

Commentary ■ ■ ■

After working this way for a short while the learners will begin to realize that it is easier to construct sentences for some distributions of stresses than others, that regularly distributed stress patterns are easier to work with and that patterns with tight groups of stresses, as in the example above, are less easy. They begin to realize that some stress patterns are quite un-English and are unlikely to occur in the language at all. They quickly reach the point where they can comment on the plausibility of patterns like these:

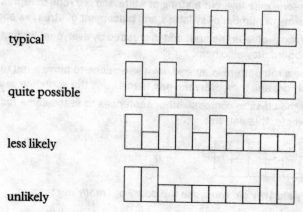

typical

quite possible

less likely

unlikely

Classroom activity 62 Exploring strong forms and weak forms

1 Put a couple of sentences on the board, like this:

   I can swim   She's going to London

2 Practise saying them with the stresses in different positions.

3 Identify different pronunciations of *can, she, is, to,* and point them out on the chart. Label them as strong and weak.

4 Ask learners to think of other words that also have a strong and weak form and collect suggestions on the board, whether or not they are suitable. Perhaps search a text to help. The list of words on the board could look something like this (though even three or four words would be quite sufficient for the exercise):

that	has	he	and	do	would
must	them	will	to	are	some

5 Use the phonemic chart to identify strong and weak pronunciations and ask learners to write them in phonemic spelling on the board beside the words.

6 In turn, practise each of the listed words in isolation in both strong and weak form. This procedure will also weed out any words that found their way into the list but which do not have a weak form. You could also ask learners which of the words can have a contracted spelling. In the list above this could apply to *has, will, are* and *would.*

7 Now ask the class to compose contrasting pairs of sentences containing the same word sequence but with differently placed stress. Practise each sentence as a piece of connected speech so that the meaning and context are as far as possible made clear through the placement of prominence. Typical learner sentences might be:

   Can he do it for them?
   Has he gone to her house?
   Some of them have come from London.
   You must do it!
   He has done it!

8 Taking any one of these sentences, invite the class to lay out a rod profile and to find how many different positions they can put the red rods in and still make a plausible utterance. This would require some discussion of context for each profile.

The 'anti-blurt' strategy

(*to blurt* = to speak suddenly, without thinking)

This strategy consists simply of thinking more carefully about what one is going to say and how one is going to say it.

From time to time most of us must wish our learners would think before they speak. Presumably this is because we feel that if they were to weed out some of their own slips before speaking then we would only be left with the more significant errors to deal with.

This deliberate attention to the planning and delivery of an utterance requires us to appeal to the learners' ability to monitor themselves both before and during speaking so that their best performance will all the sooner become integrated and automatic.

While this quality of attention has been implicit in most of this approach so far, now is a good time to re-assess the degree to which we have installed this carefulness because it is when working with rhythm, prominence and in the next section with intonation that the overall pronunciation of an utterance becomes inextricably linked to its intended and perceived meaning.

The 'anti-blurt' strategy consists simply of putting into circulation, in a game-like way, the discipline of separating the planning of an utterance from its delivery, so that structure, sounds and stream of speech qualities are all taken into account in the light of the intended meaning.

Classroom activity 63 Installing the 'anti-blurt' device

1 When you ask a question, encourage a few seconds of directed and alert thinking time, during which learners may plan, visualize and internally hear what they themselves are going to say.

2 Then, when they speak, give their utterance full value by listening to it with attentiveness and sincerity. If you, the teacher, treat your learners' output with respect, it is more likely that they will too, and so will be more prepared to invest themselves fully in what they do, and attach importance to feedback from you.

Such an attitude will also bring about more attentive listening by the rest of the class, and a more intense, supportive and useful response from them.

4 Intonation

Problems encountered in teaching intonation

Here is a summary of three problem areas in teaching and learning intonation. Each is followed by a response. I have put these thoughts at the beginning of the practical section on intonation because I think that only if we act on them will we be able to make significant improvements in the way we foster the learning of intonation.

Intonation is not as susceptible to change

Intonation seems not to be as accessible to direct cognitive intervention as the pronunciation of individual sounds or the manipulation of grammatical constructions or the learning of new vocabulary. Perhaps intonation is controlled by a different part of the brain, less accessible to conscious intervention.

Response: make use of all learning channels

This makes it all the more important to make learning a holistic experience, rather than a mainly cognitive one. That means involving the visual, auditory, tactile, physical and affective senses, and making use of the power of intuition, hunch, association and recognition. This in turn points to a curriculum based on awareness rather than one based on mechanical activities.

Classrooms impoverish intonation

There is a tendency for classwork to involve recitation, citation, exemplification of language which has little discoursal value, despite its supposed communicative content. Even activities set up to 'make the language communicative' such as roleplay can end up quoting language rather than using it, and so using intonation patterns that are in fact quite appropriate to convey the meaning *these are the words I would say if the situation were real*. Most learning situations assign dominance to the teacher, so learners are unlikely to have the context within which to produce all the elements of the intonation system. Teachers' own hierarchical relationship with learners may lead them to a limited and unnatural use of intonation.

Response: be present, be real

We need to enrich classroom language by paying attention to interpersonal relationships, especially the roles of speakers in relation to each other. This requires teachers to be authentic in themselves, not just to play the role of teacher. Activities must be real, here and now. The teacher needs to treat learners as people, and to participate as a person. She needs to value listening not just to the speech but to the speaker, and to differentiate between evaluating the language and being accepting, affirming and non-evaluative towards the person who is speaking. Be clear about your intention and about what your behaviour is saying to your learners. Be aware of the psychological learning atmosphere that is emanating from you all the time. Don't get driven by what you wish was happening, but enjoy and invest yourself in what *is* happening. Have a person-to-person rather than teacher-to-pupil relationship.

The intonation of calculation rather than communication

Another level of difficulty arises from the learners' preoccupation with language. A lot of work in class is word selection rather than sense selection, an emphasis on being right rather than on understanding others or being understood. Learners spend time working things out, applying rules, using their cognitive faculties to think, evaluate, formulate. And the intonation patterns they use, quoting intonation (proclaiming tone) and zero intonation (level tone), along with pauses for thought, may be entirely appropriate to these internal and largely non-communicative activities.

Response: treat the learner as a person

This problem already begins to change with the different attitudes described in the previous paragraph. As I become more genuine in my behaviour and attitude towards the learners, and as I permit myself to enter into the learners' world, to understand what is going on, to be *with* the learners and not only with myself, then whatever the learners are doing can take on significance. When I am only interested in the superficial topic, football or pollution or food, or in the learners' correctness of language, then I am not able to respond to learners as people, and not able to turn their preoccupation with language into a source of interest, of valuing, and of potential delight.

Components for an intonation syllabus

This section looks at different kinds of activity that you could include in an intonation syllabus:

- signs and symbols to represent intonation;
- sensitization to intonation;
- listening to pre-recorded cassettes;
- intonation from a printed text;
- learners' spontaneous speaking.

Signs and symbols to represent intonation

On the chart

The chart gives the five tones in the top right-hand corner. The four moving tones are presented in one composite symbol, so that learners have to choose and deliberately trace the intonation contour with a pointer. The level tone is shown underneath the composite symbol.

You activate these tone choices in the same way as the other symbols on the chart, by indicating them with a pointer. Sometimes you may want to indicate the tone choice alone, either as a prompt or as a response. Sometimes you will indicate the words of the tone unit before the pitch choice, at other times the pitch choice before the words. The seven modes of chart usage in classroom toolkit Level 1 apply to the use of tones as well as to sounds.

You and your learners may prefer to indicate these five pitch patterns with a hand gesture in the air, because that gives you more control over the range and degree of the movement.

On paper or on the board

Here are some ways of notating pitches on the board or on paper.

1 Simple arrows before the tone unit, in which case you need to identify the tonic syllable on which the main part of the pitch movement will take place. For example:

| ↘ NOW it's **MY** turn |

2 Pitch lines through the words. For example:

Or you could do it like this:

Or like this:

Now it's my turn

The beginning and end of tone units can be marked with a vertical line, as in the above examples.

Sensitization to intonation

Classroom activity 64 Listening to themselves – mother tongue

1 Arrange for learners to record on cassette a few sentences of themselves speaking their own language.

2 Ask them to listen to their own (and each other's) recordings and to observe any landmarks in their speech. Suggest that they listen to the way they speak and not what they say.

3 Discuss what they notice in the way of stress, pitch, length. Can they pick out the highest and lowest syllables?

You could comment yourself in a non-evaluative and supportive way about what you notice, especially intonation features. If the class is multilingual then some will not understand the mother tongue of their colleagues, but they can still comment on the intonation features.

Classroom activity 65 Listening to themselves – in English

You can do the same thing with learners speaking in English and listening to each other and commenting. You can talk to individuals about their own tape, but you can also talk to the whole class about how you hear a tape, letting them behind the scenes of what the teacher notices.

Classroom activity 66 Listening to you – target language or mother tongue

1 Read your class a few sentences of English with which they are familiar; perhaps a dialogue from the coursebook. Leave the rhythm as it should be but remove all trace of intonation, and do not even fall at the end of each sentence. If you have a monolingual group you can do this in the mother tongue also.

2 Repeat the sentences with fairly expressive intonation. Discuss the differences. Could they identify the highest pitch, or the lowest?

3 You can ask the learners to try these two contrasting activities.

Commentary ■ ■ ■

These activities give learners the opportunity to identify simple intonation contrasts such as 'same' and 'different', 'highest' and 'lowest', and then 'up' and 'down', which they may not have been consciously aware of before. It helps you to find out what they can already perceive, and gives an opportunity to the class to label intonation features. Maybe they begin to talk of 'up' and 'down' in connection with tones, and perhaps even to use arrows on the board to indicate pitch directions. Maybe they can use gestures to indicate up or down. ■

Classroom activity 67 Listening to you listening to them!

1 Record a few sentences of each learner in your class as a natural part of an oral activity.

2 Invite the class to listen to and comment on their own performances (as always in an atmosphere of mutually supportive curiosity).

3 Invite a colleague (probably another teacher) into the class to listen with you to the tape, both of you sitting in front of the class.

4 The two of you talk, as if just to each other, about what you notice about the speakers' stream of speech. You do this in a matter-of-fact and supportive way, finding the positive points and showing the way forward.

Commentary ■ ■ ■

This is a good opportunity for sharpening observations about the stream of speech and for raising self-esteem by valuing and taking seriously someone else's performance. ■

Classroom activity 68 Vowel sounds and pitch movement

When working on individual vowel sounds you can also work on pitch change.

1 Learners say long vowels and diphthongs with both a falling and a rising pitch. Ask them to identify the direction. Use the chart to indicate both phoneme and pitch direction.

2 Extend this to include all five tones. Use the games of recognition and production suggested by the seven modes in classroom toolkit Level 1.

Listening to pre-recorded cassettes

Classroom activity 69 Extending awareness using a recording

For this activity use a dialogue from your coursebook, or if possible some fairly authentic recording. This activity extends previous activities to include work on intonation. Build up the following steps on the board.

1 Play the tape. Ask learners to listen for the stresses.

2 Ask them to put the stressed sounds and syllables they hear on the board. Don't correct them.

3 Ask them to fill in the other words, and observe any word links.

4 Ask them to underline the stressed syllables.

5 Notice whether there are any stretches of three or more stresses that seem to make a short rhythm.

6 Ask them to listen for the highest and lowest pitches, or any that are quite clear, and to mark them over the text. Notice those pitches that finish with a rising tone, and those that finish with a falling tone.

7 Indicate the ones that seem most significant to the meaning. Don't be afraid to get it wrong.

8 Mark any obvious tone group divisions with vertical lines.

9 Consolidate these observations by helping the class to incorporate them into their own delivery of the sentence.

10 Practise with the tape for speed, and also without the tape for consolidation.

11 Ask the class for their observations about the meanings of the speakers, and make any links to the intonation patterns, taking into account anything known about the speakers. Do rising and falling tones seem to be referring back to the common ground or adding something new? (See 'Common ground', discovery toolkit Level 3).

Commentary ■ ■ ■

Help the class to notice whatever they can, and to talk about their observations. As you and your class become experienced in this kind of exercise the discussions may refer to attitudes, grammatical boundaries, and the interplay of common ground between the speakers.

I try to remind myself that these activities should be done with a light touch, and done *with* the class as a joint exploration, not done *to* the class as an epic of compulsively helpful teaching. I need to resist the temptation to launch into an A–Z of intonation. One very simple thing that helps create a workshop atmosphere of purposeful investigation is to arrange the lesson so that as often as possible several people at the same time are writing on the board their guess, or their observation or their solution or their attempt.

These kinds of awareness questions can help in an activity: 'Where are the pauses?' 'Where is the highest pitch?' 'Where is the lowest pitch?' 'Where are the stresses?' 'Which are the most important stresses?' 'Where is the tonic?' 'Which direction is the pitch movement?' 'Which words are joined together?' 'Which is the longest syllable?' 'Which syllables seem to disappear?' ■

Classroom activity 70 Rehearse dialogue – then listen to recording

This is similar to the previous activity but with one big difference. Using the transcript of a taped dialogue, the class take these steps:

1 Decide on stressed syllables.

2 Decide on word links, vowel reduction, and other simplifications.

3 Rehearse these, and begin to get a feel for some natural intonation choices.

4 Choose and mark the tonics and intonation contours.

5 Rehearse all these features, bring the dialogue up to a good speed, and work on the problems that emerge.

6 Perform it to each other, and perhaps record it.

Only then, when they have invested all this work in the dialogue, do they listen to the published recording of the dialogue. What do they notice?

Commentary ■ ■ ■

Because of their previous investment in the dialogue learners will hear every nuance and every deviation from their own performance. You can then ask them to point out, discuss and illustrate some of the differences between their rendering and the published recording, and draw conclusions. One conclusion might be that they feel their own dialogue sounds more 'real'. ■

Intonation from a printed text

Classroom activity 71 Texts, sense groups and reading aloud

This activity uses a printed text, perhaps a narrative from the coursebook or the class reader, or an authentic text you have used for comprehension and vocabulary.

1 The class prepares the text according to the first six steps of activity 59. This can be done individually or in small groups, but it is also very instructive done as a class activity on the board as this brings everyone together. Have learners, rather than yourself, doing the board work.

2 Ask learners to study the sense groups (already marked) and to choose an intonation pattern for each one. Then ask them to rehearse it.

3 Each learner reads a short section aloud, while the others listen to the differences and offer their observations. You could record it for playback and discussion.

Commentary ■ ■ ■

Learners' reading aloud is full of information about how they understand the text. Does their reading consist of disconnected words and phrases, or disconnected sentences? Are they quoting the text or are they interpreting it for the listener? (See 'Reading aloud and intonation', discovery toolkit Level 3.) ■

Learners' spontaneous speaking

So far the activities for intonation work have used material that is already scripted to allow the speaker to attend to intonation rather than to syntax and vocabulary.

The aim now is to make a link between the awareness of the stream of speech characteristics developed under controlled conditions, and more spontaneous speaking. Here are two activities that you can adapt to your situation:

- free speaking with sense grouping;
- telling anecdotes.

Classroom activity 72 Free speaking with sense grouping

This activity deliberately separates planning and formulating the utterance from speaking and making fluent, in order later to become better at doing both together.

1 You or someone else introduces a topic that each can respond to in their own way. I usually take something open-ended, eg talking about a picture or an object brought into the classroom.

2 Everyone is invited to make responses, though only one speaks at a time. At first the responses are best kept to a couple of sense groups. Learners think of what they want to say, and rehearse their statements internally.

3 Anyone who is ready to speak tries to say each group of words smoothly and fluently, linked together, and with some feeling. At the end of each group they pause to plan and internally rehearse the next sense group before speaking.

4 Others listen and offer feedback.

Commentary ■ ■ ■

The internal preparation includes rehearsal of the phrasing, linking, stressing and intonation contour. Delivery can be as slow or fast as the speaker likes. The aim is to do the planning and rehearsal, in order then to invest in the delivery, in 'being behind the meaning' of each utterance.

A good antidote to this activity is to do the opposite. Each person is to speak as quickly and spontaneously as possible, with the least preparation. Discuss the outcome. ■

Classroom activity 73 Relating personal anecdotes or stories

The aim of this is to take a topic where the content is known to the speaker but the precise wording is not. A story or personal anecdote would be quite suitable.

1 Start by telling a short anecdote yourself, but don't be too fluent. Leave pauses to gain attention, to let the words sink in, and to give yourself time to formulate what to say next.

2 Now invite learners to do the same. Perhaps they have already prepared an outline of what to say. Invite the others to listen and at the end to give feedback on the fluency and the use of intonation.

Commentary ■ ■ ■

This is a demanding and fruitful activity that can be done with any group provided that the previous steps of the intonation syllabus have been carried out. I find that I can learn a lot about the stream of speech and intonation by working on it side by side with my learners. ■

5 Some integrative activities and suggestions

Classroom activity 74 The 'humane dictation'

Dictations can practise many language skills including aural comprehension, sound/spelling relationships, syntax and internal retention of utterances for hearing and re-hearing. Possibly most significant of all, learners begin to discover what it is about spoken English that they tend *not* to hear. (For example, the short unstressed syllables of content words and entire one-syllable function words.)

When conducted with the right attitude dictations can be challenging and highly engaging activities. This is a format I often use, and in the commentary afterwards I have emphasized some of the special aspects of the 'humane dictation'. There are five phases:

- choosing the text;
- preparing the text;
- the dictation;
- marking it;
- finding the best mistakes.

Choosing the text

Ask the learners to select a passage for a dictation, perhaps from the class reader or the coursebook or a text written by the class. They can search individually and in small groups, and all suggestions are recorded on the board by a class member. Perhaps each group also states *why* it has chosen its excerpt. This gives learners responsibility for a decision that is usually taken by the teacher, and it gets learners thinking about why they would choose one text rather than another.

Preparing the text

Once the choice is made ask everyone to read the text and to identify any mistakes they think they might make in the dictation. Ask class members to predict how many mistakes they will make, and – betting shop style – ask them to put their name and their prediction on the board. Then ask them all to study the possible mistakes they have identified. The text is still open for them to look at. This helps them to sharpen their awareness of the kinds of mistakes they each make, and to take responsibility for working on that. I may suggest they visualize tricky spellings in their mind's eye.

The dictation

I follow a fairly conventional procedure: I read each phrase two or three times and then I read the whole thing again. But my reading remains faithful to connected speech, and I deliver the phrase in rapid colloquial speech the first time, and in more careful colloquial speech the second time for those who didn't catch it. I take my cues from the learners because I want them all to be successful.

There is no reason why it should always be the teacher who reads. There is much to be learned from the problems that arise when a learner reads. Or you can share the reading with a learner.

Marking it

Learners check their own version against the text. They can change papers to find mistakes that they have missed. There is no need to cheat since there are no marks, indeed mistakes will be treated positively.

Finding the best mistakes

Learners examine their own mistakes, and come to the board to write their total number of mistakes against their prediction. This is done in an atmosphere of supportive interest. ('You predicted nine and you only made three, what happened?' 'You predicted five and you made eight!'). Then you ask each person to select the 'best' mistake they made, to come to the board and write up both the mistake and the correction, and to tell the class the story of that mistake, ie how they made it, where the confusion came from, etc. Invite the class to discuss the merits of each mistake, and to be curious about its origin.

Commentary on the 'humane dictation' ■ ■ ■

The learning in this goes well beyond the conventional dictation in terms of choosing the text, clarifying personal criteria for mistakes, focusing on self-appraised weaknesses, discussion of criteria for selecting a dictation text, negotiating who reads and dealing with the problems that arise, examining mistakes and getting behind them, finding that mistakes are occasions for curiosity, talking openly about mistakes with interest rather than judgement, and experiencing a different kind of attitude emanating from the teacher.

There could be many kinds of follow-up activity to consolidate the awarenesses that emerge through this process. ■

Other integrative activities

Inviting visitors to the classroom

Visitors can read a short story, be interviewed, reproduce sentences previously composed by the class. Whatever the activity a prior instruction to your class is to notice as much as possible about how the visitor speaks.

Using the video camera

Use a video camera to record the class in an oral activity. Focus on face, gesture and mouth movements. Replay to notice aspects of pronunciation. Replay with the sound off to notice visual cues, and to try to lip read.

Parallel speaking

Have learners work with a tape of spoken English, aiming to speak at the same time as the recorded voice and to follow the pronunciation, rhythm, stress, intonation, etc. This is best done with individual headphones or in a language laboratory.

Practising dialogues with different intonation

After working on the coursebook dialogue, invite learners to rehearse the same dialogue but giving it a quite different meaning (perhaps bizarre or hilarious). They achieve this through pause, intonation, etc.

Adapting spelling and number games to phonemic script

You can easily construct phonemic versions of Hangman, Scrabble, Bingo, anagrams, crosswords, etc.

Non-specialized pronunciation materials

Even a simple comprehension passage offers many opportunities for phonological investigation. Learners can search any text for diphthongs, consonant clusters, schwa, silent letters, particular sounds, word stress, instances of regular rhythm, vowel reduction, word-linking, simplification, sense groups, tone unit boundaries, possible intonation patterns, etc.

Appendix 1

Further thoughts

... about using the cassette player

1 Use the cassette player at the lowest comfortable volume level. My experience suggests that playing the cassette at a higher volume has more to do with the teacher's anxiety than with helping the learner to hear better. In fact I think a higher volume can make the learner's ear lazy while the lowest comfortable volume can create attention. Higher volumes also tend to distort the sound.

2 By turning the volume right down a point can be reached where the stressed syllables are still audible, and the unstressed syllables are not. This is a striking experiment which often works, and it can be a dramatic way of illustrating that volume is a component of stress, and also of highlighting the rhythmic nature of a sentence or phrase. It may be easier if you start by turning the volume off and then gradually increase it to find the precise point at which these things can be picked up.

3 Use the tone control. If you turn the treble off, and perhaps the bass up, you emphasize the intonation and rhythmic profile of an utterance on the tape. If you turn the treble up and take the bass off you emphasize the individual sounds, especially the consonants. Of course in classrooms we often have poor quality equipment and acoustics. But if you can make some difference in the tone, then use more treble when working on individual sounds, and less treble when working on pitch contours.

4 Learners can operate the tape recorder. Why should the teacher switch it on and off and make every decision about stopping and pausing and playing the tape? Perhaps there are some times when you must be in control of it, but must it be all the time? I think it is enabling and empowering to involve everyone in the production of the lesson. My experience is that they may then take more responsibility for their learning.

5 When you are doing a speaking activity, sometimes record it on tape for use with the class later. There are plenty of activities you can do with a recording of an 'imperfect example of English', and hearing themselves can sometimes have more impact than hearing anonymous correct voices, especially when the listening is done in a psychological atmosphere that is interested and supportive rather than judgmental or competitive. And include yourself on the recording too, not because you are the teacher but simply when it is your turn.

6 However complicated or fiddly or broken the buttons on your cassette player are, try to become an expert at playing the last phrase again. You need this for repeated intensive listening to key phrases, without either repeating the whole paragraph leading up to that phrase, or getting those awful high-speed squeals while you rewind.

... about using the blackboard

1 Let learners do as much of the writing on the board as possible. There is nothing sacred about that space in front of the board. It doesn't belong to you. Inviting learners into that space is a simple psychological strategy to increase engagement and to invigorate the lesson. When learners read something out or perform a dialogue in pairs, have them come to the front. When learners have suggestions to be put on the board, get them out and give them the chalk to do it. Why do *you* have to write the learners' words on the board? What is the subtle message about power here? When you want to put a few learners' sentences on the board for intensive examination by the whole class, get them all up to write their sentences themselves.

2 Encourage several to write on the board at the same time. That way you save time too.

3 Use the board as a worktable. If a word needs changing or correcting, ask a learner, perhaps the original author to come and do it. The lesson doesn't have to stop while they come to the front. You can carry on with the next item.

4 Make it a place to collect suggestions, answers, guesses, attempts, etc but let the originator do the work and have the involvement. Don't hijack their work and so also subtly hijack their engagement in the lesson.

... about using a pointer

1 The person who points usually does so silently. The speaking (usually from others) comes before, or after.

2 Using the pointer can produce a sense of expectation and anticipation.

3 If a person working on the chart makes a mistake and you want to intervene, stop the pointer rather than the person, because this can be done with a slight and gentle movement and without speaking.

4 When you want to invite someone up to the chart try to offer the pointer to the whole class rather than choosing an individual to give it to. This promotes a sense of learner self-direction rather then yet more teacher direction.

5 Turn-taking is thus indicated by passing the pointer from one person to another. And whoever has the pointer has the focus of attention at that moment.

6 Never use it to point at a learner!

Appendix 2

Phonemic charts for other languages

The principles governing the arrangement of the phonemic chart can be applied to any language to create charts to help learners. Here are two such charts, for French and German, using the same principles for layout of vowels and consonants, and also incorporating into the layout particular features of each language. These charts have been in regular use for teaching the respective languages.

French

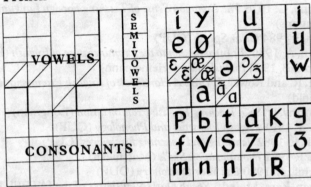

© Jean-Claude Renié and Adrian Underhill

German

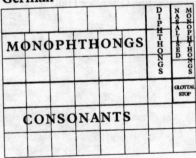

© Jonathan Marks and Adrian Underhill

Further reading

Bowen, T. and Marks, J. 1992 *The Pronunciation Book* (Longman)

Bradford, B. 1988 *Intonation in Context* (CUP)

Brazil, D., Coultard, M. and Johns, C. 1980 *Discourse Intonation and Language Teaching* (Longman)

Brazil, D. 1985 *The Communicative Value of Intonation in English* (ELR University of Birmingham)

Brown, A. 1991 *Teaching English Pronunciation* (Routledge)

Burgess, A. 1992 *A Mouthful of Air* (Hutchinson)

Catford, J. 1988 *A Practical Introduction to Phonetics* (OUP)

Crystal, D. 1991 *A Dictionary of Linguistics and Phonetics* (Blackwell)

Gattegno, C. 1976 *The Common Sense of Teaching Foreign Languages* (Educational Solutions)

Gilbert, J. 1984 *Clear Speech* (CUP)

Gimson, A. 1980 *An Introduction to the Pronunciation of English* (Edward Arnold)

Haycraft, B. 1994 *English Aloud* (Heinemann)

Hooke, R. and Rowell, J. 1982 *A Handbook of English Pronunciation* (Edward Arnold)

Kenworthy, J. 1987 *Teaching English Pronunciation* (Longman)

Roach, P. 1991 *English Phonetics and Phonology* (CUP)

Stevick, E. 1982 *Teaching and Learning Languages* (CUP)

Tench, P. 1981 *Pronunciation Skills* (Macmillan)

Underhill, A. 1980 *Use Your Dictionary* (OUP)

Vaughan-Rees, M. (ed.) *Speak Out!* (Newsletter of the IATEFL Phonology Special Interest Group)

Wells, J. 1990 *Longman Pronunciation Dictionary* (Longman)

Wong, R. 1987 *Teaching Pronunciation* (Prentice Hall)

Index

accent 51, 58, 69-70
allophone viii-ix, 44, 50
alphabet, international phonetic viii, 51, 122
   pronunciation of 122-3
articulation 2-4, 12, 33-47, 52, 124-8
assimilation 60-3, 173
assumptions xii
attitude 83, 84, 86, 132-3

box, phoneme ix, 2, 10, 22, 98
blackboard 206
breath 19, 30-3, 38-40, 42, 127
British English viii, xi

cassettes 197-9, 205
chart, phonemic viii-xi, 3-7, 9-11, 15, 21-6, 30-3, 37, 39, 41, 43, 47, 50-1, 112-13, 117, 122, 124-6, 131, 140-1, 145-7, 180-1, 196, 206
   a first lesson with 107-110
   as map x
   general applications of 96-8
   integrating 99
   introducing 99, 118-19
   seven modes of usage 100-6
co-articulation 49, 145
common ground 59, 74, 86-7, 89-91, 199
connected speech (see speech, stream of)
consonants 2-4, 20, 29-47, 97, 107
   affricate 33-5, 61
   distinguishing 29
   introducing 108, 124-9, 131, 141
   fricative 38-41
   lateral 44
   mime and gesture 128
   nasal 42-3, 47, 130
   plosive 33-5, 37, 125
   strong and weak 31, 126
   unvoiced 31, 126
   voiced 31, 126
   weak 31
context ix, 18-21, 27
continuant, post-alveolar frictionless 45
correction 132-8
   finger 136, 160-66
   techniques 137-44
Cuisenaire rods 154-9

definition 28, 52, 133
dictation 202-3
dictionary 166-8
diphthongs 22-8
   introducing 107-8, 121-2
   centring 22, 26-7
   closing 22-5
   length in 27
   mime and gesture 128-31

   stress in 27-8
   visual clues 28

element of diphthong 22-8, 122
elision 61-5, 173-4
energy 12, 142, 145
   in unstressed syllables 53-4
   profile 52, 161, 166
errors 133-4, 136

finger correction 136, 160-6
fortis 30-3, 36, 43, 126-7
   fricative 43, 47
French 207

German 207
gesture 115-22, 126-30, 138
glottal stop 37
grammatical indicator 84

head 76, 79-82

information structure 59, 85, 91
intelligibility 75, 171-2
intonation ix, 2, 80, 84-6, 88, 107, 109, 111, 194-7, 200-1, 204
   and learnability 75
   and reading aloud 91
   and rhythm 59
   and word stress 57-8
   attitude 83
   choice 75, 86
   discourse 85, 92
   form of 76
   meaning of 82-3, 85
   oblique 86, 89
   problems in teaching 195
   sensitization to 197
   syllabus 196
   theory 93
intrusive /j/, /r/, /w/ 65-7

jaw, energy in 12
   position 5, 7, 9, 11-12
juncture 68, 173

key 86, 92-3
   additive 92
   equative 92
   contrastive 92

language laboratory 140, 181, 186, 191, 203
lateral 44
length 2, 5, 16-23, 27
   mark 17, 19-20, 23
lenis 30-3, 38, 126-7
liaison 65-7, 173-4
linking /j/, /r/, /w/ 66-7
lip movement 5, 6, 13-15, 23, 25

position 3, 5, 9, 13-16
   reading 28, 169, 203
   rounding 14, 21, 23
   spreading 14, 23
loudness 52, 54, 179

metrical material 109, 176-7, 180, 182, 185
mime 115-17, 119-22, 127-31, 138, 169, 182
mistakes 109, 119, 132-3, 135-43, 149-50, 202-3
model xi, 100-4, 107, 110
   giving 101, 110
   internal imaging 110, 113-14
   non-verbal 110, 113-14, 117-19
   repeated 110-11
   single 110, 112
monophthongs 2-22, 107, 118, 122
   mime and gesture 120
   sequencing 119
   working with 118
multisensory dimensions of pronunciation xii, 135

nonsense word grouping 177, 188-9
nasal (see consonants)

onset 33, 37-8, 43, 76, 78-82, 87
   unvoiced fortis fricative 43

parallel speaking 181, 203
phoneme viii-xi, 2, 6, 11, 22-3, 25, 29, 35, 39, 49-51, 118, 146, 150-1
phonemic set viii, 27, 68, 107, 124, 145
pitch 57, 75-88, 91-3, 194-7
   variables of 77
plosive (see consonants)
pointer x, 98, 104, 106, 113, 206
prehead 76, 79-82
production 2, 4, 5, 19, 64, 73, 83, 96, 132, 153, 184, 198, 205
profile 155, 156-9, 184-5, 192-3
prominence 58, 69-70, 77-82, 87, 90-2, 171, 176-7,
pronunciation 171-2
   materials, conventional xi, 172, 204
   productive 171-2
   received xi, 57, 45, 59
   receptive 171-2
   slow down 50
   speed up 50

received pronunciation (see pronunciation)
rhotic 45, 66
rhyme 90, 109, 180-5
rhythm 59, 61-2, 64-5, 69, 72-3, 80, 90, 97, 107, 109, 176-87, 190-2

rods (see Cuisenaire rods)
RP (see pronunciation, received)

schwa 11, 182-3, 189
semi-vowel 29, 46-7, 67
sense groups 91, 164-5, 177, 185-92, 200, 201
simplification 59, 97, 173-6
slips 133-7
sounds viii, x-xi, 2, 11, 49, 101, 108, 114-16, 123, 128-9, 135, 140, 145, 147, 150, 161-2, 198
   correcting 136-43, 160-6
   in between 9
   in connected speech 58-60
   in isolation 2, 96, 101, 118
   intrusive 67
   linking 47, 66
   reduction of 173
   significant viii, 37
   simplification of 60-8, 173
   syllabus 118
speaking, learner's spontaneous 200-1
speech, careful colloquial 59, 64, 72, 85, 172, 202
   rapid colloquial 37, 59, 72, 85, 172, 202
   stream of xi, 47, 58, 61-5, 68-9, 72, 73, 97, 151, 164, 173, 200
spelling 146-9, 166-7, 204
strategy, anti-blurt 193
stream of speech (see speech)

stress 27-8, 51, 53
   a practical definition of 52
   and intonation ix, 57
   and loudness 179-80
   and lung power 51
   attributes of 52
   contrastive 70
   in compound nouns 54
   in connected speech 58, 176-7
   in derivatives 56
   in two-syllable nouns/verbs 56
   in two-syllable words 54, 152-6
   primary 54, 157-8
   secondary 54, 157-8
   sentence 58, 69
   shift in words 54
   timing 71-2, 178-9
   word 55, 109, 151-9
stress time, non-metrical 185
strong and weak forms 64, 193
study, three levels of x
sufficient 135, 137, 143, 163, 165, 180
syllable 151-2
   timing 71-2
   tonic 76-82
syllabus, rhythm (see rhythm)
symbols viii-x, 2, 22, 26, 51, 153, 196

tail 76, 78-82
target language 197
   pronunciation 171-2
tone unit 76-93, 190

tones, proclaiming 86-92
   referring 86-92
tongue movement 5-6, 26, 45, 130
   position 5, 7-16, 21-5, 44
tonic syllable (see syllable)
transactions – modes of using the chart 100, 105-6

unstress
   in the stream of speech 73
   in words 53

ventriloquism 169-70
vocabulary 148, 167, 169
vocal tract 2, 5, 30, 124
voice 30-47, 126-8
vowel 3, 5, 22, 29
   back 5, 10, 13, 16
   centre 5, 10, 16
   close 11-12
   front 5, 10, 13, 16, 24
   high 5, 9-10, 12-13, 16, 22, 24
   in-between 6, 9
   length 16-23, 27
   long 17
   low 8-10, 12, 16
   mid 5, 8, 10, 16
   neutral 5
   open 11-12
   reduction 57-8, 62-4, 173
   sounds and pitch movement 198

weak forms 64, 193
word boundary 47, 68
   stress (see stress)
words, citation form of 48
   in isolation 48-57, 145-170

Sound Foundations
Chart and Guide

Adrian Underhill

Heinemann English Language Teaching
A division of Heinemann Publishers (Oxford) Ltd
Halley Court, Jordan Hill, Oxford OX2 8EJ

OXFORD MADRID ATHENS PARIS FLORENCE PRAGUE
SÃO PAULO CHICAGO MELBOURNE AUCKLAND
SINGAPORE TOKYO IBADAN GABORONE JOHANNESBURG
PORTSMOUTH (NH)

ISBN 0 435 24093 5

© Adrian Underhill 1994

First published 1994

All rights reserved; no part of this publication may be reproduced, stored
in a retrieval system, transmitted in any form, or by any means,
electronic, mechanical, photocopying, recording, or otherwise, without
the prior written permission of the publishers.

Designed by Mike Brain

Acknowledgements

Thanks to students and teachers of International House and many other
schools who have helped to develop this approach to teaching and
learning phonology.

Key to phonemic symbols

i: see	/si:/	e egg	/eg/	æ cat	/kæt/	ɪə here	/hɪə/	ʊə cure	/kjʊə/	eə there	/ðeə/
ɪ sit	/sɪt/	ə away	/əweɪ/	ʌ up	/ʌp/	eɪ eight	/eɪt/	ɔɪ boy	/bɔɪ/	aɪ my	/maɪ/
ʊ good	/gʊd/	ɜ: her	/hɜ:/	ɑ: ask	/ɑ:sk/			əʊ no	/nəʊ/	aʊ now	/naʊ/
u: two	/tu:/	ɔ: four	/fɔ:/	ɒ on	/ɒn/						

p pen	/pen/	f five	/faɪv/	m me	/mi:/
b bee	/bi:/	v very	/verɪ/	n nine	/naɪn/
t ten	/ten/	θ thing	/θiŋ/	ŋ long	/lɒŋ/
d do	/du:/	ð this	/ðɪs/	h house	/haʊs/
tʃ chair	/tʃeə/	s so	/səʊ/	l love	/lʌv/
dʒ just	/dʒʌst/	z zoo	/zu:/	r right	/raɪt/
k can	/kæn/	ʃ she	/ʃi:/	w we	/wi:/
g go	/gəʊ/	ʒ pleasure	/pleʒə/	j yes	/jes/

Printed and bound by Fine Print Services Ltd, Oxford

94 95 96 97 98 10 9 8 7 6 5 4 3 2 1

Contents

1 **Introduction**   4

2 **Ideas behind the chart**   5
Looking at the chart   5
Using the chart   5
Guiding principles   7

3 **The design and layout of the chart**   8
Monophthongs   9
Diphthongs   11
Consonants   13
Stress and intonation symbols   18

4 **The chart in practice**   19
General applications of the chart   19
Using the pointer   20
Introducing and integrating the chart   21
Seven modes of chart usage   21

5 **A first lesson with the chart**   29

1 Introduction

Over the last twelve years I have worked with teachers and learners from many countries on the development of the *Sound Foundations* chart and its use in the classroom. I am delighted by the number of people who are contributing to the growing body of skill and knowledge in this approach to learning pronunciation.

I think there are several reasons why teachers and learners find the chart useful:

- The layout and visual nature of the chart promote insight and understanding.
- The use of phonemic symbols encourages learner independence through making dictionary pronunciation accessible.
- The chart and the approach offer a way of responding to pronunciation problems at the moment they arise.
- It does not rely on any other specialised pronunciation materials and is very flexible.
- It can help teachers to think on their feet and to extend their range of choices.

A number of in-house video films have been made in schools in different countries illustrating uses of the chart for teaching and training purposes. One such film is available from International House in London.

I would be glad to hear from teachers about their experience with *Sound Foundations*, especially about problems, solutions, and suggestions.

A full teacher's handbook *Sound Foundations, Living Phonology* is available, containing discovery activities for teachers and classroom activities for learners.

2   Ideas behind the chart

Looking at the chart

iː	ɪ	ʊ	uː	ɪə	eɪ	χ
e	ə	ɜː	ɔː	ʊə	ɔɪ	əʊ
æ	ʌ	ɑː	ɒ	eə	aɪ	aʊ
p	b	t	d	tʃ	dʒ	k	g
f	v	θ	ð	s	z	ʃ	ʒ
m	n	ŋ	h	l	r	w	j

Figure 1

The phonemic set

Every spoken language has its own set of sounds. All the sounds within this set exist in some sort of relationship to each other, each sound helping to shape the contours and boundaries of its neighbours. I refer to this set as the *phonemic set*. The chart shows the phonemic set of English as a complete and consistent system, to be worked with as one organic and interacting whole (figure 1).

Why these symbols?

The symbols which are used on the chart to represent the sounds of the English phonemic set are taken from the International Phonetic Alphabet (IPA). These are the symbols used by most learner dictionaries, so working with them will also help learners develop the skills of finding for themselves the pronunciation and stress of words in a learner's dictionary.

The layout of the chart

The 44 phonemes of standard English are presented on the chart in a significant visual relationship to each other. Built into this design are references to how and where in the mouth each sound is produced, and so there are many clues in the design that can help in recognising, shaping, correcting and recalling the sounds. Each symbol has its own box and pointing to this box selects that particular sound for attention. It can be useful to think of the box as containing all of the acceptable variants (allophones) of the sound.

The stress and intonation symbols

The primary and secondary stress symbols as used in most dictionaries are shown in the top right corner of the chart, and beside them the five basic discourse intonation patterns[1] are shown in one composite symbol.

Using the chart

Permanent display of the chart

The chart is designed for permanent display at the front of the classroom, so that it can be referred to at any moment during any lesson, and for a variety of different purposes (eg presenting, practising, diagnosing learners' perceptions of sounds, reshaping sounds, etc.).

The chart as map

The chart is not a list to learn, but a map representing pronunciation territory to explore. Like any map it can help in two ways: It can help travellers to become more familiar with areas they have already visited; and it can help travellers to be clear about which areas they have yet to explore.

---

1 ie fall, rise, fall-rise, rise-fall and level.

Learn sounds not symbols

The symbol is not the sound, just as a church or a lake on a map is not actually a
church or a lake! The aim of this approach is to experience sounds and sequences of
sound in a personal, physical, muscular way, and to use the phonemic symbol as a
visual hook for that physical and auditory experience. It is sounds that are being
studied not symbols.

Activating the chart

You and your learners can activate the chart by touching the sound boxes singly or in
succession with a pointer. This is either to initiate sounds or speech from others, or to
respond to sounds or utterances made by others. The basic rule is either *Point then
speak* (ie someone points out sounds or sequences of sounds while others say them),
or *Speak then point* (ie someone speaks while another tries to point out all or part of
what they have said). You can establish these two basic patterns within the first few
minutes of using the chart. Further below you will find seven modes of using the
chart. The even number modes correspond to *Point then speak*, and the odd number
modes correspond to *Speak then point*.

Three levels of study

The *Sound Foundations* approach enables the focus of pronunciation work to move
elegantly, and on a moment-by-moment basis, between individual sounds, individual
words, and connected speech. Thus micro and macro work can be integrated in
precise response to the learners' pronunciation needs as the lesson unfolds.

Each of the three levels invites a different focus of attention and work can take place
at any of the three levels according to the problems that arise in the lesson.

Level 1   Sounds

This level aims to develop in teachers and learners a deep and internally experienced
awareness of how they produce sounds by manipulating their vocal musculature, and
how the internal sensation of using the muscles relates to what is heard through the
ears. The development of this awareness enhances learners' ability to change and
modify how they use their musculature to produce new or different sounds.

Level 2   Individual words

Words spoken in isolation consist of a 'flow of sound' which is different from the sum
of the individual phonemes. Neighbouring sounds modify each other as the vocal
muscles join them together and take short cuts. In multi-syllable words, distribution
of energy across the syllables creates an energy profile, called *word stress*, that is
typical of a particular word when spoken on its own.

Level 3   Connected speech

Words flow together to make a stream of speech that is different from the sum of the
individual words. In connected speech sounds become simplified and reduced. The
fixed stress placement in words (word stress) is subordinated to another level of stress
chosen by the speaker to indicate the intended meaning (prominence). Intonation too
is chosen by the speaker to highlight meaning. A package of pitch and prominence is
called a *tone unit*.

Which model of English?

The phonemic symbols on the chart are generally taken to refer to standard English.
Where the target for learners is a non-standard accent then either the relevant
symbols can be given different values or adaptations can be made to the chart or to its
use.

Conventional pronunciation materials

The chart is designed to be used without conventional pronunciation materials, by exploiting material from general classroom interaction and from the course book and cassettes. However, you can easily integrate the use of the chart with specialised pronunciation materials, thereby adding a new precision and clarity to such work.

Guiding principles

For language learning and teacher training

The *Sound Foundations* chart is designed for use with learners of English at all levels. It is also designed to help you, the teacher, to develop your own awareness of pronunciation, and to discover new and practical ways of perceiving, diagnosing and responding to your learners' pronunciation needs.

Multisensory

Pronunciation is the physical side of language, involving the body, the breath, the muscles, acoustic vibration and harmonics. When attention is paid to this fact, studying pronunciation can become a living and pleasurable learning process. This approach is holistic in that it allows learners to work from their individual strengths and to develop their own, more vivid, learning styles. Pronunciation can become physical, visual, aural, spatial, and affective as well as intellectual.

Assumptions and values

The values and beliefs about learning and about people that underpin this approach are essentially humanistic, holistic and positive in their view of what learners are capable of under the right conditions. The *Sound Foundations* approach to teaching and learning goes beyond content and technique, and takes into account the psychological dynamics of learning and the creation of an atmosphere conducive to learning. An assumption that is not discussed further in this guide is that motivation and enjoyment arise naturally when the deep-seated human predisposition to learn, to experiment and to search for order is creatively engaged. These ideas are more fully explored in the book *Sound Foundations, Living Phonology*.

3 The design and layout of the chart

As you can see the chart has three main sections. The vowels are shown in the upper half, monophthongs /mɒnəfθɒŋz/on the left, and diphthongs /dɪpθɒŋz/or /dɪfθɒŋz/on the right. The consonants /kɒnsənənts/are shown in the lower half. The box in the top right contains stress and intonation symbols (figure 1a).

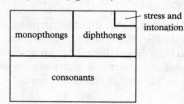

Figure 1a

To facilitate the learning of the 44 phonemes of standard English, we need to know:
- **how** each sound is produced within the vocal tract (referred to as *manner of articulation*)
- **where** in the vocal tract each sound is produced (referred to as *place of articulation*).

Figure 2 gives a summary of **how** and **where** for monophthongs, diphthongs and consonants.[2]

	WHERE	HOW
Monophthongs	The distinguishing quality of each vowel is produced by the shape and size of the resonant space in the mouth. This is controlled by the position and shape of the tongue, lips and jaw.	There is no obstruction to the escape of air through the mouth, and they are all voiced, ie the vocal cords vibrate in the airflow.
Diphthongs	As for monophthongs the distinguishing quality is produced by the tongue, lips and jaw. The difference is that there is one mouth posture at the beginning of the vowel sound, and another at the end. The resulting glide between these two tongue and lip positions gives the diphthong its characteristic 'two-sound' quality.	As for monophthongs there is no obstruction to the escape of air through the mouth, and they are all voiced, ie the vocal cords vibrate in the airflow.
Consonants	The restrictions to the airflow that make the characterisitc consonant sounds are made at one of the points of contact between the various speech organs such as tongue, teeth, lips, roof of mouth etc. All consonants involve some sort of restriction to the airflow except /w/ and /j/.	Restrictions to the airflow can be made in various ways, each giving a different characteristic sound. Restrictions can be produced by friction applied to the airflow, or by a momentary blocking of the airflow followed by a sudden release, or by diverting the airflow through the nose. The use of voicing and unvoicing also characterises consonant sounds.

Figure 2

The *Sound Foundations* phonemic chart is arranged to convey much of this information visually. We'll look at how this is done by taking monophthongs, diphthongs and consonants in turn.

---

2 **Etymological note:**
Vowel - *vocal*
Monophthong - literally *one sound*, from Greek mono = one, phthoggos = sound.
Diphthong - literally *two sounds*, from Greek di = two, phthoggos = sound.
Consonant - literally *sounding with (another)*.

Monophthongs

In the production of vowel sounds, the *vocal tract* (that is the air passage above the larynx or 'voice box') is open so that there is no obstruction to the airflow escaping over the tongue. All vowels are *voiced* (that is, the vocal cords are vibrating) so the airflow also has to drive the larynx, and the distinctive sound of each vowel depends on the shape and size of the space in the mouth. This is determined by:

1 The horizontal position of the tongue (which can be *front, centre* or *back*)
2 The vertical position of the tongue (which can be *high, mid* or *low*)
3 The lip position (which can be *rounded, neutral* or *spread*)

There is a fourth variable which is not dependent on tongue or lip position:
4 The typical length or duration of the vowel (*long-short*)

In the rest of this section we'll explore these four variables, and see how they are reflected in the layout of the chart.

Tongue position

Tongue position is the most important variable in determining the sound of a vowel. For each of the twelve English monophthongs the tongue is curved in some way, such that one part of the tongue is closer to the roof of the mouth than any other part. The monophthong section of the chart is laid out to show the approximate tongue positions for the twelve monophthong vowels. In figure 3 vowels formed at the front of the mouth are on the left. Those formed at the back are on the right. Vowels formed with the tongue high in the mouth are at the top of the diagram, and those formed with the tongue low in the mouth are at the bottom. Within this area the tongue forms the twelve vowel positions. Figure 4 gives you a rough idea of how these positions relate to the mouth.

Figure 3

Figure 4

The horizontal tongue position (front-centre-back)

The part of the tongue that is raised may be the front part, in which case it is raised towards the *hard palate* (the hard, front part of the roof of the mouth); or the back part, raised towards the *soft palate* (the softer, back part of the roof of the mouth), or the centre part, raised towards the juncture of hard and soft palate. The resulting vowels are correspondingly referred to as *front, back* or *centre* (figure 5).

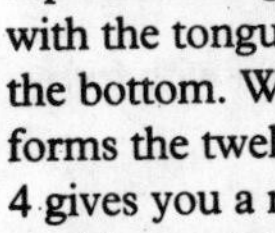

Figure 5

The vertical tongue position (high-mid-low)

From a vertical point of view the raised part of the tongue may be *high*, which means it is relatively close to the roof of the mouth, and above the level it holds in neutral position, it may be *low*, which means that it is relatively distant from the roof of the mouth, and below the level it holds in neutral position, or it may be *mid*, which indicates a neutral or middle position between these two extremes. Figure 6 shows how the monophthongs fall approximately into these three bands of high, mid and low. When high vowels /iː ɪ ʊ uː/ are formed the tongue is high in the mouth and the jaw is relatively closed. When low vowels /æ ʌ ɑː ɒ/ are formed the tongue is low in the mouth and the jaw is relatively open. So high vowels are sometimes called *closed* and low vowels *open*.

HIGH	(jaw relatively closed)
MID	(jaw approximately half-way)
LOW	(jaw relatively open)

Figure 6

The two vowels that are both central and mid /ə/ and /ɜː/ are naturally at the centre of this configuration (figure 7).

Figure 7

Summary of tongue positions relating to the chart

The top row contains the four high (or closed) vowels /iː ɪ ʊ uː/ arranged from front vowel /iː/ on the left to back vowel /uː/ on the right.

The second row contains the mid vowels /e ə ɜː ɔː/ again arranged from front vowel /e/ on the left to back vowel /ɔː/ on the right.

The bottom row contains the four low (or open) vowels /æ ʌ ɑː ɒ/ again with front vowel /æ/ at the left and back vowel /ɒ/ at the right (figure 8).

iː	ɪ	ʊ	uː
e	ə	ɜː	ɔː
æ	ʌ	ɑː	ɒ

Figure 8

So, as you can see, the arrangement of monophthongs on the *Sound Foundations* chart is a diagrammatic representation of the location of each vowel in the mouth in terms of the horizontal and vertical location of the highest point of the tongue. Each vowel is shown in a significant relationship to the others around it. The vowels that are neighbours on your chart are also neighbours in your mouth. This has important implications for building a repertoire of learning and shaping strategies.

For example, when learners confuse two English monophthongs it is quite likely that the two sounds will be neighbours on the chart, either vertically, horizontally or diagonally. Sometimes learners can be helped to arrive at elusive monophthongs by extending their tongue position further along the vertical or horizontal line from a known monophthong.

Lip position

The lips can further modify the size and shape of the resonating space, and they provide a kind of acoustic tuning to the fundamental vowel sound produced by the tongue position. Lip movement is easier to detect visually, and for many people easier to sense internally, than the movement of the tongue.

As it happens, lip rounding and lip spread in standard English coincide respectively with back and front tongue positions. Figure 9 shows a visual generalisation of this coincidence.

iː	I	ʊ	uː
e	ə	ɜː	ɔː
æ	ʌ	ɑː	ɒ

☐ lip rounding
☐ lip spreading
☐ lips neutral

Figure 9

You can immediately appreciate the importance of lip position if you say the English sound /iː/ and then while maintaining the same tongue position you round your lips. You will obtain a vowel sound which is not English but which is a definite phoneme in a number of other languages. (Note though that some speakers do not spread or round their lips very much.)

Vowel length

Vowel length, or duration, in the flow of speech can depend on a number of variables such as the stress, the speed of speech and individual characteristics of the speaker. But there are five vowels in English which are characteristically relatively longer than others when in an identical phonemic context. They are indicated by the presence of the length mark /ː/ (figure 10).

iː		uː
	ɜː	ɔː
	ɑː	

Figure 10

Summary

We have now looked at the four physical variables that govern the sound of a monophthong:

1 Horizontal tongue position (*front - centre - back*)
2 Vertical tongue position (*high - mid - low*)
3 The position of the lips (*rounded - neutral - spread*)
4 Vowel length, or duration (relatively *longer* or *shorter*)

We have also seen how information about these four variables is built into the design of the chart.

Diphthongs

The diphthongs are in the top right section of the chart, (figure 11).

ɪə	eɪ	
ʊə	ɔɪ	əʊ
eə	aɪ	aʊ

Figure 11

Diphthongs result from a glide from one vowel to another, eg from /e/ to /ɪ/. The phonemic symbol for a diphthong shows the two extremes of vowel movement /eɪ/, as in *game* /geɪm/. The starting point of the glide /e/ is called the *first element*, and the point it moves towards /ɪ/ is the *second element*.

A diphthong is perceived as one vowel not two, and therefore as one syllable and not two. For this reason each diphthong occupies just one box on the chart, like the monophthongs and consonants.

The eight diphthong phonemes are grouped vertically on the chart according to their second element. Those in the first column end in /ə/ and are called *centering diphthongs,* as the movement is towards the centre vowel /ə/ (figure 12).

Iə	
ʊə	
eə	

Figure 12

If you plotted the same diphthong movement on the monophthong section it would look like this: (figure 13).

I		ʊ
e	ə	

Figure 13

Those in the second column end in /ɪ/ and are referred to as *closing diphthongs* as the movement is towards the closed phoneme /ɪ/ (figure 14).

	eI	
	ɔI	
	aI	

Figure 14

If you plotted the same diphthong movement on the monophthong section it would look like this: (figure 15), but as you can see there is a bit more to the story this time.

	I	
e		ɔ:
	a	

Figure 15

According to phoneticians the first element of these two diphthongs is a sound that can be notated as /a/ but which in standard English does not exist as a phoneme on its own. If it did it would be somewhere between /ʌ/ and /ɑ:/ which is where I have shown it in the diagram. For practical purposes I use /ʌ/ as the first element, and I help learners to build these two diphthongs by first pointing to /ʌ/ on the chart. The results are always entirely satisfactory.

The diphthongs in the third column end in /ʊ/ and are also referred to as *closing diphthongs.* The movement is towards the high or closed phoneme /ʊ/ (figure 16).

	əʊ	
	aʊ	

Figure 16

If you plotted the same diphthong movement on the monophthong section it would look like figure 17. Once again the first element /a/ lies between two monophthongs, and again I have found that /ʌ/ is a satisfactory first element on which to build this diphthong.

	ʊ	
ə		
a		

Figure 17

The visual aspect of diphthongs

The mouth movements of diphthongs are usually visually detectable since any movement from one vowel to another involves a movement of the tongue, and often a movement of the lips and jaw as well. You can make use of this visible aspect when helping learners to discover the muscular movements required.

Consonants

Describing the 24 consonants

All consonants (with two exceptions /w/ and /j/) involve a restriction to the outflow of air, and it is the precise place and manner of this restriction that gives each consonant its unique sound.

We can describe the uniqueness of each consonant quite well using these three variables:

1　Voiced or unvoiced
2　Place of articulation (where the sound is produced in the vocal tract)
3　Manner of articulation (how the sound is produced in the vocal tract)

Variable 1　**Voiced or unvoiced**

A sound is said to be *voiced* if it requires the vocal cords to vibrate, and *unvoiced* if it does not require the vocal cords to vibrate. In English the voiced/unvoiced distinction tends to coincide with gentle and strong aspiration (also referred to as *lenis* and *fortis*). This means that voiced consonants may be uttered with weaker breath force, while unvoiced consonants may be uttered with stronger breath force. (This is partly because voiced sounds take energy from the breath in order to drive the larynx, and partly because unvoiced sounds need to compensate for their lack of voice with force and clarity in their articulation).

Variable 2　**Place of articulation**

The place in the vocal tract where the physical restriction or block to the airflow takes place is referred to as *place of articulation* ie where the characteristic vibrations of that consonant are initiated.

Variable 3　**Manner of articulation**

The nature of the physical restriction to the airflow is referred to as *manner of articulation* ie how the characteristic vibrations of that consonant are initiated.

By combining these three variables we arrive at a practical working description of how each consonant is produced. The consonants are arranged on the *Sound Foundations* chart according to these three variables, so understanding the layout will give you a useful grasp of how the consonants are made and how they can be altered.

This is how the consonant phonemes are arranged on the chart, (figure 18).

Figure 18

Now let's take the three rows of consonants one row at a time.

Row one

According to **variable 1** this row consists of four unvoiced/voiced pairs.
According to **variable 2** this row consists of four corresponding places of

articulation, with points of contact ranging from the front of the mouth at the left of the diagram, to the back of the mouth at the right (figure 19).

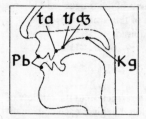

Figure 19

Each of these four places of articulation yields two consonant phonemes, one unvoiced and one voiced.

According to **variable 3** this row consists of the six *plosive* and two *affricate* sounds.

For plosives, the air stream is completely blocked or stopped by the tongue or lips, held momentarily, then the pressure is released 'explosively'. The sounds are also called *stops*.

Affricates also begin with a block to the airflow and a build up of pressure, but the release stage is a little slower, producing a sound with more friction. Hence these two sounds are termed *affricates*. But they start in the same way as plosives and can be treated as members of the plosive family. Figure 20 summarises these three variables in terms of the sounds in the first row, and shows the approximate locations of the Latin named places of articulation.

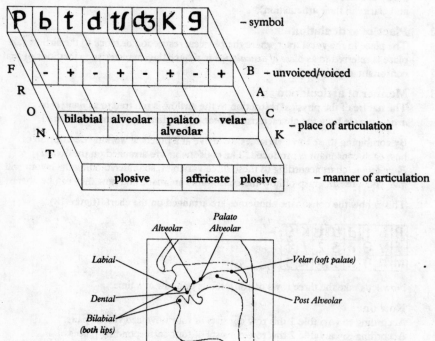

Figure 20

Row two

According to **variable 1** this row consists of four unvoiced/voiced pairs.
According to **variable 2** this row consists of four corresponding places of articulation, with points of contact ranging from the front of the mouth at the left of the diagram, to the back of the mouth at the right, (figure 21).

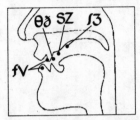

Figure 21

Each of these four places of articulation yields two consonant phonemes, one unvoiced and one voiced.
According to **variable 3** this row consists of eight *fricative* sounds.

Fricative sounds are produced when the airflow through the mouth is restricted but not completely blocked. (If it were blocked a plosive sound would be produced). Even before the sound begins there may be a slight 'airleak' through this restriction. At the beginning of the sound there is an increase in the pressure of air behind the restriction, producing an audible friction which provides the characteristic sound of that consonant. Unlike plosives, fricatives can be sustained and given longer or shorter duration. Figure 22 summarises this in an exploded version of the second row.

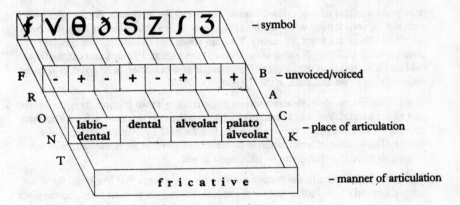

Figure 22

Row three

The third row contains the remaining eight sounds. They are more of a mixture than the other two rows, and this is reflected in their arrangement on the chart.

According to **variable 1** seven of the eight consonants are voiced. Only /h/ is unvoiced.

Taking **variables 2 and 3** together: The first three sounds /m n ŋ/, which are all voiced, all have the same manner of articulation. In each case a block to the airflow through the mouth diverts the air stream through the nose. What differentiates them is the place in the mouth at which the airstream is blocked and diverted through the nose. The different blocking places produce different resonances in the vocal tract which result in the different consonant sounds. The three places for /m n ŋ/ are points on a continuum from front to back with bilabial /m/ at the front, alveolar /n/ further back, and velar /ŋ/ at the back. Try saying the three in sequence to notice that backward shift (figure 23).

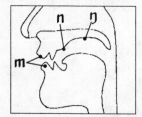

Figure 23

Notice that these three places of articulation are approximately the same as for the plosives /p/, /t/ and /k/. It is simply the different manner of articulation, nasal or plosive, that results in the different realisations.

The fourth sound /h/ requires the tongue, lip and jaw to take up whatever position is required for the vowel that follows (the term *onset* describes this phenomenon). There is no single place of articulation for /h/. Try saying the words *he, who, ha, her* and notice how the place of articulation of /h/ is determined by the following vowel. You'll notice a stronger expellation of air from the lungs (*fortis*) than is required for the vowel alone, causing friction in the vocal tract (*fricative*), which is already shaped in readiness for the following vowel.

/l/ requires a partial (though non-fricative) closure to the airstream. Air escapes over each side of your tongue while the blade is in contact with the *alveolar ridge* (the bony ridge just behind the front top teeth). You can check this by forming the tongue position for /l/ and then drawing air in through the mouth. Perhaps you can feel the cold air on each side of the tongue. This manner of articulation is referred to as *lateral* (ie the air goes over the sides of the tongue).

/r/ is frictionless because the airstream escapes freely, without friction, over the central part of the tongue. You can check this by forming the tongue position for /r/ and then drawing air in through the mouth. You can feel the cold air over the centre of the tongue. The manner of articulation is therefore described as *frictionless* and also as *continuant* since this sound can be prolonged at will.

This position is similar to the tongue position for /ʃ ʒ/ except that for /r/ the tip of the tongue is raised a little further back in the mouth, behind the alveolar ridge. So the place of articulation is referred to as *post alveolar*, ie 'a little behind' the alveolar position of /t d/ and also a little behind the palato-alveolar position of /ʃ ʒ/, (figure 24).

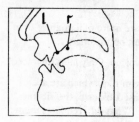

Figure 24

The manner of articulation of /w/ and /j/ is rather vowel-like, and they are often referred to as semi-vowels. Although their articulation can be described in vowel terms, they actually function as consonants in that they precede the main vowel of a syllable.

The exact starting position depends on the nature of the following vowel. The starting point of /w/ is usually characterised by rounded lips in the position of /ʊ/ gliding rapidly to the following vowel. /j/ begins with /ɪ/ of very short duration, immediately gliding to the following vowel.

The last three sounds in the bottom row /r/, /w/ and /j/ are placed together because they play an important role in linking words in connected speech.

Figure 25 summarises the information about the third row.

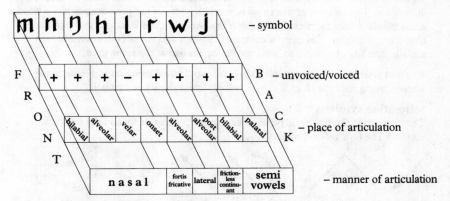

Figure 25

If you put the three variables for each sound together you arrive at the conventional name for each consonant (figure 26).

unvoiced bilabial plosive	voiced bilabial plosive	unvoiced alveolar plosive	voiced alveolar plosive	unvoiced palato alveolar affricate	voiced palato alveolar affricate	unvoiced velar plosive	voiced velar plosive
p	b	t	d	tʃ	dʒ	k	g
unvoiced labio-dental fricative	voiced labio-dental fricative	unvoiced dental fricative	voiced dental fricative	unvoiced alveolar fricative	voiced alveolar fricative	unvoiced palato-alveolar fricative	voiced palato-alveolar fricative
f	v	θ	ð	s	z	ʃ	ʒ
voiced bilabial nasal	voiced alveolar nasal	voiced velar nasal	unvoiced fortis fricative onset	voiced alveolar lateral	post alveolar frictionless continuant	bilabial semi-vowel	palatal semi-vowel
m	n	ŋ	h	l	r	w	j

Figure 26

This concludes the summary of the relationship between the way the phonemes of Standard English are articulated and their arrangement on the chart. Bear in mind that when these individual sounds are strung together in words and in the flow of connected speech, they are likely to lose clarity depending on the context, the stress patterns, the speed of speech, speaker characteristics etc.

Stress and intonation symbols

Word stress symbols

The International Phonetic Alphabet (IPA) uses the symbol /ˈ/ for primary stress and the symbol /ˌ/ for secondary stress. These symbols are displayed at the top right corner of the chart, just to the left of the intonation symbols.

You activate them by touching them with the pointer at the beginning of the syllable. to be stressed. Generally it is sufficient to use just the primary stress symbol, except when you specifically want to focus on the contrast between primary and secondary stress when it is helpful to use both symbols.

Word stress is the term used to describe the accent or emphasis given to a particular syllable of a word, and it is a more or less invariable attribute of that word when spoken in isolation. The location of this stress is as much a part of the pronunciation of a word as are the phonemes themselves. For this reason word stress is indicated in the phonemic transcription shown in learners' dictionaries. Sounds and stress both contribute to the acoustic identity of a word, so both need to be studied at the same time.

You and your learners may prefer to indicate word stress using hand gestures, but when working with the chart it can be helpful to use the stress symbols.

Intonation symbols

The chart gives the five basic types of intonation contour or tone in the top right corner.[3] The four moving tones

are presented in one composite symbol, so that teacher or learners have to choose the tone they want and deliberately trace it with the pointer. The level tone

forms the bottom part of the composite symbol.

You activate these tone choices in the same way as the other symbols on the chart, by indicating them with a pointer. Sometimes you may want to indicate the tone choice alone, either as a prompt or as a response. Sometimes you will indicate the words of the tone unit before the pitch choice, at other times the pitch choice before the words. The seven modes of chart usage (page 21) can apply to tone choice as well as to choice of phoneme.

You and your learners may prefer to indicate these five pitch patterns with a hand gesture, because that gives you more control over the range and degree of the movement.

---

3 The five intonation contours refer to the five tones identified in the discourse approach to intonation. According to this approach information that the speaker is giving as somehow additional to the common understanding between speaker and hearer is likely to have a falling tone, either \ or ⋀ . Information which is given as not new, but as referring to common understanding already exisiting between speaker and hearer is likely to have a rising tone, either ⋁ or ⁄ . The level tone is used when the speaker is not primarily concerned to communicate directly with the hearer, as for example when quoting a text or thinking aloud.

4 The chart in practice

4.1 General applications of the chart

The chart has applications in many kinds of lessons and at any language level. Here are some of the applications:

Level 1 **Individual sounds**
- Learning new sounds and sound sequences
- Shaping and fine-tuning sounds
- Using the visual cues in the chart layout to strengthen the link between aural perception and oral production
- Relating the visual arrangement of the chart to the internal muscular sensation of each sound
- Inviting learners to identify their own areas of difficulty on the chart
- Recognition and discrimination activities eg minimal pairs, odd one out, same or different, etc.
- Highlighting the pronunciation of word endings, past tenses, agreements etc.
- Prompting and correcting learners by touching the chart rather than by speaking yourself
- Inviting learners to collect their own key words for each sound

Level 2 **Words in isolation**
- Separating the sounds of a word, working on them, and then putting the word back together
- Giving feedback to learners on their word pronunciation
- Working on syllabification and word stress
- Highlighting and working on sound/spelling relationships
- Developing learners' ability to write down pronunciations of words using phonemic symbols
- Promoting self-help by relating use of the chart to use of dictionaries for checking and discovering pronunciations
- Presenting and recycling vocabulary
- Promoting better learning, retention and recall of vocabulary through precise and vivid attention to pronunciation and word stress

Level 3 **Connected speech**
- Examining small samples of connected speech for ear training, awareness raising, and practice
- Focusing on fluency by highlighting linking sounds that join words together
- Isolating important words and pronunciations from continuous speech on tape or video, and reassembling the fluency of connected speech
- Focusing on changes and modifications to consonants in the stream of speech
- Drawing attention to the effects of stress and unstress on vowel sounds
- Examining the reduction and simplification of structure words in connected speech
- Studying rhythm and the changes necessary in pronunciation to achieve a good rhythm
- Drawing attention to intonation contours and how they relate to the prominent syllables
- Practising structures without repetition by focusing on the fluency and connectedness of the students' utterance
- As an alternative way of addressing the class (eg giving instructions, asking questions, setting homework) without speaking yourself

General

- Use pronunciation work as an opportunity to change pace and re-focus attention during a lesson.
- Bring phonology alive as an active, creative, physical, joyful and integral part of all other language activities!

All of the kinds of activity outlined above can be worked on in seven different ways. These ways, or modes of work, are described in section 4.4.

4.2   Using the pointer

The attention of the group is focused on a symbol on the chart by touching that symbol lightly and deliberately with the pointer, somewhere within its box. This has the effect of selecting that symbol and bringing it forward for attention. Touching a sequence of symbols in turn makes a sequence of sounds or a word.

When you are working at higher levels of discrimination you can point to the centre of the box to indicate that a learner's sound was the exact target sound you are after, and point closer to the edge of the box to indicate that the learner's sound was *acceptable but not quite right*. You can point to another box if it was closer to another sound, or to a mix of boxes if the sound seems to be a mixture of two or three sounds. You can point outside the chart if the sound given by the learner does not exist in standard English. Learners can be helped by this kind of precise feedback. But keep the work light, and with enough supportive humour to maintain both pleasure and curiosity.

Everyone is active in this, one person pointing, others watching, recognising the sound, saying the sound internally, and retaining it until invited to say it aloud. The activity of pointing can evoke a high degree of attention from learners. In the spirit of this approach the pointer belongs to the whole class, not just to the teacher. After you, the teacher, have introduced something on the chart, you might offer the pointer to anyone who would like to come to the chart to test themselves, or test another, or get a response from another, or seek further guidance, or try something out to see if it's right or wrong. This helps the way the class manages itself in terms of turn taking and respect for the efforts of each other.

You can be very much in control by initiating tasks, by giving feedback to the learners on their efforts, and by deciding who is to have the pointer next. But the learners too can take this control once they see how to use the chart, and you can stand aside and leave them to take the initiative while you watch and listen, intervening when needed. Used with this attitude the action of pointing can help reveal learners' perceptions of problems and can encourage initiative-taking.

I use a telescopic pointer as used by speakers and presenters, but any thin stick or rod about 40 - 60 cm long would do just as well. A pen is a bit short, as then the wrist and forearm obscure part of the chart, and a ruler is a bit wide, also obscuring other symbols. But either can be used.

One final point, and perhaps the most important. The dynamic of pointing necessarily slows the speed and deepens the attention. When the chart is being used for pointing out words, learners will probably say the word slowly and with more care. As soon as they've done that I ask them to say it faster or 'in English', an invitation to retain the insight but bring the utterance up to natural spoken speed.

4.3   Introducing and integrating the chart

The aim is to use the chart not only to add impact to your normal pronunciation work, but to infuse all class work with an easy access to its pronunciation content. Before the chart can be helpful in these ways you will have to think about an initial introductory stage for the benefit of those (including yourself) who may not have used the chart before.

So, there are essentially two stages:

1 Introduction of the chart
2 Integration of the chart

1   Introducing the chart

Introducing the chart refers to the initial two or three sessions where the class are meeting the chart for the first time. Learners are beginning to identify individual sounds and gradually to recognise and distinguish them from each other. In doing this they are beginning to find out *what there is that they can pay attention to.* They are beginning to attach the aural and oral impressions and the physical sensations of individual sounds to the symbols on the chart, thereby investing the symbols with the capacity to evoke the same sounds again when the symbols are pointed out.

As learners become familiar with the workings of the chart and become able to use it, the chart increasingly becomes an instrument for all sorts of pronunciation work and for integrating that work with other language work.

Once you have read about the seven modes for using the chart outlined in section 4.4, you will probably see how in the first few moments of this introduction stage mode 1 is likely to predominate, but that it should quickly be followed by work using modes 2, 3 and 4.

2   Integrating the chart

This is the main use of the chart. Both you and the learners are becoming able to use the chart as an instrument for refining awareness of what is involved in making isolated sounds and in running the sounds together to make words. The chart provides an immediate way to test hunches and take risks. Its most important attribute is that it enables objectification of inner processes that otherwise go unseen, and this in turn makes possible a more subtle level of feedback, initially from teacher to learner, but increasingly from learner to learner and from learner to teacher.

The chart is integrated into all areas of language work at all three levels using a wide range of the applications described in section 4.1. Mode 1 will still be used from time to time, modes 2 - 5 will be in constant use, and modes 6 and 7 will increasingly be used as learners gain confidence.

4.4   Seven modes of chart usage

A vast repertoire of activities is possible. Many are specific to the chart, while others are conventional activities made more focused and precise through appropriate use of the chart. In this section I describe a way of ordering them so that they form a basis from which you can investigate the potential of the chart and adapt it to your style of teaching. It will enable you to create an unlimited range of games, exercises and techniques.

Each mode is characterised by its basic *transaction*. The transaction consists simply of a first move and a second move in response to it. Eg the transaction of mode 2 is 'teacher points' followed by 'learner speaks'. Figure 27 shows the seven possible transactions in the second and third columns. Each mode includes all the activities that are possible using that basic transaction format.

As you become familiar with the modes you will soon find that you no longer need to think about the modes separately, but that you move naturally from one mode to another. For instance if you wanted to prompt a learner to add the past tense ending /ɪd/ you might use mode 2 ('teacher points' followed by 'learner speaks') and it would take two or three seconds. If you wanted to help a learner to distinguish more clearly between two vowels you might use mode 5 for a moment to diagnose and give feedback to the learner, then mode 4 to give her the opportunity to hear one or more models, then mode 3 to give her the chance to distinguish them aurally, mode 2 for you to hear how she is doing, and back to mode 5 or 6. This might take 15 seconds or three minutes, and could involve some or all of the other learners in the group.

As you will see each mode offers its own distinctive way of approaching pronunciation problems, and in combination they make up a coherent and balanced set of options. I've put them here in an order in which you might use them, moving from more teacher control (mode 1) to more learner control (mode 7). The teacher is completely in control in mode 1. In modes 2 and 3 the teacher makes the first move. In modes 4 and 5 it is the learners who make the first move, and modes 6 and 7 are characterised by learner-learner interactions which the teacher observes (figure 27).

The seven modes of chart usage

Mode	First move	Second move
1 Sounds are introduced and attached to the chart	Teacher gives model	Teacher points
2 Teacher uses the chart to prompt learners to speak	Teacher points	Learner speaks
3 Learners use the chart to point to what teacher has said	Teacher speaks	Learner points
4 Learners use the chart to prompt the teacher to speak	Learner points	Teacher speaks
5 Teacher uses the chart to point to what learners have said	Learner speaks	Teacher points
6 Learners use the chart to prompt other learners to speak	Learner points	Learner speaks
7 Learners use the chart to point to what other learners have said	Learner speaks	Learner points

Figure 27

Options for teachers at this point
1 Read no further! Develop your own ideas through using the chart in class.
2 Study the modes in depth before starting to use the chart in class.
3 Read through the modes to get a rough idea of them, then forget about them and develop your own ideas through using the chart in class. Read more later.
4 Start experimenting with the chart in class. Afterwards think about what you did and at the same time read more about the seven modes.

I would recommend options 3 and 4, and a gentle step-by-step exploration in class.

Mode 1 **Sounds are introduced and attached to the chart**

This is the mode in which learners first meet the chart. In this mode you introduce new sounds, you invite learners to practise them, and you help them to shape the sounds. Once the sounds are provisionally acceptable you point to the symbol on the chart in order to 'attach' the sound to the chart, perhaps indicating those learner utterances that are closer or not closer to the target. Alternatively of course you can point out the symbol first and then give the model.

As soon as two or three sounds have been 'attached' to the chart in this way you can practise them further in modes 2 and 3, and then modes 4 and 5.

Although the first move in this mode is the teacher giving the model, there are many different ways of putting a model into circulation. Obviously you can say the sound (or word or sentence) aloud, but you can also use mime or gesture to evoke the sound from learners, or you can elicit the model from the learners or take it from an audio tape or from some other source.

Here are four approaches to putting new sounds or words or phrases into circulation. The first is the most conventional.

1 The repeated model

You give the model several times, and then the learners repeat it several times, both together and individually. This has become the conventional approach, and is probably familiar to you.

2 The single model

You give the model once only, requiring your learners to derive as much as they can from a single exposure, and to do as much as they can with it. When they have made the most of the single exposure you can ask if they'd like the model again.

3 The internal imaging model

This approach introduces the idea of internal imaging, a natural human faculty which can usefully be exploited in the classroom. You give the model only once, and then leave a couple of seconds for the learners to listen to their own internal registration, that is to hear it again internally in their 'mind's ear'. Only then do you invite them to say it aloud.

4 The non-verbal model

This is about evoking new sounds from your learners without giving a spoken model yourself. Options here include using mime or gesture; lifting a 'new' sound from an already known word; lifting the sound from the learner's mother tongue; using a sound spoken by another learner; or reshaping an incorrect sound offered by a learner.

Whichever type of model you use the aim of mode 1 is to put new sounds into circulation, to work on them, and to attach them to the chart so that the symbols on the chart begin to take on some personal meaning for each learner. They do not have to be perfect when attached to the chart, just the best that the learners can manage at that moment. These four types of model giving can be applied to sounds in isolation, words or short connected phrases and sentences.

Mode 2 Teacher uses the chart to prompt learners to speak

This is probably the most frequently used mode, and typically the starting point for many pronunciation, vocabulary and grammar activities. In this mode you silently point to the symbols on the chart, singly for individual sounds or in sequences for syllables and words, and you invite a vocal response from the learners (or some learners or just one learner). You help them to hear themselves critically, and to evaluate, reshape and improve what they are saying. Here are some typical activities for mode 2:

- Point out contrasting or confusing sounds for learners to practise.
- Use the pointer to initiate discovery of diphthongs by combining the relevant monophthongs.
- Combine consonants to practise typical clusters
- Combine sounds to make syllables and words.
- Select a vowel and ask learners to suggest English words containing that sound ie they say them or write them on the board or point them out on the chart.
- Present or recycle vocabulary items on the chart. (I find that the added dimension of working on and arriving at the best possible pronunciation of a word helps learners to fix it in their memories and to recall it later.)
- Practise words that will occur in a text or on tape.
- With multi-syllable words you work on word stress, linking this to the stress symbols on the chart and in dictionaries.
- Intonation can be usefully introduced at the level of single words, without necessarily worrying about meaning, to get learners accustomed to consciously controlling the pitch of their voice. You can relate this to the intonation symbols on the chart.
- While pointing out words you can either have learners say each sound as you touch it, or remain quiet until you have finished. Both ways are useful, though the first is probably better until learners are confident. In either case the word is said as a whole once you have finished pointing it out.
- You can use the chart for giving general class instructions and setting up activities that have nothing to do with pronunciation. This is an interesting way of using your authority without using your voice. It usually rivets attention.

When building up words or short connected speech utterances it's important at the end to get the learners to say it at least once with the focus on the right sounds in the right order, and a second time to say it up to speed and with an 'English flavour'.

In this way each symbol, and its position on the chart, gradually becomes a 'visual memory hook' capable of evoking for each learner their accumulating physical, oral and auditory experience of that sound. This experience is not static, but is constantly evolving as the sound is brought into play again and again, and refined, shaped, forgotten, rediscovered, and so on.

Though the most frequently used mode, and important in establishing the conventions of the chart, it becomes monotonous if overused. It invites extension and elaboration into modes 3, 4 and 5 to increase learner participation and activity, and back to mode 1 whenever new models are needed.

Mode 3   **Learners use the chart to point to what teacher has said**

In this mode you say a sound (or word or phrase) and the learners respond by silently pointing out the sound or sequence of sounds on the chart. This requires the learners to pay attention to their inner registration of your model, to listen to it again internally, and to identify the appropriate symbols on the chart.

Use of this mode could follow from work in mode 2 which has revealed (for example) that a learner is not able to distinguish between two vowels when she speaks.

- Say the sounds that a learner is confusing, and see whether she can point them out on the chart. This enables you to diagnose whether the problem is that she cannot hear the difference or cannot say the difference. If she can hear the difference you can swap roles and work on her ability to say the difference (Mode 5).
- You can do the same thing to help learners discriminate between similar sounding words, and to become sensitive to the location of word stress.
- The model comes from a tape the class is studying. The learners try to reproduce a key phrase from the tape on the chart. This draws attention to a word or phrase (even where pronunciation is not the main focus of study). In this mode the challenge of trying to reproduce what is heard other than by oral repetition forces discrimination of what is heard and provides instant feedback for both you and your learners.
- You can change the activity by not looking at the chart yourself. You turn your back to the chart so that it is clear that you cannot see what symbols the learner is pointing out. Then the class has to decide whether the learner is pointing at the right symbol by saying *yes* or *no*. If they are unanimous then you accept their decision without looking. If they are not unanimous then the class need to say both your original sound, and the sound being pointed out, in order to savour the difference. By not watching the chart you shift responsibility for discrimination onto the class.
- Whatever learners point out on the chart gives you the opportunity to follow and gain insight into their inner processing. When they get stuck there are several options: to give the model again; or to ask them to say the sound they think they are looking for; or to say clearly the wrong sound that a learner has just pointed to so that everyone is clear about the difference; or pass the pointer to another learner to try while keeping the first learner at the chart ready to take over again.

Mode 3 provides a subtle way for learners to hear oral models from you without immediately repeating it themselves. Instead they have to organise what they have heard onto the chart, while rehearsing and rehearing it internally.

Mode 4   **Learners use the chart to prompt the teacher to speak**

A learner indicates on the chart any sound or sequence of sounds (making a word or phrase) that he would like to hear you say. It may be that he is uncertain of a sound, or is confused about the difference between two or three sounds. You simply say whatever he points to, without adding any comment yourself, leaving him time to assimilate what he has heard and decide what to try next. The learner can continue to 'feed' himself sounds of his own choice in various combinations, and can stop when he has got what he wanted.

This leads easily into Mode 5 where the learner speaks the sounds first, and you then point at what you have heard, thus giving feedback. Or it can lead into Mode 2 where you point to the sounds and the learner tries to say them.

Mode 4 puts the responsibility for what happens entirely in the learners' hands. They tend to use this opportunity to focus on their own perceived areas of uncertainty, and to become clearer about what it is they are uncertain of. This gives you insight into a learner's own perception of what he is finding difficult. The rest of the class is also able to see the symbols he is requesting and to hear your response.

So in this mode learners have the opportunity to hear as many teacher-spoken models as they like, but entirely at their own discretion and their own request. This is quite interesting, in terms of the politics of the classroom, since the learner chooses what he wants to hear the teacher say (which makes a change!).

Mode 5   Teacher uses the chart to point to what learners have said

You make an offer to a learner that you will point out on the chart whatever sounds she says. The rationale for this is that learners can more quickly learn to distinguish English from non-English pronunciations if they are given feedback that is immediate and precise. The feedback should be given in a warm and supportive way, devoid of praise or blame or of 'anxious helpfulness'.

Suppose the student is aiming to make the sound /e/. These are some of the responses you can make with the pointer:

- If the sound is an acceptable /e/ you point to /e/on the chart and she knows that her intended sound was heard as such.
- If you hear not /e/ but another quite clear English sound e.g. /ɪ/ you point at /ɪ/. Now she knows she has unexpectedly made a different but also quite acceptable sound. She can use this as a basis for further attempts.
- If what she says is an ambiguous mixture of, say, /ɪ/and /e/you point at the border between two sounds /e/and /ɪ/ or indicate a mixture of the two by stirring the two boxes together with the pointer. She uses this feedback as a basis for further attempts.
- If the sound was too un-English to be able to give accurate feedback on, you can point outside the chart. Done with the right attitude this usually causes a chuckle, and can be illuminating for the learner.
- If you hear a mother tongue version of /e/ you can point near the perimeter of the /e/ box.
- This often reaches a point where a learner who is trying to disentangle the pronunciation of three different vowels by saying them and trying to make you point at them, finds that she can get you to point at two of them but every time she says the third you point somewhere else on the chart. She realises that she is not making the right sound, and tries to change it. If she is not successful then you can help her to reshape the sound, or use mode 3 to find out how she is hearing that sound, or use mode 4 to enable her to request more models of the sound(s).
- The same game can be extended so that learners can test their ability to articulate correctly any sound on the chart while you offer immediate feedback on what they say.
- Games in this mode can be extended further to include words, word stress, phrases and intonation.

The immediate and precise (and non-verbal) feedback helps learners to become aware of the discrepancy between what they say and what they think they say. Learners soon stop saying the sounds they are sure of and begin to focus on ones that elude them, using your feedback as a basis for exploration.

Mode 6 **Learners use the chart to prompt other learners to speak**
As learners become familiar with the discipline of attention to sounds you will find an increasing use for this mode. Once the transaction is in progress your job is to watch and wait, and to learn from all the evidence that surfaces about how the learners are learning. You are ready to intervene as soon as they need help which they can't provide for themselves.

This has similarities to modes 2 and 4, except that a learner takes the teacher's place. One of the learners is helping the other to solve a problem or to hear or produce a particular distinction.

- The first learner may point to symbols she is uncertain of, prompting the second learner to say them, (similar to mode 4).
- The first learner may be testing and giving feedback to the second, (similar to mode 2).
- Another family of activities work like this: Learners each prepare a word or sentence. Each comes to the chart to point out what she has prepared. The others try to say it aloud. Mistakes and problems come to light and provide a spontaneous syllabus for further work.
- As students' facility at this grows, you can invite two students to have a short dialogue with each other using the chart as the only medium of expression, and with the whole class following.
- Any appropriate mode 2 or 4 activities can be used in this mode.

Mode 7 **Learners use the chart to point to what other learners have said**
One learner is at the chart pointing out sounds or words spoken by other members of the class. You watch and wait, learning from this autonomously-run diagnostic process. You only intervene if unacceptable mistakes pass unnoticed by the class, or if there are difficulties that require you as resource.

This requires precision on the part of the learner who speaks, and careful listening by the one who is pointing out what has been said. There are three sources of mistake and each can be turned to advantage:

- The pronunciation of the speaker is unclear or not acceptable
- The learner at the chart is thrown by what was said unclearly, or hears something other than what was said.
- The learner at the chart selects the wrong symbol for a correct sound that she heard correctly.

You need to be ready to intervene at any of these points, and in particular to distinguish between the second and the third type of mistake and to exploit them fully.

Diagrammatic summary of the seven modes

So far we have considered seven basic kinds of transaction, around which are built all the activities of the seven modes. Each transaction has been seen in terms of a first move and a second move. However in order to extend this you only have to see the second move as being also the first move of a further transaction, and so on. This is one way in which the modes can flow seamlessly into each other during classroom work. Figure 28 illustrates this.

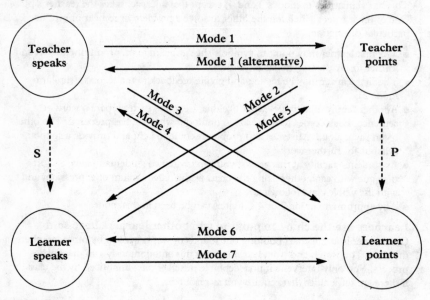

Figure 28

All of the modes can be simplified down to two basic moves. The variables are:

● who points
● who speaks
● which happens first.

In figure 28 each arrow points from the first move to the second, and is labelled with the corresponding mode. The second move can then become the first move for any of the transactions proceeding from there so that by following the arrows a single activity can be extended through several modes.

The dotted line S shows the transaction of normal dialogue, and dotted line P shows the transaction of a dialogue that takes place entirely through the medium of the chart.

5   A first lesson with the chart

Here is what I might do during a first lesson with the chart. In this case I devote a whole 45 minute lesson to it, though I could just as easily spread the same content over several lessons. This is an example rather than a recipe, and it may give you an insight into the spirit of this approach if you have not seen it used before. During this lesson I work with monophthongs, diphthongs, consonants, words, word stress, intonation and rhythm. But this is just to introduce the chart and get it into circulation. In subsequent lessons, however, I would not normally cover so much ground because I would use the chart to work on pronunciation issues arising from normal course work, perhaps five seconds here for a prompt, or two minutes there to work on a specific problem.

The numbers in brackets refer to which of the seven modes has predominated in the previous activity, and is simply to help you study the modes in more depth.

The chart hangs permanently beside the board, for easy use during each lesson, but for this lesson it is in the middle of the board, as we are going to focus on it for a longer period, and also so that we can write on the board round the chart during the activities.

Introducing some monophthongs

To introduce the chart I usually start with a few vowel sounds. I put one sound into circulation at a time eg /i:/ or /u:/ etc. either by miming it (model type 4) or by saying the sound clearly once only (model type 2). Then I leave a couple of seconds of quiet, or 'hearing time', after which the learners try it themselves. I indicate those learner responses which seem closer to the target sound, and with a variety of techniques help them to tune or shape their articulations. I try not to correct them by just repeating the model at them, though if the model is needed again, I give it. (1)

I encourage them to listen carefully to each other and to the variations between them by listening carefully myself. Although I value correctness, what I value more at this stage is their discovery that they can (re)gain conscious control of the muscles that make sounds, and that they can not only hear the difference between sounds but also feel the difference in their musculature, and even see the difference. My main aim is to help them discover that they can unlock themselves from the grip of the phonemic set of their mother tongue. (1)

Once the new sound is reasonably well established (even though it may not be 'exact'), usually after a minute or two of the class saying and listening and changing and trying, I point to the relevant symbol on the chart, making the connection between the muscular and acoustic experience of what they have just done, and the symbol on the chart which will become a visual memory hook. (1)

I repeat this for several other vowel sounds, eg /ɜ: ɑ: æ e/ etc. (1) frequently revising the sounds just studied by pointing at them in turn (2), helping them to make modifications, to rediscover ones they have 'lost', and to distinguish clearly between neighbouring sounds on the chart.

Practising sounds

Having done three or four vowels in this way I invite learners to take my place at the chart and to point to sounds we have done while the class responds (6). Then I invite the learner to point at sounds she is not sure of, and I say them myself (4). They also test each other (6,7).

Then I might invite a learner, who I think is not hearing the difference between a couple of the sounds, to point at one or the other of them on the chart after I have said them (3). Once she has got the hang of this I deliberately turn away from the chart to face the class so that the feedback has to come from the rest of the class rather than from me (3). From the earliest stages I look for every opportunity to have learners take my place as judge, as this keeps them actively searching for the criteria of Englishness, and gives me feedback on the progress of their insight. All of this proceeds at a fairly fast pace, and every activity has the dual function of providing both practice and feedback.

Introducing diphthongs

I now introduce a diphthong, but instead of saying it I use the pointer to run together the component monophthongs which we have already worked on, thus guiding the learners to discover the diphthong for themselves. After shaping the diphthong so that it sounds English, and practising it for a moment I point out the diphthong symbol on the chart which from then on acts as the visual memory hook on which to hang their growing experience of that sound (1).

I enjoy the fact that the mouth movements of diphthongs are quite visual, and so I mime the diphthong and some monophthongs and ask the class to watch closely, in order to discriminate between diphthong and monophthong, to say each and to point to the exact one on the chart (3).

The lesson may have been going on for about twenty minutes, and six or eight monophthongs and three or four diphthongs have been introduced and worked on. By now it is becoming clear to learners that the message is not *you must be perfect at this before we can move on to the next* but rather *do what you can on each of these at any given moment, and we can move forwards on many fronts at the same time. We will also come back to sounds as often as we need to.*

Introducing some consonants

Now I introduce a few consonants, again by saying them once and then giving hearing time, or by miming them. The ones to the left of the chart are generally easier to mime, though you can develop ways to mime all of them. I usually introduce both the voiced and unvoiced members of a pair at the same time so that we can focus on triggering the muscle that starts or stops the voicing (1). This means that we get 'two consonants for the price of one'.

Making words from sounds

Now after about half an hour they have worked with ten or fifteen sounds and have begun to put them together into different sequences, forming English words which they say and point out on the chart. Once again the learners are up at the chart, using the pointer and prompting and responding to each other as well as the teacher (2 - 7). Through paying attention to detail and through being alert the learners begin to discover that they can modify and control the target sounds more precisely, and that paying attention in this kind of way is engaging and enjoyable.

Words are put into circulation in different ways. I may say a word once, leave a couple of seconds hearing time, and then invite someone to come to point it out on the chart (3). Or I might point a word out on the chart and invite them to say it (2). Or a learner could say the word and others try to point it out on the chart (7).

Word stress

We may need to work on word stress in words of two or more syllables. I ask them to listen to the word once, and then to listen to it again internally in their 'mind's ear' while counting how many syllables the word contains, and which one is stressed (3). We may use the Cuisinaire rods to indicate the syllables, and to work on stressing and unstressing different syllables, savouring the difference, learning to make the difference at will, and noting which version is actually English. White rods represent unstressed syllables, red rods represent stressed syllables.

This helps to develop a more conscious control over the articulation of stress. Then the pointer is offered to anyone who would like to come to verify the pronunciation and stress of the word on the chart (6). Turns are taken until it is correct. Then I may give another word, and the learners also offer words to work on.

Intonation

I introduce intonation, not by requiring specific patterns, but by inviting the learners to experiment with their voice pitch and to produce different effects. We do this on single vowels, diphthongs, words and connected speech. In this first lesson we take simple words or phrases, like *hello*, and *nice to meet you* and I ask them to 'sound happy!' or 'sound bored!' or 'be sad!' or 'be in love!' or even 'be English!' or 'be Spanish!'. Later on, as they gain confidence, we can begin to notice and talk about falling and rising pitch movements, and relate these to the intonation arrows on the chart, just as the sounds were hooked to the symbols.

Phrases and connected speech

In the last few minutes of the lesson I use the chart to point out short English phrases consisting of several words. These are practised for their sounds, word stress, rhythm and intonation (2). The object here is to arrive at short bits of English that the learners know they are saying in a very 'English' way. The lesson ends with the students learning a couple of lines of strongly metrical verse, for example, a nursery rhyme (2).

Throughout the lesson mistakes provide starting points for further games and exercises. I view mistakes, or 'not quite right sounds', as opportunities that can guide and enrich the moment by moment emerging syllabus.

The aims of such an introduction are:

1 To establish some of the conventions for working with the chart
2 To foster a positive attitude towards phonology and a way of working which is engaging and enjoyable.
3 To work with all three levels of phonology (sounds, words, connected speech) at the same time, and to move elegantly between the three levels.
4 To help learners discover that they can relate to pronunciation not just intellectually, but also through the eyes, the voice, the ears, physically through muscular sensation, and through the feeling of being pleasurably challenged.

This introduction would have been essentially the same with only small modifications at elementary, intermediate, advanced and native-speaker level, though I would always demand the best the participants can do 'plus a bit'. What I am effectively saying to each learner is *do the best you can at this and then see if you can improve it*. My job is to provide both the activity and the psychological climate that will encourage them to do that.

iː	ɪ	ʊ	uː
e	ə	ɜː	ɔː
æ	ʌ	ɑː	ɒ
p	b	t	d
f	v	θ	ð
m	n	ŋ	h

Sound Foundations • Adrian Underhill • Heinemann

eɪ	ɪə	ɪə	✗
əʊ	ɔɪ	əʊ	
eə	aɪ	aʊ	
tʃ	dʒ	k	g
s	z	ʃ	ʒ
l	r	w	j

The Sound Foundations chart has become a popular teaching aid. It can help make the learning of phonology visual, physical, auditory and creative.

This pack contains:

Sound Foundations Phonemic Chart
Guide explaining the significant arrangement of sounds on the chart, the main concepts behind the chart and ways of using it.

Also available:

Sound Foundations
This complete Teacher's Book explores understanding and practice at three levels: Sounds, Words and Connected speech.

Other titles in the Teacher Development Series:

Learning Teaching
Inside Teaching
The ELT Manager's Handbook
Readings in Teacher Development

ISBN 0-435-24094-3

9 780435 240943